W9-ADR-158

PROPERTY OF FEDERAL EXECUTIVE INSTITUTE
OFFICE OF PERSONNEL MANAGEMENT
CHARLOTTESVILLE, VA 22903

America
Overcommitted

America Overcommitted

United States National Interests in the 1980s

DONALD E. NUECHTERLEIN

327.73
N964a

THE UNIVERSITY PRESS OF KENTUCKY

Copyright © 1985 by The University Press of Kentucky

Scholarly publisher for the Commonwealth,
serving Bellarmine College, Berea College, Centre
College of Kentucky, Eastern Kentucky University
The Filson Club, Georgetown College, Kentucky
Historical Society, Kentucky State University
Morehead State University, Murray State University,
Northern Kentucky University, Transylvania University,
University of Kentucky, University of Louisville,
and Western Kentucky University.

Editorial and Sales Offices: Lexington, Kentucky 40506-0024

Library of Congress Cataloging in Publication Data

Nuechterlein, Donald Edwin, 1925-
America overcommitted.

Includes index.
1. United States—Foreign relations—1981-
2. United States—National security.   I. Title.
E876.N84   1985   327.73   84-17409
ISBN 0-8131-1529-9
ISBN 0-8131-0163-8 (pbk.)

Contents

N.C. WESLEYAN COLLEGE
ELIZABETH BRASWELL PEARSALL LIBRARY

Figures

Preface

This book deals with the foreign policy priorities of the United States as it enters the latter half of the 1980s and contemplates its role in the world during the 1990s. The title *America Overcommitted* was suggested by an article I contributed to the *Foreign Service Journal* in 1982, which concluded with this statement: "Whether the United States remains a super-power into the 21st century depends in large measure on how it decides its international priorities in this decade and marshals its resources to defend them. Reducing the range and the cost of worldwide U.S. commitments is long overdue, and the Reagan Administration should not flinch from making the hard decisions to do so."[1] This theme was elaborated in a paper entitled "National Interests and National Strategy: The Need for Priority" that I presented to the National Security Affairs Conference of the National Defense University in October 1982. That paper came to the attention of the University Press of Kentucky, which had published my previous volume on U.S. national interests, and we agreed that it would make a provocative book.

This volume is the fourth effort that I have made to develop and broaden a conceptual framework for defining U.S. national interests in the contemporary world. The first was *United States National Interests in a Changing World* (University Press of Kentucky, 1973); the second was *National Interests and Presidential Leadership: The Setting of Priorities* (Westview Press, 1978); the third was my contribution to a 1981 publication of the Woodrow Wilson International Center for Scholars, entitled *The National Interests of the United States in Foreign Policy*. This study is the first, however, that analyzes U.S. interests and policies on a worldwide scale.

1. *Foreign Service Journal*, March 1982, p. 30

Several things need to be stated at the outset. First, this is a policy oriented work and it deals with major issues in U.S. foreign and national security policy rather than with the theory of international politics, decision theory, or the morality of American foreign policy. Second, it is urgently concerned with establishing priorities among the vast number of U.S. defense commitments and responsibilities around the globe. It is simply not going to be feasible, in my view, for the United States to pay the costs of all its forces currently stationed abroad while taking on new responsibilities in the Middle East, the Indian Ocean, and Central America. Hard choices among Europe, Northeast Asia, the Indian Ocean, and the Caribbean Basin will therefore have to be made in terms of manpower, economic resources, and military and economic assistance programs if the United States is to remain financially strong and emotionally committed to an international rather than an isolationist foreign policy. Third, this study assumes the rational-actor model for deciding what interests and policies the United States should pursue in the world, and it accepts the view that the President has the primary, although not exclusive, constitutional authority to determine the national interests of the United States and propose the policies needed to defend them. Fourth, although the study deals with policy issues and is aimed at a large audience of opinion leaders as well as serious students of international affairs, it includes a conceptual framework for analyzing policy choices that should prove helpful also to the general reader in sorting out his/her own priorities about the importance of specific regions of the world and the appropriate policies to pursue in them. Finally, this study represents my own views—not those of policy-makers, scholars or military planners—as to what U.S. national interests and policies *ought to be* in the 1980s and 1990s. In some cases I agree with official policy and in others I do not; but the important point is that readers should be able to make up their own minds about the U.S. stake in the world, not simply on the basis of the opinions and judgments contained herein but by the use of the conceptual framework suggested in Chapter 1 for establishing international priorities.

The book is divided into three rather distinct parts. Chapters 1 and 2 suggest a methodology for focusing the discussion on priorities and policy tools, using the national interest matrix that I developed earlier and that is recognized as a useful tool of analysis. Chapter 1 also sets the criteria for deciding which interests should be considered *vital* to the United States, thus requiring the urgent attention of top policy-makers. Chapter 2 describes twenty instruments of policy that are available to a President in dealing with foreign policy and national security issues. This chapter also suggests a correlation between the levels of national interest and the instruments of policy that might be employed. Chapters 3 through 8 analyze U.S. interests and policies in seven different regions of the world and suggest changes in policy that will benefit the United States and many of the countries concerned. Finally, Chapters 9 and 10 are my effort to establish worldwide priorities among U.S. national interests and policies and to review the Reagan administration's handling of U.S. priorities during its first three years in office.

This is an ambitious undertaking. I know of no other scholar who has attempted it recently. The book will not satisfy those who think that national interest is too imprecise a way to analyze foreign policy issues and international relations. It may not appeal to those who believe that American foreign policy since World War II has been misguided on ideological grounds or corrupted by unwarranted confidence in the efficacy of military instruments of power. But it should attract those who believe, as I do, that wiser choices can be made by political leaders if they decide to be more systematic in the way they assess U.S. interests and policies. I also believe that their task will be easier if we have an informed American public that appreciates the need for priorities and is willing to accept the hard choices that policy-makers must face. I do not pretend to be the leading authority in this process of getting the ends and means of U.S. foreign policy into alignment, but I do bring to the debate some forty years of experience in government and academia, the last fourteen of which have been devoted to finding a more rigorous way of getting the priorities right. I hope that this new volume will add to my earlier efforts to clarify the issues and that it will stimulate others to enter the arena.

Charlottesville, Virginia
June 1984

1. National Interest as a Basis of Foreign Policy Formulation

The term *national interest* has long been used by statesmen and scholars to describe the foreign policy goals of nation-states. Although the concept is not new there is ambiguity about its meaning, and most scholars have chosen to use their own descriptions rather than follow formulations offered by others. Today the student of international relations finds numerous definitions of national interest, most of which are not conducive to precision in the making of foreign policy. Before attempting a more adequate definition, however, it is useful to review briefly what major American writers have said about the nature and roots of the nation's interests, particularly those writing after the United States became a great power.

Charles Beard, in *The Idea of National Interest*, traced the evolution of the phrase from the first nation-states down to the twentieth century and described the historical interests of the United States in essentially economic terms. Beard was concerned with what might be called the national economic interest. He argued that the founding fathers, particularly Washington and Hamilton, had a clear perception of what the new nation's interests had to be in order to survive: self-interest rather than sentiment, and a deep appreciation of the limited means available to carry out its policies. Beard believed that the predominant national interest of the United States was economic during the first hundred years of its history and that the two major political parties defined this interest to suit their own purposes. Commercial groups in the

East were primarily concerned with overseas trade and opposed to the nation's westward expansion across a vast continent. The landed gentry of the South and West, however, favored adding vast new lands in the West in order to build the political influence of farmers and to reduce the power of eastern commercial groups. Hamilton and Jefferson were the initial spokesmen of these two forces, which dominated American politics until the Civil War and represented the basic cleavage over what America's role in the world ought to be. Beard maintained that historically national security was not a principal concern of the United States, except for a brief period during the War of 1812, because no foreign power had the capability of invading the country and forcing it to submit. The Monroe Doctrine was a feasible policy because of the British Navy's support in the Atlantic. Thus, the new nation's interests could afford to emphasize economics rather than military power.[1]

A different view of what constitutes the basic interest of the United States was provided in the post–World War II period by Hans Morgenthau, whose ideas were forcefully set forth in his widely read textbook, *Politics Among Nations*. Both in this volume and in his shorter treatise, *In Defense of the National Interest*, Morgenthau argued that power, primarily industrial and military power, was the means by which nations survived in an essentially competitive world, and that nations neglecting self-interest and national power succumbed to the influence and intimidation of other states which emphasized them. Morgenthau deplored what he termed the "utopian" view of the world held by the "idealists" and favored instead a "realistic" outlook based on national self-interest. Like Charles Beard, he claimed that the realism of the founding fathers enabled the new nation to chart a wise policy that avoided entanglements with the great powers of Europe and permitted American commerce to prosper. The difficulties encountered by the United States in its international relations during the twentieth century, he asserted, resulted from the moralism and utopianism of leaders such as Woodrow Wilson; they subordinated the self-interest of the United States to universal principles that were often unattainable and therefore proved to be deeply frustrating to the nation.[2]

---

1. Charles A. Beard, *The Idea of National Interest* (Chicago, 1934).
2. Hans J. Morgenthau, *In Defense of the National Interest* (New York, 1951).

George Kennan, a professional diplomat turned scholar, shared Morgenthau's view of the world and the need for realistic thinking as the basis of foreign policy formulation. He too criticized the utopianism of those who shared Wilson's outlook. Such views, he argued, led to serious errors in judgment about the real nature of international politics and the best way for the United States to advance its basic national interests. Morgenthau and Kennan were strong advocates of the balance-of-power principle of international relations in which great powers seek to maintain international stability and relative peace through the balancing of military and economic power, and in which no single nation could become so powerful as to threaten the security of others. Kennan became associated with the so-called elitist view of foreign policy–making, arguing that the general public neither appreciated nor cared about the intricacies of foreign affairs and that skilled statesmen and diplomats should be given wide latitude in determining U.S. national interests and the policies most likely to advance them.[3]

The theologian-scholar Reinhold Niebuhr, who began publishing his ideas on the nature of international politics during the pre–World War II period, was interested in finding a place for both idealism and realism in the formulation of United States interests. He was deeply disturbed, as were many of his contemporaries, by the shattering impact of World War I on the international order and on the idealism that had characterized the western intellectual community. *Moral Man and Immoral Society*, published in 1932, reflected a new sense of realism in Niebuhr's thinking about the behavior of states in their international relations, and he reluctantly concluded that the role of power could not be ignored as a major element controlling the relations of states. In 1953, his widely read volume entitled *The Irony of American History* elaborated the view that both moral values and power must be considered in the formulation of national interests and in the pursuit of international peace.[4]

Probably the most thorough postwar research effort on U.S. national interests was conducted by Robert Osgood, whose comprehensive *Ideals and Self-Interest in America's Foreign Relations* was published in 1953. Osgood's view was that egoism and idealism

---

3. George F. Kennan, *American Diplomacy, 1900-1950* (Chicago, 1951).
4. See also Niebuhr's *Structure of Nations and Empires* (New York, 1959).

had been competing concepts in determining U.S. foreign policy since the turn of the twentieth century, when acquisition of the Philippines in the Pacific and Cuba in the Caribbean resulted in an imperialistic trend in U.S. foreign policy. The most notable proponents of this viewpoint were Theodore Roosevelt and Alfred T. Mahan. Osgood traced the development of the two distinct viewpoints—egoism and idealism—into separate foreign policies, with the Republican party adopting the former and the Democrats tending toward the latter. He described the two points of view as follows: "National self-interest is understood to mean a state of affairs valued solely for its benefit to the nation. . . . An ideal is a standard of conduct or a state of affairs worthy of achievement by virtue of its universal moral value."[5] He went on to argue that nations, like individuals, seldom act out of either purely selfish motives or pure idealism, that most actions and policies are a blending of the two. The degree to which a nation acts out of self-interest or from idealistic motives is the key to discovering the basis of its national interest, he observed.

Another scholar who wrote extensively on national interest was Arnold Wolfers, one of a group of scholars who sought to bridge the gap between idealists and realists. Wolfers noted that the term *national interest* had become, in the post–World War II period, practically synonymous with a formula for national security and that, unless they explicitly deny it, those who emphasize national interest as the basis of foreign policy may be assumed to mean that "priority shall be given to measures of security." Wolfers believed that among scholars and statesmen there was a preoccupation with national security and military power, which he said was not surprising during the 1950s when there was a major concern in the United States about building up strategic military power; but, he argued, one did not have to be obsessed with national security in order to be realistic about the goals and interests of the United States in the world.[6]

The trend in the 1950s to associate national interest solely with national security was unfortunate because it gave a distorted view of what U.S. interests consist of and made it more difficult to use

5. Robert E. Osgood, *Ideals and Self-Interest in America's Foreign Relations* (Chicago, 1953), 4.
6. Arnold Wolfers, "National Security as an Ambiguous Symbol," *Political Science Quarterly* 67, no. 4 (Dec. 1952): 481-502.

the term in a broader context. A more comprehensive view of national interest was described by Paul Seabury in his volume *Power, Freedom, and Diplomacy*: "We might thus conceive of the national interest as a kaleidoscopic process by which forces latent in American society seek to express certain political and economic aspirations in world politics through the highest organs of state. To comprehend this process, we must not merely understand something of the formal governmental processes by which foreign policy is made, but also penetrate into the depth of the nation itself to discern the wellsprings of thought, ideology, and smaller interests that feed into the mainstreams of American policy abroad."[7]

Some scholars, however, do not believe that national interest is a useful way to analyze the foreign policy objectives of states. One of the most prominent skeptics is James Rosenau, who thinks that neither the "objectivists" nor the "subjectivists," as he calls representatives of the contending viewpoints, offer an effective rationale for using the concept as a research tool. In *The Scientific Study of Foreign Policy*, Rosenau argues that "despite the claims made for the concept and notwithstanding its apparent utility, the national interest has never fulfilled its early promise as an analytic tool. Attempts by both objectivists and subjectivists to use and apply it have proven fruitless or misleading, with the result that, while textbooks on international politics continue to assert that nations act to protect and realize their national interests, the research literature of the field has not been increased and enriched by monographs which give central prominence to the concept." Rosenau gives as another reason for doubting the utility of national interest the declining importance of the nation-state in international politics: "The ever greater interdependence of nations and the emergence of increasing numbers of supranational actors is also bound to diminish reliance on the concept. Increasingly, decision makers act on behalf of clusters of nations as well as their own."[8] Roseanau is typical of many scholars writing in the late 1960s and early 1970s who were convinced that the nation-state was declining in importance. I believe that events

7. Paul A. Seabury, *Power, Freedom and Diplomacy* (New York, 1963), 87.
8. James N. Rosenau, *The Scientific Study of Foreign Policy* (New York, 1971), 243, 248.

of the past decade have proved them wrong and that the concept of national interest remains relevant to today's world.

From this brief review of some of the principal writings on the subject, it is apparent that there is no general agreement among scholars on how to define the term national interest or what policies should flow from its definition. In fact, there is no common conceptual framework in which serious discussion can take place. It is desirable, therefore, that this study of U.S. national interests begin with an effort to provide such a framework, for if we can be more precise about definition, especially about degrees of interest that should guide policy formulation, we may find greater utility in the term than has been the case during the past forty years.

Definitions of Interest

For purposes of defintion, it is well to draw a distinction between the nature of *national interest* and *public interest*. The *public interest* may be viewed as the well-being of the American people and American enterprise within the territorial boundaries of the United States; the *national interest*, on the other hand, is concerned with the well-being of American citizens and enterprise operating *outside* the United States and thus beyond the administrative jurisdiction of the U.S. government. This is especially important when the rights of Americans are endangered by the policies of nations that are antagonistic to those of the United States. Obviously, the public interest and the national interest are not mutually exclusive. Indeed, the public interest is heavily influenced by the nature of the international environment in which the United States interacts, particularly when there is a threat of war; similarly, the national interest is strongly influenced by the degree of social stability and political unity prevailing within the country at any specific time. For purposes of this discussion, it is useful to think of the public interest as the concern of federal, state, and local government—with the President sharing his authority with Congress, the courts, and the fifty states—and the national interest as the concern only of the federal government, with the President exercising the principal authority and responsibility for the nation's international welfare.[9]

9. The President's primary role in setting U.S. foreign policy objectives has

Strategic interests are second-order interests and derive from a clear perception of national interests. They are concerned with the political, economic, and military means of protecting the nation against military threats and are defined to a large degree by geography, availability of scarce resources, military technology, and the limitation of damage which could be inflicted on American territory or that of key allies. Occasionally, strategic interests tend to determine national interests, rather than the reverse, and in such cases confusion and overemphasis on military security often result. *Private interests* are the activities of U.S. groups and companies operating abroad whose business is not of major concern to the entire United States.

The national interests of the United States may therefore be defined as follows: "The country's perceived needs and aspirations in relation to other sovereign states constituting its external environment." U.S. national interests are the product of a political process in which the country's elected national leadership arrives at decisions about the importance of specific external events that affect the nation's political and economic well-being.[10] Clearly, the determination of national interests is influenced, especially in a representative democracy, by the needs and aspirations of interest groups, bureaucratic structures, and various political factions; but ultimately the President has to make a judgment about the extent to which the national interest is involved in a specific international issue or crisis. On important issues, the President has to persuade a majority of members of Congress, particularly the Senate, that his view of the national interest is correct and should have their support in the form of policies that he believes are needed in order to defend it. An excellent illustration of this check-and-balance relationship in determining a national interest was the congressional controversy over President Ronald Reagan's policies in Central America during 1983 and 1984.

The United States, like most great powers, has both changing and unchanging national interests, some of which it has pursued

been well established by precedent and decisions of the courts. See Edwin Corwin, *The Presidency: Office and Powers* (New York, 1957).
    10. This definition of U.S. national interests was first used in my article entitled "The Concept of 'National Interest': A Time for New Approaches, in *Orbis* (Spring 1979): 73-92.

consistently—although with varying degrees of intensity—over long periods of time, and others which it has pursued for short periods and then altered because of changing world conditions, or domestic political considerations. The United States has four basic, relatively unchanging, national interests, and all of its interests and foreign policies can be fitted into these four categories: defense, trade and commerce, the building of a stable world order, and the promotion of American values abroad. These long-term interests are defined as follows:

1. *Defense of Homeland*: Protection of the people, territory, and institutions of the United States against potential foreign dangers. This is usually referred to as the national defense interest, and it has been pursued with varying degrees of intensity throughout American history as the U.S. government has perceived foreign dangers arising and threatening the people, borders, and internal security of the country.

2. *Economic Well-being*: Promotion of U.S. international trade and investment, including protection of private interests in foreign countries. This may be called the national economic interest. It was historically the most important interest of this country because geography made it possible for the nation to concentrate its energies on trade and commerce rather than defense of its territory.

3. *Favorable World Order* (international security): Establishment of a peaceful international environment in which disputes between nations can be resolved without resort to war and in which collective security rather than unilateral action is employed to deter or cope with aggression. This is also referred to as the international security interest, and it came to prominence after the United States achieved great power status early in this century. This interest is also concerned with questions of alliance systems and world balance of power.

4. *Promotion of Values* (ideology): Promulgation of a set of values that U.S. leaders believe to be universally good and worthy of emulation by other countries. The emphasis given by Congress and the President to "human rights" in U.S. foreign policy during the 1970s and 1980s underlines the enduring role of this basic interest, even though it received less attention from the U.S. government in the early post–World War II period than other interests cited above.

The problem of correctly defining U.S. national interests lies not primarily in identifying these broad enduring interests, but rather in assessing the *intensity* of the interest—or stake—at different moments in history, and the desirability of using influence and pressure to defend or enhance certain national interests in preference to others, and at the expense of other nations. For example, the United States has long had an interest in freedom of the seas, for both economic and defense reasons, but the willingness of the government to use military force to protect that interest has changed over time as its perception of defense and economic interests has altered.

In sum, we are concerned with the intensity of interest the United States feels in specific issues relating to its four basic national interests, and with the basis for determining which threats are so important to its defense, economic, world-order, and ideological interests that it would contemplate the use of economic and military sanctions to prevent encroachment by a foreign power. It is the intensity of concern about any basic interest at a given period of time that forms the basis of policy-making in foreign affairs. These intensities, or degrees of interest, constitute a different category that we will call "transitory," because they are subject to change depending on the government's perception of their urgency at any given time.

The term *transitory*, as used here, does not imply that an interest is present at one period of time and not at another; rather, it suggests that certain specific issues falling under any of the basic interests may receive more attention from policy-makers at some times than at others. The degree of interest involved usually depends on the President's perception of the international environment within which the United States conducts foreign policy and on his judgment of the political climate in the United States. Looking at transitory interests in this light, we can visualize a four-tiered scale of priorities as a basis for defining more precisely the amount of value the nation, acting through its government, attaches to specific foreign policy issues. This scale of priorities may be defined as follows: (1) *survival* interests, where the very existence of the nation is in peril; (2) *vital* interests, where probable serious harm to the security and well-being of the nation will result if strong measures, including military ones, are not taken by the government within a short period of time; (3) *major* interests, where potential serious harm could come to the nation if no action is taken to counter an unfavorable trend abroad; and (4) *peripheral* (minor) interests, where little if any harm to the entire nation will result if a "wait and see" policy is adopted. Another way to measure the intensity of an interest is to use a time dimension: survival interests require the immediate attention of the President; vital interests require urgent planning in the executive branch; major interests require serious study; and peripheral ones suggest "watchful waiting." It is the job of the President and his principal advisers to decide when an international issue is at the *vital* level, especially if it is likely to approach the survival level. The Cuban missile crisis in 1962 is an example.

A *survival* interest exists when there is an imminent, credible threat of massive destruction to the homeland if another state's demands are not quickly met. Such crises are easy to detect because they are dramatic and involve an armed attack, or threat of attack, by one country on another's territory. Hilter's invasion of Poland in September 1939, Japan's bombing of Pearl Harbor in 1941, North Korea's attack on South Korea in 1950, and the Soviet Union's intervention in Afghanistan in 1979 are examples of a survival interest for the states being attacked. Except for the bombing of Pearl Harbor and possibly the raid by Pancho Villa into New Mexico in 1916, the United States has not had its own territory invaded or bombarded since British forces entered Washington, D.C., in 1814. All other major powers that entered World War II were either invaded or (like Great Britain) heavily bombed. Thus, the United States alone among the major powers has not experienced having its homeland destroyed. But the threat of massive destruction on the United States has existed since the introduction of long-range bombers in the 1950s and the development of Soviet intercontinental ballistic missiles and submarine-launched missiles in the 1960s and the 1970s.

The Cuban missile crisis in October 1962 was the most dramatic example of the United States having a near-survival interest at sake. This occurred when U.S. reconnaissance planes discovered that Soviet medium-range missiles were being installed in Cuba and appeared to carry the threat to the United States of massive destruction even though the Soviet leader, Nikita Khrushchev, did not specifically threaten to use them. Today, every major city and military installation in the United States is a target of Soviet missiles, and the survival interest of the United States is potentially at stake if there should occur a military confrontation between U.S. and Soviet military forces anywhere in the world. Survival interests usually are limited to the defense of a nation's homeland.

A *vital* interest differs from a survival one principally in the amount of time that a country has to decide how it will respond to an external threat. Vital interests involve economic, world-order, and ideological issues as well as defense of the homeland ones and may ultimately be as crucial to a country as direct threats to its independence. But threats to vital interests are potential rather than imminent dangers to a country's well-being, and they therefore provide policy-makers with time to consult allies, bargain with the adversary, employ political and economic measures to change a trend, and engage in a show of military force to convince an adversary that its course of action could be extremely costly.

In the final analysis, a vital interest is at stake when an issue becomes so important to a nation's well-being that its leadership will refuse to compromise beyond the point that it considers to be tolerable. If political leaders decide they cannot compromise an issue beyond what has already been done and are willing instead to risk economic and military sanctions, the issue is probably vital. Examples are President Harry Truman's decision in June 1950 to confront North Korea over its invasion of South Korea; President Dwight Eisenhower's decision in 1958 not to accept Syrian domination of Lebanon; President John Kennedy's decision not to accept Soviet missiles in Cuba or elsewhere in the Caribbean; President Richard Nixon's decision to take the United States off the gold standard in August 1971 and force its trading partners to accept a devaluation of the dollar; President Nixon's decision in October 1973 to alert U.S. forces when the Soviet Union threatened to send paratroopers to Egypt; and President Jimmy Carter's ill-fated decision to try a rescue mission of American hostages in Iran in 1980. Although ideological interests usually do not reach the vital interest level, they nevertheless provide an undergirding for other interests and occasionally may reach that level in their own right. The Reagan administration's policies in Central America during 1983 were couched in strong ideological terms, but the real issue was President Reagan's belief that a vital world-order interest was at stake in preventing Communist-sponsored revolution from taking over all of Central America.

In sum, vital interests include defense, economic, world-order, and occasionally ideological issues in U.S. foreign and national security policy.

It is important to emphasize here that a vital interest is *not* defined by the kind of policy actions a president takes in a crisis or serious international dispute; the actions are only symptomatic of the intensity of the interest. Sometimes a leadership may conclude that an issue is vital (that is, has reached the intolerable point) but that no dramatic action is warranted—or possible. The fall of the Shah of Iran is an example of President Carter's dilemma. Conversely, there may be cases where force is used even though the issue involved is not viewed as intolerable; this may result from a calculation that the risks of using force are low and the benefits will be considerable. This was probably the situation when President Reagan decided to invade the island of Grenada in October 1983. A vital interest is reached when a country's leadership becomes convinced that serious harm threatens the country and that it needs to act quickly to relieve the pressure applied by another state to have its way in an international dispute. The policy action taken, or not taken, to defend the interest is a separate issue and is discussed in Chapter 2.

A *major* interest is one that a country considers to be important but not crucial to its well-being. These are issues or trends that can be negotiated with an adversary—whether they are economic, political, or ideological. Such issues can cause serious concern and even harm to U.S. interests and policies abroad, but policy-makers usually come to the conclusion that negotiation and compromise, rather than confrontation, are desirable—even though the results can be painful. Examples of major interests for the United States are the Arab oil embargo in 1973 and the decision of OPEC to greatly increase the world price of crude oil; the Sandinista revolution in Nicaragua in 1979; the Siberian gas pipeline to Western Europe, which became a serious political and economic issue within NATO in 1982; and the Soviet invasion of Afghanistan in 1979. Each of these cases presented a potentially serious challenge to U.S. national interests, but in each one the

President decided that he could live with the outcome even though it entailed considerable pain.

Ultimately, the difference between a major and a vital interest comes down to what is *tolerable:* if the President and his National Security Council believe they can accommodate to an adverse situation, the issue probably is a major interest; if the situation becomes so distressing that they are ultimately unwilling to compromise, then the issue is probably vital. In the case of American diplomats held hostage by Iran in 1980, President Jimmy Carter decided that a continuation of the situation was intolerable, and he authorized a rescue mission. When the mission was aborted, however, Mr. Carter did not follow up with additional military pressure on Iran but instead continued the negotiation track— suggesting that for him the hostage issue was not firmly at the vital interest level. Secretary of State Cyrus Vance's resignation over this issue is a rare example of a key policy-maker's deciding to leave office when his view of the national interest was rejected by the President. In this case, President Carter moved toward the view of his National Security Adviser, Zbigniew Brzezinski, who considered the hostage issue to be a vital interest to American worldwide prestige and therefore requiring strong action. The hostage issue also highlights the importance of context in deciding the level of interest. President Carter had always to consider that the use of U.S. forces in Iran might result in a Soviet countermove in northern Iran and a potential U.S.-Soviet military confrontation. President Lyndon Johnson faced a similar dilemma in Vietnam: his decision not to invade North Vietnam was motivated by his unwillingness to risk China's intervening in that war—as it had done in Korea in late 1950 when U.S. forces approached the Yalu River—China's border.

A *peripheral* interest is one which does not seriously affect the well-being of the United States as a whole, even though it may be detrimental to the private interests of Americans conducting business abroad. These are issues that bear watching by the State Department and other government agencies, but they are a lower order of political, economic, or ideological magnitude. Examples are the imprisonment of American citizens on drug charges, isolated cases of infringement on U.S. business interests, the harassment of local political figures who are friendly to the United States, and the expropriation of U.S. private property with compensation. Although the detention of a political opponent by a friendly government would usually be viewed as a peripheral U.S. interest, the imprisonment or assassination of opposition leaders is clearly of greater concern. The murder of Benigno Aquino in the Philippines in 1983 was viewed as a major ideological interest by the Reagan administration and was responsible for the cancellation of a presidential visit to Manila.

Use of the National Interest Matrix

The heart of this conceptual framework for assessing national interests is the matrix shown in Figure 1. The national interest matrix comprises the four basic interests of nation-states on the vertical plane and the four intensities of interest on the horizontal one.[11] The policy-maker's task is to decide how large a stake the United States has in a specific international issue or crisis affecting its four basic national interests. Then he should estimate the intensity of interest that other countries have in the same issue, for each basic interest. Comparing the levels of interest at stake for the principal countries involved, a calculation can be made as to whether the issue is likely to be negotiable or whether it will probably lead to an armed confrontation. These calculations about the intentions of other countries are, of course, subjective judgments made by diplomats, intelligence specialists, scholars, and journalists who have detailed knowledge of the countries involved. Policy-makers, however, especially the President and his National Security Council, need to calculate carefully the degree of the U.S. interest at stake and decide whether it is *desirable* to negotiate an issue even though U.S. defenses, economic well-being, alliances with other countries, or sense of values may be seriously affected.

An illustration of how the national interest matrix may be employed as a decision-making tool is the Falkland Islands (Malvinas) controversy in the spring of 1982, in which Argentina and Great Britain went to war. In this case, the principals were Argen-

11. This national interest matrix was developed in a previous volume: Donald E. Nuechterlein, *National Interests and Presidential Leadership: The Setting of Priorities* (Boulder, Colo., 1978), 11-18.

Fig. 1. National Interest Matrix

Basic Interest at Stake	Intensity of Interest			
	Survival	Vital	Major	Peripheral
Defense of Homeland				
Economic Well-Being				
Favorable World Order				
Promotion of Values				

tina, which claimed sovereignty over the Malvinas, and Britain, which occupied the islands in the last century and retained control over them for 150 years. The United States had important interests in the crisis because of its close ties to the antagonists, and Venezuela had strong views because it is a Latin American state and has a border dispute with neighboring Guyana, a former British colony. Figure 2 is an approximation of the stakes that these four countries had in the Falkland Islands crisis in 1982.

Fig. 2. The Falkland Islands War, 1982

Basic Interest at Stake	Intensity of Interest			
	Survival	Vital	Major	Peripheral
Defense of Homeland		Argentina	Britain	Venezuela United States
Economic Well-Being			Britain United States	Argentina Venezuela
Favorable World Order		United States Britain	Argentina Venezuela	
Promotion of Values		Britain Argentina	United States Venezuela	

These countries' interests may be summarized as follows. *Defense-of-homeland interests*: Argentina was convinced it had a *vital* defense interest because the Falklands were claimed as Argentine sovereign territory. Britain's defense interest was at a somewhat lower level because of the islands' distance from the homeland. Neither the United States nor Venezuela (one of Argentina's most vigorous supporters) had important defense interests at stake in the South Atlantic. *Economic interests*: Britain and the United States had *major* economic interests in the conflict because of investments and trade with Argentina that could be jeopardized by war. However, neither Argentina nor Venezuela believed that its economic well-being would be affected by Argentina's seizure of the islands. *World-order interests*: The United States concluded that it had a *vital* world-order interest at stake because of its strong ties to Great Britain in the NATO context and because of its displeasure with Argentina's blatant use of force. Argentina had a lesser world-order interest, however, and was willing to risk the displeasure of the United States and the world community by violating the United Nations Charter. Venezuela's world-order interest was influenced primarily by its own dispute with Guyana and its antipathy to colonialism. Britain's was at the *vital* level because it could not tolerate the loss of prestige that would have resulted from capitulation to Argentina's demands. *Ideological interests*: Both Britain and Argentina had vital ideological interests in this controversy: Britain wanted to defend the right of 1,700 islanders to remain British citizens, and it was determined not to be humiliated by a country it considered to have been pro-Nazi during World War II; Argentina had a strong historical need to repossess the Malvinas, which it charged were illegally taken by the British in the 1830s. The United States and Venezuela, supporting opposite sides in the conflict, had lesser ideological interests at stake.

Nearly all of these considerations about the interests of Britain, Argentina, the United States, and Venezuela in the Falklands crisis were predictable in April 1982 when Argentina invaded the islands. The only factor that was not entirely clear in advance was whether the Thatcher government would view the Falklands as a crucial (vital) world-order interest. If it did not, the Buenos Aires regime would have been correct to conclude that a quick seizure of the islands would convince London to negotiate the transfer of sovereignty rather than undertake a risky military effort and the expenditure of substantial funds to retake the islands, even though it might wish to uphold the principle of self-determination. In addition to miscalculating British interests, Argentina was wrong in thinking that the United States would have only a modest interest in this crisis and that it would reluctantly accept Argentina's seizure of the islands if that move were quick and decisive. The Falkland Islands War also demonstrated how serious the consequences can be of miscalculation of national interests in an international dispute. Argentina clearly underestimated the world-order interests not only of Britain but of the United States, and consequently suffered defeat and a great loss of prestige. The United States also may have miscalculated Argentina's intensity of interest by not appreciating the risks the Galtieri government was willing to take to achieve a vital interest.

A rule of thumb for analyzing the placement of countries on the national interest matrix is that if any country that is party to an international dispute has a survival or vital defense interest at stake, that country may well go to war rather than submit to political, economic, and military pressure. If the defense of one's homeland is not at issue, however, but there are vital economic, world-order, or ideological interests at stake, armed conflict may still be expected, especially if any participant has two basic interests ranked at the vital level. If one country's interest is vital and the opposing country's interest is less than that, it is probable that a negotiated settlement can be worked out between the parties. However, if two countries to a dispute each have a vital interest in the outcome, there is a strong possibility that hostilities will result unless outside influence is brought to bear on the parties to negotiate rather than fight.

Distinguishing between Vital and Major National Interests

In assessing the national interests of sovereign states, a crucial factor is appreciating the difference between a vital interest and a major interest. The policy implications of choosing between them are enormous because a country must be prepared for an armed confrontation, if all other measures fail, when its leaders decide that the issue at stake is vital. Policy-makers normally do not have difficulty identifying a survival interest, because these are cases where there is an imminent danger of attack on the homeland and a crisis atmosphere has already occurred. The Cuban missile crisis in October 1962 is an example. Similarly, policy-makers have little difficulty sensing what issues are at the peripheral level, and they put them aside for further study. The real decision is whether a foreign policy problem is *vital*; that is, whether the stakes are sufficiently high that the policy-maker does not believe the basic issue can be compromised significantly. If the President and his national security advisers believe that compromise will prove to be intolerable for the country's well-being, the issue is probably a vital one.

Clearly, the term *vital interest* is used so loosely by many policy-makers, military planners, and politicians that it has often become confusing—even dangerous—when applied to specific issues. Too often a military or political leader will call something vital if he thinks it is very important, without regard to the consequences. That is why it is essential that policy-makers and scholars consider specific criteria when they decide whether a national interest—be it defense, economic, world-order, or ideological—is indeed at the vital level.

The following definition and list of criteria represent my effort to promote greater precision in the use of the term. *An interest is vital when the highest policy-makers in a sovereign state conclude that the issue at stake is so fundamental to the political, economic, and social well-being of their country that it should not be compromised—even if this may result in the use of economic and military sanctions.*[12] In arriving at such a judgment, national leaders base their assessment on many factors, including hunches. But a much more rigorous standard is required if the United States is to avoid the kind of miscalculations that occurred during the Vietnam War, and in the Lebanon peacekeeping operation in 1982-83. Listed in Figure 3 are sixteen criteria for assessing whether or not an issue is vital to the United States. Eight of these are value factors and eight are cost/risk factors, which too often are underestimated or overlooked altogether in crucial policy deliberations. This listing does not suggest any priority or relative importance.

Proximity of the Danger. Americans still think in geographical terms when assessing the importance of a foreign threat to the national interest. Despite the fact that intercontinental bombers and ICBMs can fly thousands of miles to reach a target, public opinion views a threat from a neighboring country as more dan-

12. *Orbis*, 85.

Fig. 3. Criteria for Determining Vital Interests

Value Factors	Cost/Risk Factors
Proximity of the danger	Economic costs of hostilities
Nature of the threat	Estimated casualties
Economic stake	Risk of protracted conflict
Sentimental attachment	Risk of enlarged conflict
Type of government and human rights	Cost of defeat or stalemate
Effect on the balance of power	Risk of public opposition
National prestige at stake	Risk of United Nations opposition
Support of allies	Risk of congressional opposition

gerous than one from a more distant country. Americans reacted strongly to Soviet nuclear missiles in Cuba in 1962 even though the Soviet Union had a limited ICBM capability that could threaten several U.S. cities from silos in the U.S.S.R. The proximity of danger is a criterion that applies primarily to defense and world-order interests. The United States and the Soviet Union, for example, are clearly more concerned with dangers in their immediate neighborhoods—as far as defense interests are concerned—than with those in distant areas. Eastern Europe is to the Soviet Union what Central America, Mexico and Canada are to the United States; these are areas where the superpowers view their defense to be at least at the vital level.

Nature of the Threat. Under this category an international issue may involve any of the four basic interests. For the United States, the danger could be a Soviet and Cuban military threat to a Caribbean or Central American country (defense), an Arab oil embargo (economic), the toppling of a friendly South American government by Marxist groups (world-order), or a flagrant disregard for human rights by an ally, such as the Philippines (ideological). It is rare, however, that an ideological interest would be so threatened that the United States would feel compelled to use great pressure to change another government's human rights policy. "Nature of the threat" becomes ambiguous for policy planners in dealing with the world-order category because the American public distinguishes between overt acts of aggression (such as the Korean case in 1950) and conflicts that are essentially internal (such as Vietnam, Angola, and Iran). Much public dissatisfaction with President Lyndon Johnson's definition of the U.S. interest in Vietnam stemmed from his inability to demonstrate overt aggression by North Vietnam, or that its Communist ideology was a threat to the United States. Similarly, the nature of the struggle for power in El Salvador in 1983-84 made it difficult for President Reagan to convince Congress that the United States should support that country militarily.

Economic Stake. Investments, trade, and commerce are important factors conditioning the level of interest the United States has in other states. Worldwide investments and trade carried on by U.S. firms and the effect this has on various segments of U.S. society make economic factors highly important considerations for policy planners. Rarely, however, have economic factors alone caused the United States to resort to war. The economic stake clearly affects two of the basic U.S. national interests: economic well-being and world-order. For example, a vital economic interest seemed to be at stake for the Nixon administration in August 1971 when the United States took strong economic measures against its trading partners, who thereafter referred to Nixon's "shocks." Middle East oil has always been vital to the economies of Western Europe; but only in the 1970s, because of the decline in U.S. oil production, did it appear to be vital also to the United States. Had the Arab oil embargo continued a few more months into 1974, and had Europe been more cooperative in forging a joint policy, it is likely that strong economic countermeasures would have been taken against Saudi Arabia and other Persian Gulf states.

Sentimental Attachment. The United States, more than most states, is influenced in its attitude toward other countries by the sentiments of the immigrants who came to the United States before and after World War II. The "ethnic vote" seems to exert more influence on Congress and on policy-makers than the numbers of voters involved. Historically, many Americans have felt a sentimental attachment to Great Britain because the two countries share similar values and institutions. The small Jewish minority in the United States has had an overriding influence on U.S. policy in the Middle East. Similarly, in 1975 the Greek lobby brought very strong pressure to bear on Congress to cut off all aid to Turkey, because Turkey had sent troops to Cyprus to protect the Turkish minority. Conversely, lack of sentimental attachment to the Vietnamese made it difficult for President Johnson to obtain a commitment from the American people to defend South Vietnam. Although some scholars and statesmen argue that sentiment should have no place in the determination of national interests, democracies find it difficult to ignore this factor because their peoples have a strong voice in influencing foreign policy. Sentiment is important in determining U.S. national interests in the Middle East, and it has also influenced U.S. policy toward Southern Africa. The rapidly growing Hispanic population in the United States insures that it will exert a strong influence on U.S. interests and policies in Latin America.

Type of Government and Human Rights. This factor is linked to sentimental attachment and flows from the ideological underpinnings of American society: namely, belief in representative government, individual rights, religious freedom, and so forth. This factor poses a dilemma for U.S. policy-makers: they have to trade off world-order and economic interests, on the one hand, and ideological interests on the other. Military assistance and economic aid to authoritarian regimes, for example, have been justified on the grounds that U.S. support is essential to the containment of Communism. Since the Vietnam War, there has been increasing sentiment in Congress and among the public for the executive branch to give greater attention to the type of government and its record on human rights when committing U.S. aid funds and making defense commitments to other countries. President Carter's human rights policy won wide acceptance from the American public, even though its implementation was criticized, and the Reagan administration has continued this policy by quieter means.

Effect on the Balance of Power. This factor should be viewed on two levels: the strategic balance between the Soviet Union and the United States (defense interest), and the regional balance of political forces in any part of the world (world-order interest). On the strategic level, the superpowers are constantly assessing the effectiveness of their nuclear missile forces in order to decide whether the other side has gained, or will gain, an advantage and thus will be in a position to pressure the other to make political concessions. The Strategic Arms Limitation Talks, which began in 1969, were motivated in part by each side's need to avoid miscalculations that could lead to war, and to keep a close watch on the other's technological developments. A regional balance of power is more difficult to assess, however. Unlike the strategic balance, which depends largely on the superpowers' decisions to produce or limit the weapons that maintain a strategic balance and thus deterrence, a regional political balance depends on the willingness of countries to cooperate with one another and with the superpowers to insure that no single country will dominate the politics of a whole region. The regional balance resembles the classical balance of power politics practiced by European statesmen in the eighteenth and nineteenth centuries. The degree of political change in any part of the world and the affect this has on the feeling of security, economic well-being, and ideological aspirations of the superpowers conditions the amount of attention they give to a specific region. After the Vietnam War, the focus of U.S. world-order interests shifted from the Far East to the Middle East, largely because Middle Eastern oil, Iran's revolution, and the Soviet invasion of Afghanistan suddenly made this area appear to be a U.S. vital interest for balance of power reasons.

National Prestige at Stake. All states are interested in the image they project to other states in the international arena, but national prestige is more important to major powers and superpowers than to small states. President Charles de Gaulle talked about the grandeur of France, and former Secretary of State Dean Rusk referred to the credibility of U.S. commitments abroad. Both were concerned with the respect showed to their countries by others, and the esteem that France and the United States were accorded in international relations. This factor is no less true for Communist powers: Soviet leaders have gone to great lengths to gain respectability in international organizations and are extremely sensitive to charges that the U.S.S.R. has broken international agreements. Prestige is difficult to measure because it has to do with perceptions and subjective judgments. For example, does a country use its power wisely? Does it respect the legal rights of other states? Does it aid its allies when they need help? Is it realistic in the pursuit of goals? Nations lose prestige when they take a stand on an international issue but do not carry through to a successful outcome—for example, Britain's humiliation in the Suez crisis of 1956, the Soviet Union's retreat in the Cuban missile crisis of 1962, the ouster of the United States from Vietnam in 1975. On the other hand, nations usually gain international prestige when they win wars, bring peace to a troubled area, or achieve significant gains from diplomatic negotiations.

Support of Allies. Most major powers have allies whose loyalty is valued and whose views are usually considered before a decision is made to take strong action against a third state. This factor is particularly relevant when an economic or world-order interest is at stake. When the Nixon administration was formulating a policy to deal with the Arab oil embargo in 1973-74, the unwillingness of NATO countries to go along with strong retaliatory measures was a factor in moving U.S. policy toward compromise rather than confrontation. Similarly, when President Reagan sought European support for his economic sanctions against Poland and the Soviet Union in 1982, European leaders exerted a moderating influence on his policies. When President Carter wanted NATO support for his Persian Gulf policy in 1980, the allies were reluctant to take a strong stand. This was because the European NATO countries' national interests differ from those of the United States in many economic and world-order issues. On the defense of Western Europe, however, European and American interests remain essentially convergent. Superpowers probably have less need of support from other countries because they have independent sources of power to bolster their policies; however, in the 1980s, the United States seems to desire the support of allies to legitimate many of its actions abroad. The Lebanon crisis of 1982-83 is an example.

Economic Costs of Hostilities. If an economic or world-order issue is so important that hostilities could occur, such a confrontation may take several forms—including a trade embargo, economic sanctions, and limited armed combat. In all such instances, the state taking the measures will incur economic costs. When the United States imposed a trade embargo on Cuba, it affected U.S. business interests and shut off the supply of Cuban sugar to U.S. markets. The economic costs of armed intervention in Korea were predicted with reasonable accuracy, and President

Truman asked Congress to raise taxes and impose controls on the economy; in the Vietnam case, however, President Johnson greatly underestimated the costs of the war, and this led to huge budget deficits and inflation by the end of the decade. In the Arab oil embargo of 1973, the economic consequences of a trade war and military intervention appeared to be very great for all Western countries. The probable costs of armed intervention or embargoes on trade must be carefully calculated by policy-makers before a determination is reached that the issue at hand is vital.

Estimated Casualties. If armed intervention is considered to be a likely consequence of a political confrontation, policy-makers should be reasonably clear about the manpower needs of a limited war, the level of hostilities expected, and the probable casualties. In advising the President what the manpower needs would be for armed intervention in Vietnam, Secretary of Defense Robert McNamara grossly underestimated the size of the force needed to contain North Vietnamese–sponsored warfare in South Vietnam. In a free society, the size of the military force and the potential casualties need to be calculated with reasonable accuracy because these factors are crucial in predicting public reaction. If a local conflict involves the possibility of direct confrontation between the superpowers, policy-makers would also have to estimate the U.S. civilian casualties that might result if limited war should escalate into general war. This could occur today in the event of a U.S.-Soviet confrontation in the Persian Gulf or in Central Europe. At a lower level of risk, President Reagan, in deciding to put U.S. Marines into Lebanon in 1982, was keenly aware that the potential for casualties was a serious question for many members of Congress. Reaction to the bombing of the Marine barracks in Beirut in November 1983 demonstrated this.

Risk of Protracted Conflict. If a country is not fighting for its own homeland (defense interest), it is generally reluctant to use military force for world-order or economic interests unless the conflict is expected to be of short duration. This is even more true for free societies than for totalitarian or authoritarian states, because public opinion is likely to play a larger part in determining how long the country's armed forces should fight. It is generally true that any government believing it can accomplish its objectives through the limited use of force over a short period of time is more likely to undertake such action than if it knows in advance that the conflict will be long and costly. Both President Truman and President Johnson were initially supported by the American people when they intervened in Korea and Vietnam, respectively; had these conflicts ended satisfactorily within six months to a year, both presidents would have been acclaimed. As it was, neither could end the war before leaving office, and each saw his party defeated in the ensuing general election.

Risk of Enlarged Conflict. When the deployment of a limited military force in a combat zone is contemplated, the risk of an enlarged conflict is often underestimated. For the most part, avoiding such situations requires good intelligence in order to clearly appreciate the intentions of other countries that will be affected by an intervention. Had Josef Stalin known in June 1950 that Harry Truman would use U.S. forces to repel a North Korean attack on South Korea, would he have given his blessing to North Korea's plan? Conversely, had Truman known that China would intervene in that war if U.S. forces were permitted to move to the Yalu River, would he have given General MacArthur the authority to cross the 38th Parallel? Many military leaders and some politicans have charged that the Vietnam War could have been won in the first six months had President Johnson been willing to use sufficient force—including the mining of Haiphong Harbor—to cripple the North Vietnamese economy. This thesis is debatable, however; such massive U.S. intervention in North Vietnam in 1965 would most likely have triggered a Chinese intervention, and President Johnson wanted no repeat of the mistake in Korea.

Cost of Defeat or Stalemate. This factor is linked to the discussion above but adds another element: even if the issue at hand is deemed to be vital, will the limited use of conventional force bring about the desired result? This is a very difficult question. The value attached to an issue may be high, but the potential level of warfare may also be high, thus raising the question whether the objective is important enough to risk war. It is clear that if the basic interest involved is defense-of-homeland, the likelihood of

N.C. WESLEYAN COLLEGE
ELIZABETH BRASWELL PEARSALL LIBRARY

taking that risk is higher than it would be for a world-order interest of aiding a friendly country far removed from one's homeland. In the case of Vietnam, it is unlikely that President Johnson
would have ordered half a million U.S. troops to that country had
he known in 1965 that the war would end in stalemate rather than
in a negotiated victory for the United States. Similar calculation
difficulties plagued President Reagan in 1983 and 1984 in deciding
how to deal with the internal political problems of Lebanon.

Risk of Public Opposition. An open democratic society must
always calculate this cost, because even though public opinion
may support a limited war when it starts, it quickly loses patience
if the conflict is not brought to a speedy conclusion. Although
public opinion does not generally operate as a brake in Communist or other totalitarian states, the leadership of a Communist
government must take into account the views of party members,
even though the party is tightly controlled. In the 1980s, risk of
public opposition assumes large proportions for major Western
countries, including the United States, and it is likely to be
exploited by the Soviet Union. The United States was so bruised
emotionally by the Vietnam experience that Congress blocked
President Ford from sending any kind of aid to non-Communist
factions in Angola in 1975. Opinion polls show that the American
public would not currently favor defending any country in the
Middle East and that many Americans even question defending
Western Europe. The debate in Congress in early 1984 over U.S.
aid to El Salvador is indicative of opposition by powerful segments of opinion even on vexing problems close to U.S. borders.

Risk of United Nations Opposition. Condemnation by other
states, particularly if the issue is taken to the United Nations
Security Council, is a cost that decision-makers must calculate
when contemplating whether an issue is vital. Major powers and
superpowers often ignore international opinion, but they do
want the approval of allies and friends. When President Carter
tried to deal with the American hostage issue in Iran, he sought to
enlist the international community in those efforts. When
Moscow found itself condemned by the United Nations for its
intervention in Afghanistan in 1979, it also sought support from
friendly countries such as India. The consistent opposition of

Third World countries in the United Nations to policies that Washington feels are in the U.S. interest has greatly reduced the esteem Americans hold for this international organization.

Risk of Congressional Opposition. The "bottom line" for any president contemplating the use of force to defend a vital interest is whether Congress will vote against the action, either in a joint resolution or a cutoff of funding. Traditionally, Congress has gone along with the President's judgment on what is in the national interest, even when it had serious doubts about the wisdom of a policy. The Vietnam War was a watershed in this regard, and since then Congress has become bolder in advising the President when it disagrees with his judgment. The War Powers Act of 1973, passed over President Nixon's veto, was a dramatic curtailment of presidential authority to define vital interests without congressional interference; subsequently, presidents have consulted more closely with congressional leaders when an international issue approached the vital level, particularly when it was possible that U.S. forces might be engaged in combat. In the 1980s it is clear that no president will be able to send forces into dangerous situations abroad without first exploring with congressional leaders the conditions under which they will be used if war should result. Congressional authorization in 1983 for President Reagan to keep Marines in Lebanon is an example. Although some constitutional lawyers think that the War Powers Act is an unconstitutional infringement on the President's authority in foreign affairs, there is little likelihood that this legislation will be repealed in the foreseeable future.

The value and cost/risk factors described above may be evaluated by policy-makers in a number of different ways in order to ascertain whether foreign policy and national security issues are vital national interests. A simple way to do this is to rate each factor as high, medium, or low. If the sum of the value factors is high and the sum of the cost/risk factors is low or medium, the level of interest is likely to be closer to *vital* than to major. Another way is to attach numerical scores to the sixteen factors and compare the totals of the value and the cost/risk categories. Some factors may be more important than others, and weights would have to be added to those which are considered to be of overriding importance. For example, during the Vietnam policy debates within the Kennedy and Johnson administrations, American prestige/credibility was accorded an extremely high value by some policy-makers, while the nature of the threat was given lesser value. Conversely, in weighing the pros and cons of U.S. intervention in Iran to secure the release of fifty-two Embassy hostages in 1980, the Carter administration apparently gave greater weight to the risks involved and less to American prestige.

An important qualifier should be added to this discussion in order to reduce misunderstanding about the utility of the national interest matrix as a tool of analysis. I do not claim this to be a scientific formula to assist policy-makers to arrive at "correct" decisions about foreign policy. The value of this conceptual framework is that it provides for systematic analysis of specific foreign policy issues; it should therefore lead to better judgments about levels of interest for the United States and its antagonists and, one would hope, to wiser policies than would otherwise be the case. This framework will not eliminate mistakes in judgment by policy-makers, but it will provide them with a better methodology for deciding whether an international issue is so crucial to the United States that the nation must be prepared to take strong action. A careful use of this framework will most likely result in greater use of diplomacy and in less propensity to employ force to deal with issues that are borderline between major and vital interests.

Summing Up

A number of conclusions may be drawn about considerations that American policy-makers ought to take into account when assessing the degree of national interest that the country has in specific foreign policy and national security issues.

First, although all nation-states have four basic national interests that guide their decisions and policies, the two that are most likely to determine whether a country will engage in war are military threats to its homeland (defense) and serious dangers to its external environment (world-order). Nations today rarely go to war primarily for economic or ideological reasons. States do join alliances and defense arrangements in order to enhance their feeling of security against a common threat and/or to obtain military facilities and economic resources that they cannot provide themselves. The United States joined the North Atlantic Pact and sent forces to Europe in order to build a balance of power there that would contain Soviet ambitions and create a more favorable world order (international security). Defending Western Europe continues to be a vital U.S. interest.

Second, correctly assessing what are vital national interests is the key to wise statecraft and requires the best thinking of a nation's political leadership. There is no substitute for careful analysis and wise judgment in ascertaining the true value and likely costs involved in a specific foreign policy issue. A U.S. president must be certain that an issue is truly vital before he commits his country to a course of action that might involve the use of force. Furthermore, the process of deciding on a course of action should take into account not only one's own national interests but also a clear appreciation of the interests of other states having a stake in the outcome of a dispute. Failure to appreciate the intensity of an antagonist's interest, or an ally's stake, can lead to blunders in foreign policy and disasters in war. Examples are Britain's invasion of Egypt in 1956, America's intervention in Vietnam in 1965, and Argentina's seizure of the Falkland Islands in 1982.

Third, no country, especially one with a freely elected government, should risk taking responsibility for defending another country unless there is a strong likelihood that its own electorate will support the use of armed forces, if that should be required. No one doubts the United States commitment to defend West Germany or France; but the Vietnam case is a dramatic example of U.S. political leaders deciding that an issue was a vital interest and failing to appreciate that the public and Congress would think otherwise. Lebanon in 1983-84 is another, less dramatic, case.

Finally, the number of vital interests that the United States is willing to sustain in the 1980s and 1990s may well decline as the costs of defending them increase and the value of doing so decreases. The same may be true for the Soviet Union because of the growing risk that nuclear confrontation could result from local conflicts getting out of hand. Wars by proxy may be a way of reducing the risk while sustaining the value, but this type of warfare requires a clear understanding by the superpowers of the limits of national interests. In 1983, the superpowers were groping for a new understanding of how broadly each side defined its vital world-order interests in this post-Vietnam period and post-Brezhnev era. The uncertainty of the answers made the international environment a more contentious arena.

2. Instruments of Foreign and National Security Policy

Defining the nature and intensity of the national interest in specific cases is a crucial first step in formulating foreign and national security policies. The national interest matrix described in Chapter 1 provides a framework for doing so. The next task of the policy-maker is to select the instruments of policy that are appropriate to the level of interest at stake and to resist using instruments solely because they are available. Taking no action is also a policy, and it may be useful in certain circumstances. Occasionally, a country's interest may be high, but its government lacks the means of defending it appropriately. If this occurs regularly, a nation may lose its independence or simply be ignored by other states. Alliances are born of such needs and vulnerabilities, as the North Atlantic Pact in 1949 proved in the case of the West European governments.

Major powers, especially superpowers, have a large variety of political, economic, and military measures that they may employ to influence the leaders of adversary states. These range from diplomatic recognition of a new government to preparation for and warning about the imminence of nuclear war. Since this study deals with U.S. national interests, the twenty policies described in this chapter are instruments available to the President and his National Security Council. They are listed (Figure 4) in ascending order of influence and pressure that may be brought to bear on another country's foreign policy decisions. The first eleven may be classified as political/economic instruments of

Fig. 4. Instruments of Foreign and National Security Policy

1. Diplomatic relations
2. Scientific and cultural exchanges
3. Humanitarian assistance
4. Technical assistance
5. Information and propaganda
6. Economic and financial assistance
7. Economic and trade policy
8. Military assistance
9. Covert actions
10. U.N. Security Council debate
11. Trade embargo and economic sanctions
12. Military show of strength
13. Increased military surveillance
14. Suspension of/break in diplomatic relations
15. Quarantine/blockade/mining of ports
16. Local use of conventional forces
17. Partial mobilization/evacuation
18. Local use of tactical nuclear weapons
19. Threatened use of strategic nuclear weapons
20. Limited use of strategic nuclear weapons

policy; the last nine are military instruments. Each will be discussed briefly, and thereafter an attempt will be made to illustrate how policy tools may be correlated with the degrees of U.S. national interests described in Chapter 1.[1]

Political and Economic Instruments

Diplomatic Relations. The granting of diplomatic recognition to another government and the inauguration of diplomatic relations gives one country a means of influencing the decisions of another by opening a direct communications channel with its top officials.

1. This discussion is not intended as an exhaustive survey of a President's policy options for influencing the decisions of the leaders of other countries. Nor is it intended as an analysis of the literature on this subject. Rather, these twenty policy tools are described briefly to show the kinds of influence or pressure that can be brought to bear in dealing with a foreign policy or national security issue, and the correlation that should exist between the instruments used and the intensity of interests at stake. *Whether* a President should take any action in a specific case is a different consideration and is discussed in Chapter 9.

A government's interests and policies may then be explained formally and any displeasure noted over the policies pursued by the other state. Once diplomatic relations are established, a country may send a large number of its personnel to carry out not only the normal diplomatic functions of an embassy but also the various programs which accompany the other instruments of policy described below. The withholding of diplomatic recognition from a new government is a strong form of pressure, equivalent to a break or suspension of relations. The United States used this policy from 1949 until 1972 to pressure the People's Republic of China to alter its unacceptable policies. The U.S. constitution gives the President the exclusive authority to decide when diplomatic recognition will be accorded another state and the acceptance of another country's ambassador. A President must, however, obtain Senate confirmation of his ambassadors to other countries. The Department of State and the Foreign Service are the formal institutions by which the United States carries on diplomatic relations with other countries.

Scientific and Cultural Exchanges. Following the establishment of diplomatic relations, the United States and other countries inaugurate exchange agreements under which scientists, academics, students, and cultural leaders are sent abroad for conferences, performances, lecturing, and research. This constitutes a modest level of political influence because the purpose of the programs is to demonstrate the capabilities of the United States in many nonpolitical areas. The Olympic Games fit this category because prestige is gained by countries whose athletes win medals. For the United States, sending of scholars and scientists abroad and accepting other countries' students and cultural leaders has been an important part of diplomacy since the Fulbright-Hays Act was implemented in the early post–World War II period. That legislation, which has permitted thousands of students to study in the United States (and abroad), was supplemented by other congressional actions that also enable many cultural groups and individual performers to go abroad. The United States Information Agency and its U.S. Information Service posts abroad run these officially sponsored programs, and they facilitate scientific exchanges and conferences as well. These exchanges promote a better appreciation abroad of the United States and its intellectual and scientific achievements, and they provide a greater receptivity for U.S. policies among foreign elites.

Humanitarian Assistance. Another important, relatively nonpolitical program that the President uses to further U.S. interests is humanitarian aid for the victims of such natural disasters as floods, earthquakes, and famines. These are usually short-term relief programs to aid the victims of disasters occurring in foreign countries. This aid is offered on a nonpolitical basis to countries that need short-term help and does not entail a large outlay of funds. Humanitarian aid is administered by the Agency for International Development (AID) in cooperation with the Departments of State and Defense.

Technical Assistance. This program, begun by President Truman and known originally as the Point Four program, sends American experts in various fields to underdeveloped countries to help them improve their education, agriculture, transportation, medical, and other facilities in order to improve living standards and promote modernization. Like scientific and cultural exchanges, this program emphasizes human resources rather than financial assistance and brings Americans directly into contact with counterparts in many fields of assistance. The U.S. technical specialists are recruited from federal and state government agencies, as well as universities and private organizations. They live for varying lengths of time in a foreign country and, although they are not officially part of the U.S. diplomatic mission, they function under general policy guidelines issued by the U.S. ambassador. Peace Corps volunteers are part of this category. Although the purpose of having American specialists reside in foreign countries is to provide technical assistance, the granting or denial of such assistance is a modest form of political influence. The Agency for International Development also administers most of these programs.

Information and Propaganda. Unlike humanitarian and technical assistance, U.S. information programs—sometimes called propaganda because they promote appreciation of U.S. foreign policy—are clearly political in nature and designed to influence the opinion of foreign leadership groups. This is done in many ways, through speeches by U.S. officials, books, television clips, movies, and conferences on political subjects, and through broadcasts of the Voice of America. American USIS libraries in other countries are informational and cultural, but specific books and articles that are translated and distributed to foreign nationals through the libraries fit the propaganda category if they are essentially political in content. The Voice of America, whose programs are beamed primarily to countries that restrict the free flow of information to their citizens, is both political and cultural in its content. Recently there has been controversy within the U.S. Information Agency, which controls the Voice of America, over the amount of political news to be carried in broadcasts to Communist countries. Careerists in the agency prefer that the Voice not be a propaganda tool of the U.S. government, while political appointees of the Reagan administration have sought to make the Voice of America, as well as other segments of USIA, more responsive to the ideological objectives of the administration. The debate centers on the assertion that since the Voice of America is a U.S. government operation, it should not try to compete with commercial and nonpolitical news outlets, but instead serve the foreign policy interests of the United States.

Economic and Financial Assistance. As tools of policy, financial assistance and economic aid to another country carry the assumption that the recipient state is sufficiently important to the United States to be assisted by a considerable commitment of U.S. economic resources. Most countries that received large U.S. economic assistance in the past were allied with the United States in mutual security pacts and thus were important to its world-order interests. Others, among them Nigeria and Indonesia, have not concluded mutual security treaties with the United States but are nevertheless considered to be strategically important and therefore worthy of assistance to help them maintain non-Communist regimes.

It is naive to view an economic assistance agreement between the United States and a foreign country as having no political strings attached. If there were no political objectives that Washington and the recipient country could agree upon, it is not likely that Congress would approve the funds. Nonpolitical aid is more likely to be channeled through international organizations, such as U.N. agencies and the World Bank, or private corporations. One reason that the American public and Congress have become disenchanted with large economic and financial assistance programs is that there is too little correlation between U.S. aid and the progress of many recipients toward democratic government. That is why "human rights" amendments were attached to foreign aid legislation in the 1970s and why Congress required the State Department to include human rights considerations in the aid programs that are currently in progress. It is no longer sufficient that the recipient country be a good ally of the United States.

Although economic assistance programs are administered by the Agency for International Development, the Department of Agriculture is also involved through the PL 480 Food for Peace program, and the Treasury Department is instrumental in arranging for credits and low-interest loans to countries that are approved for economic assistance.

Economic and Trade Policy. This instrument of policy has to do with making it easy or difficult for another country to trade with the United States and to obtain international financing for economic development. Whereas U.S. economic and financial assistance, cited above, is provided to allied countries that do not have the resources to build substantial military forces of their own, economic and trade policy involves decisions affecting both developed and developing countries that depend on the U.S. market for trade and on U.S. financial institutions for credits. Mexico, Brazil, Argentina and a few European countries are examples. In addition, the United States maintains import quotas on many foreign products: for example, sugar, coffee, oil, meat, and dairy products. How these quotas are employed to protect domestic producers can have a great effect on the economies of certain countries that depend on these commodities for their economic well-being. Although the United States officially follows free trade policies in industrial goods, many exceptions have been made—notably in steel, automobiles, and machinery—in order to protect domestic industries hard hit by the economic recession of the early 1980s. Another area of economic policy that has generated resentment from European allies is the overvalued dollar, which remains the primary currency of international exchange. U.S. monetary and fiscal policies that affect the value of the dollar and harm other currencies can have serious repercussions on relations with many countries. The inability of their leaders to persuade President Reagan to reduce the huge U.S. budget deficits in 1983 and 1984 was a source of serious political concern to the British, French, and West German governments. Perhaps the most dramatic example of the use of economic policy by a U.S. President was the so-called "Nixon shocks" of August 1971, when President Nixon suddenly announced that the United States would no longer convert dollars into gold and would adopt floating exchange rates. That action signaled to all U.S. trading partners that the U.S. economic interest had moved near the *vital* level and that strong action was required to preserve the nation's economic health. President Reagan's Caribbean Basin economic plan, which became law in 1983, is another example of trade policy used for political purposes—in this case to help friendly neighbors to the south by facilitating their trade with the United States.

Economic and trade policy is decided in the State, Commerce, and Treasury Departments and is normally coordinated with the White House.

Military Assistance. This category of action covers all forms of military assistance, including advisers, training teams, grant-aid equipment as well as the military aircraft, ships, tanks, and other hardware that the United States sells to other countries. The decision to give or sell military equipment abroad is based on a decision by the President that doing so is in the national interest, and it must be approved by Congress. The key consideration is that the recipient country is so important to the U.S. national interest that its military forces should be provided with U.S. military equipment and, if necessary, U.S. advisers. Normally the United States does not give or sell military hardware to another country unless that country is an ally, or unless the U.S. government is convinced that its security is a *major* national interest to this country. For example, neither Saudi Arabia nor Egypt is a formal U.S. ally, but President Reagan decided to sell AWACS planes to the Saudis and advanced fighter planes to the Egyptians because they are friendly to the United States and are willing to assist in the defense of the Persian Gulf. Saudi Arabia is

rich enough that it can buy whatever U.S. military equipment it
needs; the issue for Washington is whether the sale is politically
desirable. In the case of Egypt and most other underdeveloped
countries receiving U.S. military aid, the question is not only
whether granting the aid is desirable, but also how much the
United States should pay.

The problem with military assistance as an instrument of policy is not with allies but with many Third World countries that
desire U.S. equipment and advisers to help them defend against
hostile neighbors. Sudan is an example. This country has little to
offer the United States in terms of bases, or armed forces that
could be used abroad; but Sudan is a close friend of Egypt, and it
feels threatened by Libya and Ethiopia—both of which are friendly to the Soviet Union and receive large amounts of Soviet military aid. But should that make Sudan a very important country
for the United States? El Salvador and other Central American
countries are examples of states close to the U.S. border that have
not previously been given much U.S. military assistance. However, with Nicaragua being armed by the Soviet Union and Cuba,
and providing significant aid to Salvadoran guerrillas, the Reagan
administration had to decide how deeply U.S. interests were
involved and to what extent U.S. military forces should assist the
Salvadoran government to cope with its insurgency. Clearly,
military assistance has a large potential for escalating the degree
of U.S. interest, and policy-makers therefore have an obligation
to limit military aid to the level of interest and not permit the
interest to be driven by a desire to save an investment.

Determining which countries should be given or sold U.S.
military equipment and the amount and nature of the material is
the responsibility of the State Department, which determines the
policy, and the Department of Defense, which administers the
programs. On major arms sales, the President and the respective
committees of Congress are involved.

Covert Actions. Covert actions or operations should be dis-
tinguished from intelligence-gathering activities in that they are
policy actions, decided at the highest level of the U.S. government, intended to influence the decisions of another country. But
they are actions for which the U.S. does not wish to take official

responsibility, and government leaders normally do not comment on them. In the spring of 1983, for example, it was widely reported that the United States was covertly aiding Nicaraguan guerrilla forces operating from Honduras, but Washington was officially silent in response to questions on this issue. All major powers engage to some extent in covert actions, and the Soviet Union's KGB reportedly has the largest such operation in the world. For the United States, the Central Intelligence Agency was given responsibility by the National Security Act of 1947 for carrying out covert actions, and presidents have issued executive orders and other instructions spelling out the controls they want placed on these highly sensitive actions. In the late 1970s Congress decided to place oversight of covert operations in the hands of the Senate and House Select Intelligence Committees. They regularly review proposals approved by the President, after he and the National Security Council decide that a specific covert action is important to the national interest. These special congressional committees have strict security rules and command access to all classified information; they are in a position to veto proposed operations if they feel strongly that they are too risky. The key element in covert actions, from a policy standpoint, is whether their objective is so politically important to U.S. national interests that the U.S. government should risk the embarrassment of having the operation exposed—particularly if it fails. When a covert operation is unsuccessful, as was the Bay of Pigs invasion of Cuba in 1961, the repercussions can be very humiliating. The famous U-2 flight that was shot down over the Soviet Union in 1960 was a bizarre example because President Eisenhower at first denied that the CIA plane was on a spy mission, even though the Kremlin had downed the plane and captured its pilot. In 1984, U.S. covert aid to the Nicaraguan "contras" was so openly discussed in the American press and Congress that "covert" lost much of its meaning. One advantage of a successful covert action is that it may avoid the necessity for the U.S. government to take stronger, more open, more dangerous actions in foreign countries.

A prime question for U.S. policy-makers is whether the use of covert action should be restricted to *vital* national interests or whether they should occasionally be employed also for *major* interests. That usually depends on the risk involved, and recent presidents have tended to limit such activities to only the most important national interests.

U.N. Security Council Debate on a Threat to Peace. Although the United Nations is not held in high esteem by most Americans and has not in recent years been significant in furthering U.S. interests abroad, it nevertheless serves as an important forum when the U.S. government decides that a vital interest may be at stake in an international dispute. Taking an issue to the U.N. Security Council and asking for a debate on a "threat to peace" is a dramatic way of signaling to the world that a vital interest may be at stake and that strong action may be employed to defend an interest. President Kennedy's decision to release aerial intelligence photographs of Cuba, during the 1962 United Nations debate on the missile crisis, was a way of dramatizing to the world his reasons for preparing for war. Another example was President Reagan's decision to release tapes at the United Nations during the debate on the Soviet downing of a Korean airliner in September 1983.

The United States has utilized the U.N. mechanism on many occasions to demonstrate its concern about international events. Other countries have used the Security Council as a forum to attack U.S. policy: for example, Panama's decision in 1964 to appeal to the U.N. after rioting and bloodshed broke out in the Canal Zone. Taking a dispute or crisis to the U.N. Security Council does not commit a country to follow up with military action, but it does signal to an antagonist that the level of national interest is approaching the vital level and that armed forces might be used if an acceptable solution to the problem is not found through negotiations. In this sense, a U.N. debate becomes a dramatic diplomatic signal by the country bringing the complaint.

Trade Embargo and Economic Sanctions. The institution of a trade embargo and/or economic sanctions is a powerful tool of foreign policy because it imposes an economic hardship on another state. This condition prevailed in 1983 between the United States and Iran, Cuba, Libya, Vietnam, and several other countries the United States considers to be hostile. President Reagan's economic sanctions on Poland following the impositionof martial law there in 1981 made it extremely difficult for the Warsaw government to obtain assistance from Western banks and all but closed American markets to Polish exports. These sanctions were eased somewhat in 1983. Suspension of trade with Cuba during the early 1960s shut off the important U.S. sugar market to Cuban exports and had a serious effect on that country's economy. A similar measure was adopted regarding Nicaragua's sugar quota to the United States in 1983. A trade embargo is not usually imposed unless the President concludes that the government of another state has flagrantly violated U.S. laws or international agreements and is considered to have committed an unfriendly act. The Reagan administration's decision in 1982 to ban the sale of equipment for building the Siberian gas pipeline from the Soviet Union to Western Europe was an economic sanction that proved adverse to U.S. interests among its NATO partners, and the decision was modified later that year. Economic sanctions may affect important domestic interests and prove to be politically embarrassing. President Carter's decision to ban the sale of additional grain to the Soviet Union, following the Soviet invasion of Afghanistan, was highly unpopular with American farmers, and candidate Ronald Reagan exploited this fact in his 1980 presidential election campaign.

Economic sanctions and a trade embargo are decided by the President and his National Security Council, and the decisions are implemented by the State, Commerce and Treasury Departments.

Military Instruments

Military show of strength. When a president wants to demonstrate deep concern about an international issue that might become a crisis, he can order U.S. naval forces to proceed to the troubled area, alert U.S. Air Force units, and place the Army's airborne divisions in a higher state of readiness. These actions show possible intent to use these forces but do not commit a president to do so. When Richard Nixon alerted U.S. forces in October 1973, following receipt of a threatening message from Soviet General Secretary Brezhnev, the implication was clear: if Moscow moved airborne troops into Egypt, the United States might counter that airlift with its aircraft and thus risk a war with the Soviet Union. The crisis passed when Washington persuaded Israel to accept a cease-fire. Similarly, in early 1983, American AWACS planes were sent to Egypt and a carrier task force was ordered to the Gulf of Sidra when intelligence information showed that Libya might try to invade Sudan or support an insurrection there—in an effort to topple the pro-Western government. In response to the Soviet invasion of Afghanistan in December 1979, the United States expanded its Indian Ocean forces and concentrated additional naval power in the region of the Persian Gulf—in anticipation that Moscow might try to destabilize Iran and establish its influence in this vital oil region. The Soviet move also prompted President Jimmy Carter to declare a few weeks later that the Persian Gulf was a "vital" American interest.

A military show of strength, particularly if there is a strong possibility of armed clashes, lies at the threshhold of war and should not be used as a tool of policy unless an interest is clearly *vital*. To use it as a bluff can be dangerous if an adversary challenges it. This happened in Laos in March 1961 when President John Kennedy dramatically warned the Soviet Union to restrain Laotian Communist forces from approaching the Mekong River. After alerting U.S. Far Eastern naval and air units to be prepared for war, the President backed off this bellicose line, and the Pathet Lao continued their advance—to the dismay of all the countries in Southeast Asia.

When a President decides on a military show of strength, it is carried out by the Department of Defense. The Navy is most often initially called upon for these missions because warships can be deployed easily in many parts of the world, and they convey an important political message without arousing the tensions that accompany the deployment of troops.

Expanded military surveillance. This policy action is often, but not always, part of a military show of strength; it heightens the tensions and signals an antagonist that its military moves are being closely monitored. Like a show of strength, it dramatizes concern and suggests intent to use force without committing a country to do so. President Kennedy's use of U-2 flights during the Cuban missile crisis was a clear warning to the Soviet leadership that he knew what military preparations they were conducting in Cuba and that he was preparing to use force. After the Iran-Iraq war erupted in 1980, the President dispatched AWACS planes to Saudi Arabia as a warning to the Iranian government that the United States would act if Iran invaded Saudi air space or interfered with tanker traffic in the Strait of Hormuz. During the Falkland Islands crisis, U.S. reconnaisance planes patrolled the British air and sea routes in the South Atlantic to warn against possible Soviet efforts to interfere with the British war effort.

Although the Defense Department carries out military surveillance operations, the Central Intelligence Agency is also involved in keeping Soviet and other hostile forces under increased surveillance during times of crisis.

Suspension/Break in Diplomatic Relations. A suspension or break in relations is the strongest diplomatic measure available to a government to show displeasure with the actions of another state. Traditionally, it was the final action taken before declaring war. Since World War II, this has occurred occasionally even though the action no longer usually leads to hostilities. Most Arab states, for example, broke diplomatic relations with the United States during the Arab-Israeli War of October 1973, to show displeasure over President Nixon's decision to resupply Israeli military forces. The United States broke diplomatic relations with Libya in 1981 to show its displeasure over that country's support for international terrorists. Diplomatic relations were broken between Iran and the United States after the Teheran Government condoned the capture of the U.S. Embassy in 1979 and approved the capture of fifty-two U.S. diplomats. Even though a rupture in diplomatic relations does not suggest that war is imminent, it does mean that hostile policies and perhaps limited conflict could occur. After the United States broke relations with Libya, an aircraft carrier of the U.S. 6th Fleet was ordered into the Gulf of Sidra to demonstrate that the United States considered it to be international waters. The fact that U.S. planes shot down two Libyan aircraft that had launched an attack was clear evidence that breaking diplomatic relations was a prelude to a more forceful military policy.

A suspension or break in relations is carried out by the State

Department after the President decides that tensions with another country have reached a dangerous level. Such a break is usually accompanied by a decision to instruct private American citizens to leave the country in question because their safety cannot be insured.

Blockade/Quarantine. A blockade is an act of war under international law, and nations therefore rarely impose one unless they are ready for armed conflict. During the Cuban misile crisis in 1962, the United States imposed a selective blockade on ships entering Cuba's harbors and called it a "quarantine" in order to avoid the legal ramifications of a blockade. President Kennedy stated that the quarantine was to prevent war materials from entering Cuba and to prevent the Soviet Union from completing its missile bases on the island. Although the United States claimed that it intended to prevent only military goods from reaching Cuba, the Soviet Union protested that this was a hostile act; yet it did not order its ships to run the naval barrier that the U.S. established. The quarantine brought on the most serious crisis in U.S.-Soviet relations that has occurred since World War II. The mining of Haiphong Harbor by U.S. forces in the spring of 1972 was an equally daring action by President Nixon, who was convinced that only strong military action would cause the Hanoi government to negotiate seriously about ending the Vietnam War. A blockade or quarantine does not necessarily mean that hostilities will commence; but the flash point has been reached, and the contending parties know that hostilities could occur at any time.

The Navy is the instrument by which a quarantine or blockade is implemented, after the President determines that very strong action is required to demonstrate that a vital interest is at stake.

Localized Use of Conventional Forces. When a government decides to send its military forces to another country, it must plan for the probability that they will be engaged in hostilities even though they may initially be sent to serve in a peacekeeping role designed to prevent hostilities. The decision to introduce forces into another country is an act of war unless the host government requests them and supports their presence on its soil. Most U.S.

interventions since World War II have been at the request of other countries: President Truman's decision to send U.S. forces to aid South Korea in June 1950; President Eisenhower's dispatch of U.S. Marines to Lebanon in 1958; President Kennedy's sending of combat teams to Vietnam in 1962; President Johnson's use of U.S. forces in the Dominican Republic in 1965; and President Carter's dispatch of peacekeeping forces to the Sinai in 1979. Except for Truman's decision in 1950 and Kennedy's in 1962, these deployments of U.S. military forces abroad were essentially peacekeeping actions. The same was true of President Reagan's decision in August 1982 to send U.S. Marines to Beirut; their purpose was to prevent further bloodshed in Lebanon's civil war and to facilitate the withdrawal of Israeli, Syrian, and PLO forces from Lebanon. The Soviet Union used its forces in Hungary in 1956 and in Czechoslovakia in 1968 to install a new political leadership in two Warsaw Pact countries. In neither case did the Soviet Union claim that it sent forces at the request of the host government. In December 1979, the Soviet Union sent its forces into Afghanistan to rid the country of a leadership that had refused to cooperate with Moscow. The sending of combat forces to another country is usually a sign that a vital interest is at stake, but the deployment of peacekeeping troops to a trouble spot does not necessarily mean that the defense of that specific country is a vital interest. Lebanon, for example, is not a U.S. ally and is not a vital interest, either; however, peace in the Middle East and the defense of Israel are U.S. vital interests, and President Reagan's decision to send Marines there in 1982 was a signal that he believed the continuing war in Lebanon could endanger the peace of the whole area.

Armed intervention usually is accomplished by U.S. Marines, the U.S. Army, or both. The U.S. intervention on a large scale in Vietnam in 1965 began with the dispatch of Marines and was followed a few months later by large contingents of the Army. Although the Navy and Air Force usually support armed interventions, they do not by themselves undertake them.

Partial Mobilization and Nuclear Alert. If conventional military forces are introduced into a region and there is a strong possibility that they will be fighting against the troops of another major power, a President would have to adopt many precautionary measures. One of these is to call up reserve units; another is to place controls on the U.S. economy and allocate scarce materials; still another would be to request increases in the defense budget and a renewal of conscription. The President would also put all U.S. forces in a state of readiness appropriate to the increased tensions and the possibility of a larger war. All these measures are precautionary, but they convey a significant message to other powers: a vital interest of the United States is engaged and its government will use whatever force is required to insure that the interest is protected. These measures do not preclude diplomatic negotiations to try to resolve the crisis before war occurs, but they clearly show that the United States is deadly serious. President Truman's actions following the outbreak of war in Korea in June 1950 are a classic example of the use of this policy tool. President Kennedy's response to the Berlin crisis in 1961 and his bold actions during the Cuban missile crisis in 1962 also fit this category. President Johnson, however, did not choose to take many of these actions when he escalated the Vietnam conflict in 1965, largely because he did not wish to provoke China's intervention—as President Truman had done in Korea in 1950 by authorizing General MacArthur to take his troops to the Yalu River. President Nixon alerted U.S. forces during the Arab-Israeli conflict of 1973, but the fighting stopped before Soviet or U.S. forces were deployed.

Since the United States abolished military conscription during the Nixon administration, a President can no longer on his own authority induct additional recruits into the Armed Forces in time of danger. Furthermore, he must obtain from Congress the authority to declare a national emergency in order that the economic policies contained in this category can be implemented. Finally, Congress can monitor presidential actions under the 1973 War Powers Act and may terminate a military action after sixty days. Mobilization would be carried out by the Federal Emergency Management Agency (FEMA) and the Department of Defense, with control being exercised by the White House through the National Security Council.

Localized Use of Tactical Nuclear Weapons. There is much debate today about whether the use of tactical (battlefield) nuclear weapons is a viable military action. So long as the United States had a near-monopoly on these kinds of weapons, they could be justified as contributing to NATO's nuclear deterrence of the Soviet Union. The basing of substantial numbers of U.S. tactical nuclear weapons in Europe (about 6,000 in 1983) made it possible over the years for NATO to compensate for the large superiority in conventional forces enjoyed by the Warsaw Pact. Even though the Soviet Union now has substantial numbers of these weapons, and could retaliate in kind if they were used first by NATO forces, tactical nuclear weapons have not lost deterrent value; Moscow cannot assume that NATO would refrain from using them if the Soviets launched a massive conventional attack on Western Europe and threatened to push to the English Channel. That would quickly become a survival interest for NATO. President Brezhnev sought to exploit this point in 1982 by pledging never to use nuclear weapons first and asking NATO to do the same. So long as NATO conventional forces are substantially smaller than those of the Warsaw Pact, however, a mutual pledge against "first use" would increase the danger to West European security.

Obviously, no American president and no European prime minister would seriously consider using any of these nuclear weapons unless a "survival interest" were at stake in Europe. This means that West German and American leaders would have to make an agonizing decision, probably within forty-eight hours of the outbreak of a conventional war, either to be conquered by Soviet armies or to grant NATO military commanders authority to use battlefield nuclear weapons. The only other places where tactical nuclear weapons might be used by the United States would be in the Persian Gulf, to stop a Soviet-led attack on the Strait of Hormuz, or in Korea if the Soviet Union aided in an attack there. President Carter and his Secretary of Defense, Harold Brown, warned Moscow in 1980 that the use of U.S. nuclear weapons could not be ruled out if Kremlin leaders decided to take advantage of turmoil in Iran to try to gain control of the oil-rich Persian Gulf.

In the mid-1980s no U.S. president can contemplate the actual use of tactical nuclear weapons, either in Europe or from aircraft carriers operating in the Indian Ocean, without taking into account the strong possibility that even the limited use of tactical nuclear weapons could quickly escalate into an intercontinental nuclear war. Therefore, nuclear weapons of any kind should not be threatened or used for anything less than a *survival* interest.

Threatened Use of Strategic Nuclear Weapons. Many argue that employing this policy option is either suicidal or pure bluff. Yet strategic deterrent strategy has long been based on threatened nuclear retaliation on Soviet territory if Moscow attacks Europe with conventional forces. The real question is whether this is a rational policy option in the 1980s, when Moscow enjoys at least parity in strategic nuclear weapons with the United States, including a reliable second-strike capability that could devastate significant parts of the United States. On the one side, it is argued that war between the United States and the Soviet Union has been averted for nearly forty years because of the fear of nuclear weapons being used if the superpowers engage in conventional war. On the other side, critics charge that it is insanity for Moscow or Washington to threaten the other because both will be destroyed if the threat is carried out.

Whether one believes that a threat to use strategic nuclear forces against the homeland of a superpower is a rational or a lunatic option, the fact remains that both U.S. and Soviet military strategy envisages conditions under which such weapons would be used and calculates the devastation that would result. The difference in these views is that until the Reagan administration assumed power in 1981, Soviet leaders believed that their homeland could survive a nuclear attack, while most American planners were never persuaded that either side could sustain a nuclear exchange and have its institutions and much of its population survive. Defense Secretary Caspar Weinberger's strategic guidance to the military services, beginning in 1982, envisioned the likelihood that the United States not only could survive but indeed prevail in a nuclear war, a calculation that is challenged by many U.S. civilian as well as military leaders.

For West Europeans, the crucial issue in 1983 was whether they should proceed with plans to deploy medium-range nuclear missiles capable of itting targets in the Soviet Union—to balance Soviet medium-range SS-20 nuclear missiles already deployed in Eastern Europe and capable of striking every major city in Western Europe. American Pershing II missiles, which were deployed in West Germany late in 1983, are viewed by the Kremlin as first-strike weapons because the warning time from launch to impact is about seven minutes. U.S. cruise missiles, scheduled for deployment in Italy, Britain, Belgium, and Holland, are slower and therefore are not perceived as quite so threatening to the Soviet Union. President Reagan offered in November 1981 to cancel deployment of both weapons if Moscow dismantled its more than 300 SS-20 missiles already aimed at Western Europe. Britain and France each have an independent nuclear capability, primarily in submarines; so the introduction of Pershing II and cruise missiles would extend a nuclear retaliatory capability to West Germany and other NATO states—although the U.S. President would control their use. Clearly, no European or American leader would contemplate threatening to use these weapons unless a *survival* interest were at stake.

Limited Use of Strategic Nuclear Weapons. The final awesome step a president could take before all-out nuclear war occurs is a limited demonstration of intention to engage in nuclear war—in order to convince an enemy that the United States will not capitulate. Former Secretary of State Alexander Haig—in trying to clarify an alarming remark by President Reagan in 1981 to the effect that the United States might be prepared to fight a nuclear war (which many Europeans concluded would be fought in Europe rather than in the United States and the Soviet Union)—stated that NATO planners had long considered a warning nuclear shot as a way to convince Moscow not to assume that a conventional attack on Western Europe would go unanswered if NATO forces were losing. One reason that President Reagan wants the B-1 bomber in the U.S. nuclear arsenal, despite its enormous cost, is that it is a strategic weapon which can be controlled after launch, whereas an ICBM or submarine-launched missile cannot under current technology be destroyed or diverted from its target, once fired. The intercontinental bomber is a means of demonstrating U.S. capability and intent to use nuclear weapons without actually dropping them. Carrier-based bombers stationed in the Indian Ocean or the Mediterranean have a similar capability; they can fly near Soviet territory and drop a small nuclear bomb at sea or in a desert to demonstrate that the United States is at the survival level of interest and that the two sides must stop the confrontation before they are destroyed. The "hot-line" established between the White House and the Kremlin following the Cuban missile crisis presumably would be in regular use during such a confrontation.

Summing Up: Correlation of Interests and Instruments

This discussion leads to a number of conclusions about the significance of policy tools in support of national interests. First of all, none of the first eleven policy instruments entails the use of force or threatened use of force. They are political, economic, and psychological measures that can be used to persuade the leaders of another country to do what the U.S. government desires, but they do not employ or threaten to use American military power. In general, these eleven instruments of policy are employed to support *major* interests of the United States abroad, although the last several may signal that the issue is approaching the vital level.

The last nine policy tools clearly entail an escalating use of U.S. military pressure to achieve a desired result in relations with an adversary state. They are employed to defend or enhance *vital* and *survival* interests. We may therefore conclude that the threshhold between a *major* and a *vital* interest rests somewhere near options 11 and 12: a trade embargo and a military show of strength.

If a vital interest is defined as an international issue that cannot be negotiated beyond a certain point because the consequences would be intolerable to a country's well-being, a show of military power might then be used to demonstrate determination not to compromise. Whether a military show of force and increased military surveillance are measures a President *should* take when he does not consider the issue to be vital, and does not plan to use force, is a crucial matter; for unless a President engages in bluff, one must conclude that these steps are demonstrations of intent to use force. President Reagan's decision to send a carrier task force into the Gulf of Sidra in 1981 was a military show of strength that was backed up with military action. A military show of force as bluff, however, is dangerous because an unintended war may result if the bluff is called by an adversary.

Figure 5 is an attempt to establish a correlation between the twenty instruments of policy and the degree of national interest at

Fig. 5. National Interests and Instruments of Policy

Basic Interests				Intensity of Interest	Policy Tools
Defense of Home-land	World Order	Economic Well-Being	Promo-tion of Values	Peripheral	Diplomatic relations
				Peripheral	Scientific and cultural exchanges
				Peripheral	Humanitarian assistance
				Peripheral	Technical assistance
				Peripheral	Information and propaganda
				Major	Economic and financial assistance
				Major	Economic and trade policy
				Major	Military assistance
				Major	Covert actions
				Major	U.N. Security Council debate
				Major	Trade embargo and economic sanctions
				Vital	Military show of strength
				Vital	Increased military surveillance
				Vital	Suspension of/ break in diplomatic relations
				Vital	Quarantine/ blockade/ mining of ports
				Vital	Local use of conventional force
				Survival	Partial mobilization/ evacuation
				Survival	Local use of tactical nuclear weapons
				Survival	Threatened use of strategic nuclear weapons
				Survival	Limited use of strategic nuclear weapons

stake. The implication of this juxtaposition of interests and policy tools is that policy planners and decision-makers should employ only those measures of influence, pressure, and force that are commensurate with the level of national interest involved in a specific foreign policy or national security issue. To overreact in the use of economic or military pressure may make a crisis worse than intended and result in an unwanted war; to underreact to provocation or external pressure may lead an opponent to conclude that your national interest is not high, or that you lack the will to defend it. President John Kennedy cited this problem after his meeting with Nikita Khrushchev in Vienna in June 1961: the Soviet leader did not believe the American President would use force in Berlin, Laos, or Cuba.

Matching the intensities of interest in foreign policy issues with the instruments of policy available to a President is an essential way of thinking through the problem of how the United States ought to react to serious issues and crises. The process should entail three steps, as suggested in Figure 5: first, an assessment of which basic interests are most affected; second, a determination of the intensity of interests, especially if any of them is at or near the vital level; third, a selection of the appropriate policy tools. The horizontal lines suggest the instruments of policy that are appropriate for each basic interest, with defense-of-homeland embracing all of them. The chart suggests that the first eleven instruments of policy are appropriate responses when any basic interest is affected at the *major* level. If the interest in question is U.S. values (ideology)—for example, the Soviet shooting-down of a Korean commercial airliner in September 1983—the U.S. government is justified in using any policy tools up to and including a trade embargo to show displeasure. If the interest at stake is economic well-being and the intensity is believed to be *vital*, the policy instruments employed could include any of the first thirteen, including increased surveillance and a show of strength. If the interest involved is world order and a decision is reached that the intensity is *vital*, appropriate policy tools could include suspension of diplomatic relations, a quarantine or blockade of ports, and local use of U.S. conventional forces to convince an opponent that things have reached the intolerable point and force will be used. The Reagan administration's policy toward Nicaragua in the summer of 1983 suggested it had decided on this level of intensity; U.S. military forces were then introduced into Honduras, and the U.S. Navy sent aircraft carriers and other warships to the waters off Nicaragua.

Figure 5 also suggests that a partial mobilization of U.S. reserves, evacuation of policy-makers to command posts, and threats to use nuclear weapons should be limited to the *survival* level of interest. This means that these instruments of policy should not be employed unless there is a direct threat to the U.S. homeland, not simply to U.S. forces stationed abroad. Mobilization of reserves and preparation to use nuclear weapons, therefore, is the threshhold between a vital and a survival interest and must be calculated with extreme care. The Cuban missile crisis was instructive in this regard because President Kennedy wanted to demonstrate to Chairman Khrushchev that the Soviet leader had seriously miscalculated in thinking that the United States would accept Soviet missiles so close to U.S. territory. Through his actions Kennedy signaled that he believed the provocation to be near the survival level and that he would go to war to force the Kremlin to dismantle the missiles. No other crisis—Berlin, Middle East, Taiwan, Vietnam—reached this level of intensity because no other threat directly affected the U.S. or the Soviet homeland.

As the United States decides what its national interests are during the coming decade and builds its economic and military strength to defend them, it is essential that political leaders clearly understand for what ends this growing power should be used. A clear lesson of the 1960s is that U.S. military and economic power should not be squandered on secondary interests, such as Southeast Asia,which are not central to the defense and security of North America and Western Europe. That lesson ought not to be relearned in the 1980s.

3. North America: The Neglected Heartland

Since World War II the United States has been so extensively involved in world security that it has lost sight of the crucial importance to its defense, economic, world-order and ideological interests of the twenty-odd countries that comprise North America. Policy-makers have used the concept of Latin America or the Western Hemisphere to describe an area that is considered to be of special geographical interest to the United States. Yet, by using "Latin America" to describe the countries of this hemisphere, Americans totally ignore Canada—our most important defense outpost as well as trading partner—and the English-speaking islands of the Caribbean. Even the term "Western Hemisphere" is ambiguous because it suggests that all countries in both North and South America are roughly equal in terms of U.S. interests. Clearly they are not. By no stretch of the imagination is Argentina, Chile, or Brazil as important to the United States as is Canada, Mexico or Venezuela. Nevertheless, the Monroe Doctrine legacy with its blanket pledge of protection for all of the former Spanish and Portuguese colonies lingers on. This concept was reinforced by the Rio Pact of 1947, which bound the countries of Latin America together with the United States into a Western Hemisphere security treaty. Canada is not a member of this treaty; instead it joined the North Atlantic Pact in 1949.

No other major power in the world takes its neighbors so for granted as does the United States. This is the product of our geography, our huge size and population compared with other North American countries and, until recently, our invulnerability to attack from overseas. An added factor is that the U.S. economy has been so dynamic and is growing at such a rapid pace that all North American countries have become dependent on it for their economic well-being. History has played a part. From 1814 onward, the United States was confronted in this continent by no other great power, and the country could grow and prosper because Great Britain found that its own national interest was served by encouraging the ex-colonies to carve out a continental nation and eventually to ally itself with Britain against hostile European powers. U.S. wars against Mexico in the mid-nineteenth century, and against Spain as the century ended, left the United States as the overwhelming power in North America. As a result, it fought in two world wars without ever having to worry that its homeland would be invaded.

Emerging from World War II as the preeminent world power, the U.S. and its leaders set about creating a new world order while paying less attention to U.S. interests in North America, except for agreements with Canada to create a North American defense zone and for continued occupation of the Panama Canal Zone. Having secured its defense to the north as well as in the Caribbean, American foreign policy gave a low priority to the economic and political problems of Latin America, particularly to countries on our own doorstep. That remained the case until 1960, when Fidel Castro turned Cuba into an anti-American Marxist state and preached revolution throughout Latin America. To underscore how much Washington took its North American interests for granted, the State Department's Office of Canadian Affairs is still part of the Bureau of European Affairs, although in September 1983 the bureau added Canada to its nomenclature. The Joint Chiefs of Staff in the Pentagon are more realistic: in their directorate for defense planning, Canada is part of the Western Hemisphere. To date, no department of the U.S. government has an Office of North American Affairs. That symbolizes the United States' blind spot about the priority of its national interests.

If one draws a circle around North America that includes Hawaii in the West, Canada and Alaska in the North, Greenland in the northeast, and Panama, Colombia and Venezuela in the South, the area included in the circle constitutes the defense-of-homeland interest of the United States. Although this circle includes two countries in South America (Venezuela and Colombia), their bordering on what President Reagan in 1982 renamed the Caribbean Basin and their large trade and cultural ties to North America make them a part of this North American community of interest. It is no coincidence that this circle of countries is also the most important U.S. economic interest. Canada is by far the largest U.S. trading partner, Mexico is third (behind Japan), and Venezuela is in the top ten. Most of the Central American and Caribbean countries have their primary trading relationships with the United States. Canadian trade with the Caribbean and Mexico is growing significantly, and Canadian tourism in that area and in the United States is enormous. The impact of the Spanish language and culture on the United States today is staggering, and illegal migration of Spanish-speaking people to the United States is nearly uncontrollable.

The obvious conclusion that must be drawn from the history of North America during the last twenty years is that not only the United States but all of this area is rapidly becoming one huge melting pot of language, culture, trade, tourism, and sports. It seems inevitable that the economies of North America will be further integrated in the coming decade, and the question then will be, should a political integration of the North American countries follow? Regardless of the answer, this area is the most important priority of U.S. interests anywhere in the world and will remain so.

U.S. Interests in North America

U.S. national interests in two basic categories—defense-of-homeland and favorable-world-order—are at the *vital* level or higher when viewing the North American continent and adjacent areas (see Figure 6). For example, Canadian air space is nearly synonymous with U.S. air space in terms of defense against Soviet intercontinental missiles and long-range bombers. Any threat to Canadian territory by the Soviet Union would be viewed as a *survival* defense interest by U.S. leaders. On the other hand, a reduction in U.S.-Canadian trade relations would be viewed as a major, not a vital, interest because it would not be shattering to the American economy. A case in point was the Trudeau govern-

Fig. 6. U.S. National Interests in North America

Basic Interest at Stake	Intensity of Interest			
	Survival	Vital	Major	Peripheral
Defense of Homeland	Canada	Central America	Venezuela	
	Mexico	Caribbean Is.		
Economic Well-Being		Canada	Central America	
		Mexico	Venezuela	
			Caribbean Is.	
Favorable World Order		Canada		
		Mexico		
		Central America		
		Venezuela		
		Caribbean Is.		
Promotion of Values		Canada	Central America	
		Mexico	Caribbean Is.	
		Venezuela		

ment's decision in 1980 to restrict U.S. private oil companies' exploitation of Canada's energy resources. This decision was painful for some U.S. commercial interests, and Canada's western provinces lost considerable U.S. private investment and other business as a result; but neither the Canadian nor the U.S. economy was seriously damaged. Nevertheless, if the Canadian government adopted a comprehensive protectionist trade policy against U.S. exports, this would quickly escalate into a vital U.S. economic interest. To the south, the United States has a vital interest in insuring that the security of the Caribbean Islands, Central America and Mexico are not upset by revolutionary forces aided by Cuba and the Soviet Union.

The United States is no exception to the rule that all major powers have a deep interest in preventing hostile political forces from gaining control of countries on their borders. In early 1983, for example, Soviet party leader Yuri Andropov commented in an interview with the West German magazine *Der Spiegel:* "Would the United States not care what kind of government rules in

Nicaragua? Nicaragua is an enormous distance from America. We have a common border with Afghanistan, and we are defending our national interests by helping Afghanistan."[1] Mr. Andropov drew the analogy to show that his country's national interest in a neighboring country is just as legitimate as the U.S. concern over what is happening in Central America. Within the whole Caribbean Basin area, however, some countries clearly are more essential to U.S. security than others. This was the nub of the debate within the United States over how to deal with subversion in El Salvador, Honduras, Guatemala, and some Caribbean island nations. The security of this region was raised to large proportions in Washington during 1983 and early 1984.

In 1978, the Carter administration achieved ratification of the new Panama Canal treaties by persuading enough senators that the canal was a *major* U.S. interest, not vital, and that the U.S. government should therefore take the risk that Panama would itself protect the canal because it was in its own interest to do so. Cuban-supported subversion of all of Central America was a different matter, however. Even before the Carter administration left office in January 1981, it abandoned its belief that Nicaragua would become a democratic state, following the revolution against the Somoza dictatorship in 1979. The Reagan administration viewed the new Sandinista government's support for Marxist revolutions in El Salvador and elsewhere as a *vital* U.S. interest, but many members of Congress disagreed and believed they had as much right to determine the intensity of U.S. interest in that region as the State and Defense Departments, and the President himself. In sum, during 1981 and 1982, there was no agreement within the American government about the level of national interest in specific parts of the Caribbean Basin, particularly when the issue was social justice within the countries concerned. In the absence of a clear Soviet and Cuban military threat, many Americans simply doubted that the United States should be involved.

Few Americans doubt that the United States has vital interests, even a survival one, in Canada. This commitment goes back to 1940, when President Franklin Roosevelt held a historic meeting

1. *New York Times,* 24 April 1983, p. 10.

with Prime Minister Mackenzie King in Ogdensburg, New York—following the fall of France to German armies—and concluded an agreement that the two countries would cooperate to defend North America against attack by the Axis powers. After the war, the two countries continued their close defense relationship by joining the North Atlantic Pact in 1949 and concluding the North American Air Defense Accord of 1958, which established a joint military command to provide for the air defense of North America. Canada is the largest customer for United States exports and is the source of a huge amount of tourism. Private U.S. companies have invested nearly $40 billion in Canada. Together, the two countries constitute a zone of 260 million democratically governed people. American presidents and Canadian prime ministers meet frequently on both official and unofficial visits, and their foreign and defense ministers are in constant contact. Although there are occasional serious policy differences in the economic and environmental areas, and occasional differences in the way the two countries view events in other parts of the world, on defense matters and relations with the Soviet Union the two countries have a strong mutuality of interests. Americans may be divided on whether and how to use U.S. forces to defend distant parts of the world, but there is little doubt among most of them that a military threat to any part of Canada would be a threat to U.S. territory. This strong bond was reinforced in April 1983 when Prime Minister Pierre Elliott Trudeau, during a visit to Washington, D.C., said Canada would approve the testing of cruise missiles on Canadian soil—despite strong public protests by peace demonstrators in Canada. The Prime Minister tied this pledge to continued efforts by the U.S. government to reach arms control agreements with the Soviet Union, on which he said the Reagan administration had demonstrated its good intentions.

In sum, Canada and the United States form one of the strongest bonds of friendship on basic defense and foreign policy matters existing between neighboring countries anywhere in the world today. Even though there are strains in economic relations, and interest groups in both countries carp at each other for exploiting the relationship, the United States and Canada are deepening the close strategic relationship that began over forty years ago. This is because their defense interests as well as their world-order and ideological interests are in basic harmony and will continue to be so in the foreseeable future.[2]

The consensus that exists in the northern part of North America does not, however, extend to the southern region— Mexico, Central America, the islands of the Caribbean, and the northern tier of South America. These countries have as one of their primary national interests a resistance to U.S. encroachments on their sovereignty; the history of U.S. military intervention in this area since the turn of the century (longer in the case of Mexico) makes them suspicious of U.S. intentions—especially since their economies are closely tied to U.S. markets. Whereas U.S. defense and world-order interests in Central America are rising rapidly, because of Marxist revolutionary inroads made with the support of Cuba and the Soviet Union, there is no correspondingly strong interest by most of these countries to draw closer to the United States. Nevertheless, Latin Americans living in the Caribbean Basin have a strong cultural and economic attraction to the United States. This ambivalence in their view is reflected in the changing ethnic composition of the U.S. population—which is becoming increasingly Hispanic.

Whereas Canadians have memories of U.S. efforts to incorporate their lands into the United States—dating back to the Revolutionary War and the War of 1812—they know that the U.S. government will not send U.S. troops to Canada unless there is an attack from outside North America; but this Canadian confidence is not shared by the people and governments south of the U.S. border. They remember covert U.S. intervention in Guatemala in 1954, covert U.S. involvement in the Bay of Pigs invasion of Cuba in 1961, and *overt* U.S. military intervention in the Dominican Republic in 1965. Revelations in the spring of 1983 about covert U.S. support of anti-Sandinista groups operating within Marxist Nicaragua reinforced the concerns of leaders throughout the region that the United States was preparing once again to intervene in

2. This is not to say that the Canadian government never criticizes the United States. For example, the *Washington Post* carried an article on May 15, 1983, entitled, "Trudeau Criticizes U.S. View of the Soviets," which reported that Canadian Prime Minister Trudeau had publicly deplored President Reagan's strong criticism of the Soviet Union and its leaders, saying that it "justifies fears that he is warlike."

Central America to force the ouster of the Sandinista government. The U.S. invasion of Grenada in October 1983 further
heightened these fears. For the United States, the challenge was
to define accurately the level of U.S. interests in the southern
sector of North America and then to devise policies that would
enhance those interests, while at the same time allaying the fears
and building the confidence of political opinion in the countries
located in the Caribbean Basin area.

President Reagan's Definition of U.S. Interests
in Central America

On April 27, 1983, President Reagan made an extraordinary
effort to focus U.S. public attention on these issues by addressing
a joint session of Congress—a rare occurrence in U.S. political
history. Because Mr. Reagan's address was so explicit on defining
the U.S. stake in this region, his arguments are quoted here at
some length.

The President began his congressional address by saying that
in the past, presidents had addressed joint sessions of Congress
in order to resolve crises, but that he had sought this forum in
order "that we can prevent one." He said that "too many have
thought of Central America as a place way down below Mexico
that can not possibly constitute a threat to our well-being," and
that he had decided to go before a joint session of Congress
because "Central America's problems do directly affect the security and well-being of our own people." Putting U.S. priorities
in geographical perspective, he said that Central America "is
much closer to the United States than many of the world trouble
spots that concern us." Pointing out that El Salvador is closer to
Texas than Texas is to Massachusetts, the President asserted that
"nearness on the map does not even begin to tell the strategic
importance of Central America, bordering as it does on the Caribbean—our lifeline to the outside world." He cited the statistic that
two-thirds of all U.S. foreign trade and petroleum pass through
the Panama Canal and the Caribbean, and that in a European
crisis "at least half of our supplies for NATO would go through
these areas by sea." It was well to remember, he reminded his
audience, that in World War II, German submarines sank more

tonnage in the Caribbean then they did in the entire Atlantic Ocean and that "they did this without a single naval base anywhere in the area." Today, the situation is different, he asserted: "Cuba is host to a Soviet combat brigade, to a submarine base capable of servicing Soviet submarines, and to military air bases visited regularly by Soviet military aircraft. Because of its importance, the Caribbean Basin is a magnet for adventurism," the President warned.

President Reagan underlined his view with this statement: "If the Nazis during World War II and the Soviets today could recognize the Caribbean and Central America as vital to our interests, should not we also?" The President reassured his country and Latin America that he was not contemplating the use of American combat forces in Central America, because they were not needed and not requested. But he made it clear that economic and military assistance was required in far greater quantities if the countries of the region were to stop the Marxist revolutionary offensive "threatening the governments of every country in Central America." He asked rhetorically: "Are democracies required to remain passive while threats to their security and prosperity accumulate? Must we just accept the destabilization of an entire region from the Panama Canal to Mexico on our southern border? Must we sit by while independent nations of this hemisphere are integrated into the most aggressive empire the modern world has seen?"

In conclusion, Mr. Reagan summed up his belief that the United States needed to become very serious about the depth of its national interests in the Caribbean and Central America:

> In summation, I say to you that tonight there can be no question: The national security of all the Americas is at stake in Central America. If we cannot defend ourselves there, we cannot expect to prevail elsewhere. Our credibility would collapse, our alliances would crumble and the safety of our homeland would be put at jeopardy. We have a vital interest, a moral duty and solemn responsibility. This is not a partisan issue. It is a question of our meeting our moral responsibility to ourselves, our friends and our posterity. It is a duty that falls to all of us—the President, the Congress

and the people. We must perform it together. Who among us would wish to bear responsibility for failing to meet our shared obligation?[3]

President Reagan's dramatic enunciation of his conclusion that the United States has a vital interest at stake in Central America set off a national debate in the United States—as it was designed to do—around the issue of what policies the government would be permitted to pursue in support of those interests. Congress was divided, reflecting divisions in the American public. The issue was debated along partisan lines, with Democratic law-makers—particularly from New England and the eastern sea-board—challenging the President's definition of U.S. interests south of the border, particularly his policies for defending them.

Congressional Democrats chose Connecticut Senator Christopher J. Dodd to reply on national television to President Reagan's April 27 address. His view of U.S. interests in Central America did not differ significantly from those of the President, but his recommended policies to support these interests were quite different. Senator Dodd started by agreeing with the President on the fundamental defense and world-order interests of the United States in Central America:

> We will oppose the establishment of Marxist states in Central America. We will not accept the creation of Soviet military bases in Central America. We will not tolerate the placement of Soviet offensive missiles in Central America— or anywhere in this hemisphere. Finally we are fully prepared to defend our security and the security of the Americas, if necessary, by military means. All patriotic Americans share these goals. But many of us in Congress, Democrats and Republicans alike, disagree with the President because we believe the means he has chosen will not fulfill them. Those of us who oppose the President's policy believe that he is mistaken in critical ways. To begin with, we believe the Administration fundamentally misunderstands the causes

3. Taken from the text of the President's address as carried by the *New York Times*, 28 April 1983, p. A12.

of the conflict in Central America. We cannot afford to found so important a policy on ignorance—and the painful truth is that many of our highest officials seem to know as little about Central America in 1983 as we knew about Indochina in 1963.[4]

For Senator Dodd and many fellow Democrats, U.S. ideological and world-order interests in Central America called for approaches different from those proposed by the Reagan administration. Dodd argued that "instead of trying to do something about the factors which breed revolution, this administration has turned to massive military buildups at a cost of hundreds of millions of dollars." The Senator denounced the administration's "ever-increasing military assistance, endless military training, even hiring our own paramilitary guerrillas . . . a formula for failure." Dodd predicted that "if we continue down that road, if we continue to ally ourselves with repression, we will not only deny our own most basic values, we will also find ourselves once again on the losing side." The Senator's proposed policy was for unconditional negotiations to stop the guerrilla fighting in Central America: "First, we should use the power and influence of the United States to achieve an immediate cessation of hostilities in both El Salvador and Nicaragua. . . . Second, the United States should use all its power and influence to work for negotiated political settlements in Central America. In El Salvador, the rebels have offered to negotiate unconditionally. Let us test their sincerity. . . . Third we must restore America's role as a source of hope and a force for progress in Central America. We must help governments only if they will help their own people." Finally, he argued, "this approach would permit the United States to move with the tide of history rather than stand against it." Senator Dodd emphasized the U.S. ideological interest in these terms: "Two centuries ago, our nation raised the light of liberty before the world—and all of this hemisphere looked to us as an example and an inspiration. In this Capitol building, from which I speak tonight, men like Daniel Webster, Henry Clay, and Abraham Lincoln once spoke of an America leading the way to human progress and human rights—and people everywhere listened

4. Ibid., A13.

with hope. There is no greater or larger ideal than the one which was forged here in the early days of this Republic. That ideal of liberty is our greatest strength as a nation; it is a powerful and peaceful weapon against tyranny of any kind anywhere in this hemisphere."[5]

The significance of the Dodd critique of Reagan's prescription for policy in Central America is that although he and fellow Democrats did not quarrel with the President's view that Marxism should not be allowed to topple governments there and that Soviet and Cuban military influence had to be checked, he did differ sharply with the President's view that the problems of Central America, and by inference also those of the Caribbean, were primarily matters of security rather than essentially social and political issues. Dodd also believed that the ideological interest of the United States demanded that the government put more emphasis on human rights and social justice than the President seemed willing to do. Republicans and some Democrats criticized Dodd's rebuttal of the President, particularly because he received television time immediately after the President addressed the joint session of Congress. Nevertheless, the early part of his address made it plain that there was bipartisan support for the President's declaration that Central America is a *vital* interest of the United States and that measures should be taken to prevent the spread of Castroism in that area. That part of Dodd's speech was largely overlooked in the press commentaries that followed.

Because a clear definition of U.S. interests in the Caribbean and Central America was crucial to focusing American public attention on this priority area, the President's address served the useful purpose of generating much analysis and commentary in the press and on television, as well as in Congress. One of the reasons President Reagan raised the issue of Communism in Central America shortly after taking office in 1981 and then promptly put it aside as a foreign policy priority was that Secretary of State Alexander Haig's alarmist rhetoric frightened many Americans into thinking the administration was preparing to repeat the Vietnam scenario of twenty years earlier. They feared he wanted to send large numbers of military advisers and eventually deploy American combat troops to "save El Salvador."

5. Ibid.

When it became clear in the spring of 1981 that the public and large segments of Congress were against getting into another Vietnam-type adventure, Mr. Reagan backed off and agreed to limit the number of military advisers there to only fifty-five. By 1983, however, it was clear that the government of El Salvador could not control the guerrillas, who were supported by large arms shipments from Nicaragua and Cuba, without increased military assistance and large economic grants as well. Despite the large turnout for the Salvadoran elections in March 1982, which elected a constituent assembly, the internal security situation had grown worse. Washington then had to decide whether to make a greater effort to curb the guerrillas or accept the likelihood that another Central American state would be taken over by Marxist-Leninists. The President's April 27, 1983, speech was designed to gain public support for a tougher policy in Central America and congressional support for increased economic and military budgets to deal with the problems of that area.

Within a week of the President's address, the Democrat-controlled Select Intelligence Committee of the House of Representatives voted to cut off covert assistance to groups fighting against the Marxist government of Nicaragua, on the grounds that no U.S. aid should be given to any group trying to overthrow the Sandinista government. This view did not prevail in the final legislation, however. The Reagan administration argued strongly that covert assistance was being given to groups that were trying to stop Nicaragua's supply of weapons to guerrillas trying to overthrow the government of El Salvador. In the Senate, where Republicans held the majority in 1983, the Select Committee on Intelligence postponed a decision on a cutoff of covert aid to anti-Sandinista groups until the end of the fiscal year, to give the Central Intelligence Agency and the White House a few months to come up with detailed proposals to show how covert aid in Central America would enhance the national interests of the United States. Senator Goldwater, chairman of the committee, told the press, "I think it is perfectly plain to the president that we want a redefined position on Central America. . . . We want him to tell us in plain language just what it is he wants to do relative to Nicaragua and the other countries."[6] In effect, the key commit-

6. *Washington Post*, 7 May 1983, p. A8.

tees of both houses of Congress told the President that they wanted a better justification of his interpretation of U.S. interests in Central America and clearer policies before approving additional funding for covert activities.

The *Washington Post* was generally favorable to the President's call for efforts to prevent the collapse of El Salvador, but it cautioned that the United States should not try to dictate the solution. "In brief, just as the United States cannot walk away from Central America because the region is too important, so it cannot take charge and dictate a solution because of the immense weight of its past involvement, which Latins remember more keenly than Americans do. That leaves the administration with a requirement to conduct a continuing policy but a limited one. . . . No American policy that swims against the Latin current will get very far. And as high as the stakes are for the United States, they are higher for the Latins whose plain self-interest is to slow down the Marxist revolutionary train before it reaches them."[7]

The New York Times, another influential newspaper in official Washington, entitled its editorial response to the Reagan speech, "The Issue Is Salvador, Not the Alamo." It agreed with the President that the United States has "legitimate, important interests" in Central America but asserted that "they do not justify open-ended commitments." The *Times* believed that the President had overstated the crisis in Central America and wondered why he had promised *not* to use American troops if the stakes were as high as he thought. "Washington's political dilemma in Central America has been plain. With Cuba and probably Nicaragua lost to the Soviet bloc, any President will do his utmost to prevent the loss of another country. Yet, after Vietnam, every Congress will fear pouring lives and billions into a new quagmire. Both branches respond to the same electorate." The *Times* suggested that the Reagan administration's responsibility in these circumstances was to teach the American people that "Central America is neither the Sudetenland nor South Vietnam: neither the place to draw rigid lines against big-power aggression nor the certain graveyard of good intentions . . . that our concern for who rules those backward nations arises naturally from history and geography . . . that direct intrusions of Soviet power can be met directly

7. *Washington Post*, 29 April 1983, p. A28.

and by other means but that Marxist-Leninists who would serve Soviet purposes are nonetheless unwelcome and worth resisting."[8] In sum, the *New York Times* supported the President's objectives but asked him to tone down his rhetoric, adopt policies that would not scare the American people, and strive to achieve bipartisan support in Congress.

Secretary of Defense Caspar Weinberger and the Joint Chiefs of Staff attached great importance to U.S. security in the Caribbean and Central America, and these views strongly influenced President Reagan's appraisal of U.S. national interests there. In his *Annual Report to the Congress* dated February 1, 1983, the Secretary of Defense made this assertion:

> Central America and the Caribbean are now clearly the target of a concerted Soviet-inspired penetration effort. We recognize, of course, as we did in Europe and Japan just after World War II, that we must promote economic and social development, which will encourage political stability and diminish opportunities for subversion. The President has strengthened that effort with his Caribbean Basin initiative. Nevertheless, we cannot wait for the attainment of all possible social and political improvements in each of these countries. We must address the fact that many countries are now under attack by guerrilla forces that the Soviet Union sustains either directly or through its intermediaries. If the trend of Soviet expansion we have witnessed over the last 20 years is permitted to continue, the long-term consequences for the United States would be disastrous. The further spread of Soviet military outposts throughout the world would increasingly threaten to cut into the lifelines of the Western alliance and make it even more difficult and costly to defend essential U.S. national interests.[9]

Differentiation among U.S. Interests in North America

The foregoing discussion of U.S. interests in the southern sector of North America suggests that of the four basic national

---

8. *New York Times*, 29 April 1983, p. A30.
9. Caspar W. Weinberger, *Annual Report to the Congress, Fiscal Year 1984*, (Washington, D.C.: Government Printing Office, 1983), 28.

interests outlined in Chapter 1, little doubt now exists that the Caribbean Basin is a vital defense-of-homeland interest. There is bipartisan support in Congress for the view that the United States should not tolerate the implantation of Soviet military bases or Soviet forces in that area. Similarly, there is little debate that Canada, Mexico, Venezuela, Colombia, and Panama constitute a vital economic interest of the United States. President Reagan's Caribbean Basin Plan, which envisages much closer economic links between the United States and the countries of the Caribbean and Central America—including a free trade zone for many commodities produced in these countries—is indicative of the growing economic relationships in North America.

It is the U.S. world-order and ideological interests south of the border that are questioned by Congress, the press and intellectual circles in the United States. Concerning ideological interests (promotion of values), the issue comes down to one of priority: the Reagan administration argued that questions of social justice and human rights for the impoverished people of Central America, while important, were not the overriding interest of the United States. Congressional Democrats, however, argued that without great attention to human rights violations and social and economic injustices, there was little likelihood that U.S. policy would make headway in curbing Marxist-Leninist influence in the region, despite ever increasing amounts of economic and military aid. The Democrats generally believed that military organizations in Central America were a principal source of the trouble and that granting them additional military assistance would more likely drive people into the Communist ranks than give them hope of a better life. The Reagan administration believed, on the other hand, that Soviet-Cuban penetration of Central America was so far advanced that only a combination of large economic and military assistance to existing governments could possibly turn the tide, and that even then it would require years of effort. For the Republicans, the ideological issue was Communism first, and human rights second; for the Democrats, the issue was human rights and economic hope first.

The world-order interests of the United States were equally ambiguous. The issue, in a nutshell, was the degree to which it was in the U.S. interest to insist that governments in the North American region maintain friendly relations with Washington, regardless of their ideological orientation. Although Communist governments in Cuba and Nicaragua were the major source of this concern, there was also frustration in Washington over the policies of the Mexican, Panamanian, and Columbian governments, which maintain good relations with the United States but do not cooperate with Washington on many important economic and political issues. Mexico's unwillingness to adopt tougher policies on Fidel Castro's support of Salvador's insurgents, Columbia's unwillingness (or inability) to curb the flow of illegal drugs to the United States, Panama's attitude on running the canal and providing military facilities to the United States, and (prior to October 1983) Grenada's decision to let Cubans enlarge an airport to accommodate long-range aircraft—all of these issues have little to do with Communism and much to do with nationalism in Latin American states. The key questions for the United States are the extent to which it should be willing to permit a hostile country like Cuba to increase its influence in this region, and how important it is to insure that these countries continue to be run by governments whose principles are compatible with U.S. political and economic interests. This issue also affects Canada; the possible secession of Quebec in 1980 posed a serious question for some U.S. policy-makers because it was unclear whether an independent Quebec would cooperate with NATO in preserving the security of North America and Europe and continue the close economic ties which the province has fostered with the northeastern part of the United States. That problem was largely resolved when Quebec voters turned down a referendum proposal to give its leaders authority to negotiate independence from Canada.

The Special Case of Cuba

The most crucial world-order dilemma for the United States is the problem of Cuba. This has been so since Fidel Castro gained control of that island by force in 1959. The irony is that Cuba was "lost to Communism" during the conservative administration of President Dwight Eisenhower. Basically, the Eisenhower cabinet thought in 1958 that the corrupt Cuban dictator, Fulgencio Batista, had outlived his time and that Cuba was in need of significant social reform. This Republican administration, which prided itself on its realistic foreign policy, was persuaded that a charismatic Cuban revolutionary named Dr. Fidel Castro, who had returned from exile in Mexico and set up a guerrilla base in the Cuban mountains, could be induced to follow a friendly policy toward the United States if the latter acquiesced in his taking control of the government. President Eisenhower did not consider Castro a threat to vital U.S. interests in the Caribbean. Once in power, the Castro leadership proceeded to confiscate American private investments without paying compensation, to round up and execute political opponents, and to start an intense anti-American propaganda campaign while opening up relations with Moscow. Within a year, the Eisenhower administration realized it had made a serious mistake, and the President ordered planning for the covert Bay of Pigs operation to begin, under the direction of the Central Intelligence Agency.

From the time John Kennedy entered the White House in January 1961 until Ronald Reagan followed him twenty years later, the question of what to do about Cuba has been a key foreign policy problem for all U.S. Presidents. In terms of national interests, the question has always been whether Cuba constituted a threat to *vital* U.S. interests and needed to be contained by military force, or whether Castro constituted only a *major* threat to U.S. interests and should be ignored until he decided to seek better relations with Washington. Different Presidents have viewed Cuba each way: John Kennedy was not willing to use American armed forces in support of Cuban exiles who tried at the Bay of Pigs to precipitate a national uprising against Castro, but he threatened nuclear war with the Soviet Union when it tried in 1962 to install nuclear missiles there. In 1970 Richard Nixon threatened retaliation if the Soviets built a submarine base in Cuba, but otherwise he left Castro alone. When Cubans were sent to Angola in 1976 to help a Marxist faction come to power, the Ford administration wanted to use covert aid to support the anti-Communist Angolan factions. Congress banned such aid out of fear that Angola might become another Vietnam. The Carter administration tried to improve relations with Castro, but by 1980 it came to realize that Castro's links with the Sandinista revolution in Nicaragua and his aid to revolutionaries in El Salvador were undermining the U.S. position in Central America. Furthermore, Carter was humiliated in 1980 when he charged that the Soviet Union had established a "brigade" of troops in Cuba, only to have Moscow inform him that the troops had been there since 1962 to train Cubans to defend their territory. Mr. Carter quietly dropped the issue. In sum, the United States treated Cuba as a major, not a vital, national interest from 1962 until 1980 because it did not appear to be a military threat to U.S. friends in North America. That situation changed when the Reagan administration came to power and concluded that Castro was intent on establishing Marxist regimes throughout Central America. This was reinforced by Mr. Reagan's view that the Soviet Union was prepared to support Castro's ambitious plans with large amounts of military assistance. For the Reagan administration, Castro constituted a serious threat to U.S. economic and world-order interests in the Western Hemisphere, and it was therefore a vital U.S. interest to prevent him from expanding his revolutionary influence in Central America and in the Caribbean.

There was little doubt in 1983 that U.S. national interests in North America were perceived by the President and Congress as vital, particularly as they affected the defense interests of the United States and the general security of Canada, Mexico, Central America and the Caribbean countries (including the northern rim of South America). Indeed, Canada and Mexico are *survival* interests in defense terms because of their long, unmilitarized borders with the United States and the relatively free flow of persons, both legal and illegal, across the U.S. border. In time of national emergency, it would be imperative for the United States to have the close cooperation of both countries in order to provide for the defense and internal security of the continent. The North American area is to the United States what Eastern Europe is to the Soviet Union: a vital defense zone which it will not permit to be turned into a base of operations by a hostile power. This applies also to a surrogate for the Soviet Union (or any other hostile world power), particularly Castro's Cuba.

Policy Tools to Support U.S. Interests

This analysis of U.S. national interests in North America leads to certain conclusions about U.S. policies toward our neighboring countries. The United States has such a high degree of interest— in all categories—in the North American area that Washington should not compromise with military threats to any part of this region. It means that the U.S. government should take strong actions to insure that the economic, social, and democratic value systems enjoyed within the United States are promoted in countries within North America. This level of interest mandates that the United States cannot follow a "benign neglect" attitude in the Caribbean Basin area, even if there were no security threat posed by Castro's Cuba or the Sandinista regime in Nicaragua. Just as the Soviet Union cannot accept an anti-Moscow regime in Eastern Europe, so the United States should not be expected to countenance an anti-American regime in its neighborhood—particularly if such a regime invites the Soviet Union to establish a large military presence. This level of interest has little to do with the fact that the United States is an open political system and the Soviet Union is not; it has much to do with the reality that any great power has the right to expect that its immediate neighbors will not become a hostile military base or source of insurgency against it.

The specific policies that the United States ought to follow in upholding so high a level of national interest in North America are suggested by Figure 5 (in Chapter 2): "National Interests and Instruments of Policy." If the level of interest for North America under "Defense of Homeland" is judged to be at least *vital*, the United States should be prepared to employ all measures, including a blockade and conventional military forces, to prevent a hostile outside power from threatening the countries and sealanes in this area. In the case of Canada and Mexico, the United States would be justified in undertaking general mobilization and employing all measures, including a threat to use nuclear weapons, if either country were threatened with attack. This is because their territory, their air space, and the waters off their shores are at the survival level of interest to the United States. Those who argue as the Catholic Bishops of the United States did in their Pastoral Letter adopted in May 1983, that there is no moral justification for using nuclear weapons even in self-defense, must be prepared to concede surrender rather than defend the territory of North America in case of a Soviet missile threat. The United States is pledged by the North Atlantic Pact and the Rio Pact to protect Canada and Mexico in case they are threatened by a Communist power, and conventional forces alone may not be capable of deterring or repelling a potential aggressor against North America. President John Kennedy, a Catholic, clearly saw this issue during the Cuban missile crisis and was prepared to use U.S. nuclear weapons to prevent the Soviet Union from placing its own nuclear missiles in Cuba. Would a U.S. president do less today if the United States, Canada, or Mexico were similarly threatened by the Soviet Union?

In economic terms, the United States has a vital interest in preserving its current trade with the North American countries, which constitutes nearly 40 percent of its total foreign trade, and its access to the energy resources and raw materials of Canada, Jamaica, Mexico, and Venezuela. Mexico in 1983 was the largest foreign supplier of crude oil to the United States; Canada provided oil, natural gas, and essential minerals and wood products for American industry; and Venezuela provided both oil and iron as well as aluminum for the American market. President Reagan's decision in August 1982 to launch a crash program to save Mexico from financial collapse, following the world-wide recession and a decline in world oil prices, was indicative of a U.S. vital economic interest at stake in preserving economic stability in its southern neighbor. Economic relationships with Canada are so closely linked to U.S. economic well-being that any American President would assist Canada to avoid economic calamity if that situation should arise. In terms of policy tools, President Reagan indicated by his Caribbean Basin Plan, which Congress approved in 1983, that the United States is prepared to treat the countries of Central America and the Caribbean islands as part of the U.S. economic area. Congress also gave the President authority to continue certain covert support to the non-Communist governments and anti-Communist guerrilla groups so long as this aid was not used for the express purpose of toppling the Nicaraguan regime and did not prove highly embarrassing to the United States.

What was more questionable was whether, and under what circumstances, the United States should be prepared to use forces to defend vital world-order interests in the Caribbean and Central America. As the *New York Times* put it in commenting on President Reagan's April 27, 1983 address to the Congress: "If the stakes are as high as he says, why on earth not [send U.S. combat troops] instead of assuring the Congress that he had no intention of doing so."[10] Clearly, if Central America is a vital interest for the United States, it follows that limited American military action should be employed to prevent Cuba and Nicaragua from using their forces to bring down the governments of neighboring countries, such as Costa Rica, Honduras, Guatemala, and El Salvador. This possibility was raised by the retiring U.S. Commander of the Southern Command, Lt. Gen. Wallace Nutting, who told the *Washington Post* that Central America is at war and the United States, whether it likes it or not, "is engaged in that war." Nutting said the United States may ultimately have to send troops if the military aid to El Salvador is not enough.[11] President Reagan probably did not believe that Cuba would ever be so reckless as to send its own forces to Central America to fight; but if Castro should make such a decision, with Soviet support, this action would clearly call for U.S. military action, including a blockade of Cuba, the prevention of Cuban air shipments to Nicaragua or other sites in the area, and the possible threat of direct military action against Cuba if it did not stop the armed intervention. Short of outright Cuban intervention, however, the use of American military forces in Central America or the Caribbean would be counter-productive because it would rekindle old fears of "Yankee imperialism" in Latin America and turn moderate Latin American opinion against the United States and possibly into sympathy with pro-Castro forces.

In the "Promotion of Values" category, there is no national consensus in the United States about how strongly the U.S. government should insist that progress on human rights and social justice must accompany aid. Supporters of United Nations Ambassador Jeane Kirkpatrick argue that it is naive to think that Central American countries, which have never known democracy and social justice, can suddenly transform their societies into models of American-style democracy. They believe democratization will be a slow process and must be built on the progressive groups that already are at work, rather than by turning these countries over to revolutionaries who would engender more hardship than they would eliminate. These self-styled "realists" point to the experience of Nicaragua: the Sandinistas came to

10. *New York Times*, 29 April 1983, p. A30.
11. *Washington Post*, 25 May 1983, p. 1.

power by promising a more democratic society and then turned the country into an increasingly authoritarian system based on the Cuban model. Liberal-minded individuals, on the other hand, believe as Senator Dodd stated in his reply to President Reagan that there is little hope of providing peace and stability in Central America unless a dramatic change takes place in the political and social systems of the corrupt and unjust societies existing there. They argue that the United States has a responsibility—a vital interest—in promoting rapid progress in this direction.

At the beginning of 1984 it seemed likely that the more liberal of these viewpoints would prevail in Congress and that the Reagan administration (and succeeding ones) would be directed to give a high priority to human rights and social justice. There was declining support, however, for the position that the United States should cut off aid to any country that does live up to the American definition of what constitutes "progress toward human rights." Thus, the U.S. ideological interest in Central America and the Caribbean will hover near the vital level. It will never again revert to the "benign neglect" that occurred after World War II.

Summing Up

The early 1980s convinced most American political leaders that North America, long neglected as a priority in U.S. worldwide interests, had assumed huge proportions in terms of the four basic interests of the United States. Still unresolved was the relative priority this heartland area should receive in terms of resources and attention of top policymakers, compared with U.S. interests and commitments in Western Europe, the Middle East, East Asia, and South America. President Reagan signaled his view of the national interest in Central America by addressing a joint session of Congress in April 1983 and making it clear he would not permit the government of El Salvador to be overthrown by Communist forces. He also suggested a tougher anti-Communist policy toward the entire Central American region by replacing the Assistant Secretary of State for Inter-American Affairs, Thomas Enders (who reportedly believed that both a military option and a political option should be followed) and the

U.S. Ambassador to El Salvador, Dean Hinton (who had expressed independent views in public about the duration of the struggle there). Yet Congress was slow to act on Mr. Reagan's aid requests for the area and was more cautious still about the use of either covert operations or military power to uphold U.S. interests there. The ambiguity of the U.S. view was highlighted by action in the House of Representatives in April 1983 to substantially increase military and economic aid to Israel—to nearly $3 billion a year—while limiting aid to El Salvador to less than $100 million. The growing awareness of U.S. vulnerability to nonmilitary security threats from the south was signaled by Congress's belated recognition of the need for comprehensive immigration legislation to tighten the restrictions on the flow of illegal immigrants into the country. There was also new willingness in Washington to increase efforts to curb the flood of illegal drugs into the United States because of the serious effects of the drug trade on crime rates and our public health. Senator Alan Simpson, sponsor of the Senate's immigration bill, asserted that the legislation was needed because "the first duty of a sovereign nation is to control its borders—and we don't."[12]

At the end of 1983, there was growing public and congressional recognition that the United States could no longer take the countries of Central America and the Caribbean for granted, that the danger of doing nothing was too great. The report of the "National Bipartisan Commission on Central America," known also as the Kissinger Commission, was published in January 1984 and raised public consciousness about the political, economic, social, and security dangers in this vital region. Although the report did not produce a bipartisan approach in Congress, it did legitimate the Reagan administration's determination to pursue a much stronger policy to cope with Cuban- and Nicaraguan-supported insurgencies in Central America, and it laid the groundwork for the next administration to launch a long-term strategy toward the area. The fact that Congress was not willing in the early months of 1984 to deny the administration's aid requests for El Salvador suggested that the U.S. public mood was gradually shifting toward action to prevent the further spread of Marxism-Leninism in

12. *New York Times*, 19 May 1983, p. 1.

Central America. The Reagan decision to send U.S. military forces into Grenada in October 1983, following the assassination of Prime Minister Maurice Bishop, was generally supported by the American public and Congress, and it caused Cuba and Nicaragua to become more cautious in pushing their ambitions in Central America. Long-range policies would have to await the outcome of the November 1984 presidential elections, however.

4. Western Europe: Cradle of American Civilization

The United States recognized that Western Europe is an enduring vital national interest when France fell to German armies in June 1940. President Franklin Roosevelt understood that the collapse of French forces meant that Hitler held supreme power on the continent and that this represented so dramatic a shift in the world balance of power that it could prove intolerable to the United States. At a commencement address in Charlottesville, Virginia, on June 10, 1940, Roosevelt stated: "This perception of danger has come to us clearly and overwhelmingly; and we perceive the peril in a worldwide arena—an arena that may become so narrowed that only the Americans will retain the ancient faiths." He called on the country to forsake isolationism with this admonition: "Let us not hesitate—all of us—to proclaim certain truths. Overwhelmingly we, as a nation—and this applies to all the other American nations—are convinced that military and naval victory for the gods of force and hate would endanger the institutions of democracy in the western world, and that equally, therefore, the whole of our sympathies lies with those nations that are giving their life blood to combat against these forces." [1] The President's policy in support of this U.S. interest was to send urgent aid to Great Britain in the hope that that last bastion of democracy could hold out against the German

---

1. *The Public Papers and Addresses of Franklin D. Roosevelt*, vol. 9, *War and Aid to Democracies* (New York, 1940), 260-61.

onslaught. Implicitly, Roosevelt knew that the United States eventually would have to enter the war in order to defend a vital interest in Europe. Lend-Lease aid to Britain, the transfer of fifty American destroyers to the Royal Navy, and the escorting of merchant ships bound for Britain were all results of Roosevelt's perception that if Britain fell, the United States would have to fight Hitler in North America. So strong was Roosevelt's conviction that Nazism was a threat to U.S. vital interests that he persuaded the country to extend Lend-Lease aid also to the Soviet Union after it was attacked by Germany in June 1941—six months before the United States itself entered the war.

After the war ended in 1945, the American people and Congress demanded the demobilization of U.S. forces and once great American armies in Europe were sent home, except for the occupation forces stationed in West Germany and Italy. Lend-Lease was halted, and the United States took little interest in the war-shattered economies of France, Britain, Belgium, the Netherlands, Italy, and Germany. However, by 1947 it was clear to U.S. policy-makers that unless steps were taken to stimulate the economic recovery of Western Europe, the Communist parties in those countries would very likely achieve power through the electoral process because of the desperation of their populations. Thus, the Truman administration decided in early 1947 that the United States had a vital interest in bolstering the European economies through the Marshall Plan. Then, in 1949, the administration responded to a proposal of the Europeans to form a North Atlantic Pact to defend the Western countries against military and political intimidation from the Soviet Union. Moscow had not demobilized its forces in Eastern Europe but used them to bring to power Communist parties in Poland, Rumania, Hungary, and Bulgaria. The Communist coup in Czechoslovakia in February 1948, against a democratically elected government, so shocked the Western democracies that President Truman asked Congress to rearm America. Soviet imposition of the Berlin Blockade that spring convinced Truman and other Western leaders that Party Secretary Josef Stalin would use force to expel American, British, and French forces from Germany if he thought they could be intimidated. When the Berlin Airlift proved the blockade ineffective, Stalin lifted it in 1949. The events of 1948-49 insured that the United States would not leave Europe as it had done after World War I, when it reverted to isolationism. By 1950, United States national interests were inextricably tied to the security and economic well-being of Western Europe. That commitment has lasted for thirty-five years, one of the most successful multination alliances in history.

The National Interests of West European Countries

The decision of ten West European countries and two North American ones to conclude the North Atlantic Pact in April 1949[2] was based on a convergence of their national interests resulting from a perceived common threat. Two years later, as a result of the Korean War, the signatories deepened their mutual commitment by establishing a joint military command, Supreme Headquarters Allied Powers Europe (SHAPE), and asking President Truman to name an American as its commander. He brought General of the Army Dwight D. Eisenhower out of retirement to become the first NATO Supreme Commander, and the post has been held by an American ever since. The convergent national interests that made this historic alliance possible can be summarized under the four basic national interests discussed in Chapter 1: defense of homeland, economic well-being, security of Western Europe and adjacent areas, and preservation of a western, democratic value system.

In 1949, there existed a strong convergence, a community of interest, on all four of these basic interests among the twelve original signatories of the North Atlantic Treaty. Regarding defense, there was agreement on the urgent need for the military power of the United States to be projected over Western Europe, to prevent Soviet encroachment upon and intimidation of its war-weakened countries. For economic well-being, there was urgent need to establish economic cooperation and growth, even though the Marshall Plan had laid the groundwork for economic recovery from the war. On building security (world order) around the periphery of member states, NATO was in agreement that the Baltic and Mediterranean areas, and even the Middle East,

2. The original signers of the North Atlantic Pact were the United States, Canada, Iceland, Norway, Denmark, Britain, France, Italy, Portugal, the Netherlands, Belgium, and Luxembourg. Greece and Turkey were added in 1951, West Germany in 1955, and Spain in 1982.

needed to be protected in order to prevent the Soviet Union from endangering Western Europe's flanks. Finally, all treaty signatories believed in 1949 that Western democratic values were seriously endangered by a Soviet Communist ideology that appealed to minorities in all West European countries and threatened to upset the political stability of some.[3]

This consensus on national interests in 1949 enabled NATO to expand its membership, in the 1950s, to include Greece, Turkey, and the Federal Republic of Germany. It thus built an alliance system that effectively contained Soviet ambitions from the Baltic to the eastern Mediterranean. Spain, whose geography was an important link in the Western defense chain, was denied NATO membership for over thirty years, until 1982, because its government's value system was incompatible with the ideological interests shared by member states.

NATO suffered a severe strain at Suez in 1956 when France and Britain, frustrated by Washington's lack of diplomatic support, invaded Egypt without consulting the United States. They were thereafter humiliated before the world and lost much national prestige. The alliance changed significantly as a result: whereas Britain and France had until that time been key partners with the United States in exerting worldwide influence, the Suez Crisis clearly reduced the power and influence of the two European powers. From 1956 onward, Washington exerted an increasingly dominant role in the alliance, which caused growing resentment in parts of Europe against United States policies. During the 1960s, leaders in Western Europe questioned U.S. military involvement in Southeast Asia, and by 1968 they had serious doubts about the wisdom of American foreign policy generally. European confidence in American leadership was further shaken by the forced resignation of President Nixon and by Washington's inability to prevent the Arab oil embargo in 1973. It probably reached a low point in 1979 when the Carter administration failed to prevent the collapse of a pro-West regime in Iran.

By 1982, the crisis of confidence within the alliance had reached

---

3. The Communist parties of France and Italy, strong and militant in the early postwar period, were part of the coalition governments of those countries immediately after the war. By 1949 the Communists had been ousted from power, but they had mounted serious campaigns to disrupt the economies of France and Italy and to force their way back into the governments.

major proportions. A new conservative American President was determined to end what he considered to be the military and economic weakness of the alliance and to punish the Soviet leadership for its role in the suppression of freedom in Poland as well as its continued occupation of Afghanistan. Mr. Reagan's opposition to the West European legs of the Siberian gas pipeline, especially the credits granted by NATO countries for its construction, led in 1982 to his imposing economic sanctions on the export of U.S. licensed equipment by European firms, touching off a serious rift within the alliance. A worldwide recession contributed to the problem because some European governments desired to continue East-West trade in order to avoid even higher unemployment at home. The U.S. government's refusal to reflate its economy made it unlikely that European economies could recover from recession as soon as some countries, particularly those governed by social democratic parties, desired.

In sum, the national interests of Western Europe and the United States were clearly divergent in the autumn of 1982, and the European leaders were looking for ways to loosen the tightly knit organization of the NATO alliance. Furthermore, the clever diplomacy of the new Soviet leadership headed by Yuri Andropov in exploiting European fears of American military policy contributed greatly to the reevaluation by Europeans of NATO's value to them.

Looking at the four basic national interests of the NATO countries at the end of 1983, one could conclude that divergence between Western Europe and the United States was growing and that divergence *among* the European NATO states on economic policy was also increasing.

Regarding defense of Europe, there was serious divergence within NATO over how to deal with the Soviet Union. The mammoth buildup of Soviet conventional and nuclear forces in Eastern Europe during the ten preceding years, particularly the deployment of three hundred medium-range SS-20 nuclear missiles aimed at Western European cities, shattered the hopes of those Europeans who believed that detente would result in a leveling-off of the Soviet arms buildup and in a reduction of Soviet control in Eastern Europe. The Soviet military buildup also had the unfavorable effect of intimidating some elements of European society and persuading peace groups to campaign against the American counterpart of the SS-20 missiles, even though European governments had pressed the United States in 1979 to find a counterweight to this new Soviet weapon. A growing number of Europeans, especially among the young, believe that U.S. arms are as great a threat to their homelands as are Soviet forces and that the Reagan administration is not serious about arms limitation with the U.S.S.R. Although this sentiment did not constitute majority opinion in Western Europe, it did signify a serious erosion in the basic underpinnings of the NATO alliance—the *form* of American military protection against Soviet power.

The divergence in interests was also significant in the economic arena. Whereas West European countries generally followed the U.S. lead in economic policy during the 1950s and 1960s, the detente policies of the 1970s produced a growing split between those governments (particularly the Federal Republic of Germany) that believed trade and financial credits for Eastern Europe and the Soviet Union were good for the economic well-being of the West, and those (particularly Britain and the United States) that had serious concerns about whether such trade and financial assistance would create a Western dependence on Eastern markets and eventually result in political dependence as well. By 1983, few Europeans or Americans believed that detente and increased trade had any real effect on the Soviet Union's determination to expand its military machine and to project its power and influence outside Moscow's postwar sphere of influence. The Soviet role in the suppression of the Solidarity free trade union in Poland was the straw that broke the back of pro-detente advocacy in the United States and caused President Reagan to respond with tough economic sanctions against the East European countries. The process of finding a new consensus between Europe and the United States on trade with the East, as well as on trade among NATO countries, was a painful readjustment and threatened to lead to more protectionism among alliance countries. The economic summit conference held in Williamsburg, Virginia, in May 1983 did little more than paper over these differences.

Regarding regional security outside the NATO area (world-order interests), 1983 found similar divergencies among NATO members. Middle East oil was the most notable case in point because European countries, with the exception of France, did not see any reason to provide military forces to a U.S.-led Middle East Rapid Deployment Force whose purpose was to insure that oil supplies from the Persian Gulf were not interrupted. As a result, there was opposition in the United States to having American ground and air forces added to the U.S. Navy's Indian Ocean presence at a time when European NATO countries were far more dependent on Middle East oil than was the United States. Only France, among the European NATO countries, keeps a significant naval presence in the Indian Ocean, although Britain retains a military training role in Oman and several patrol ships in the Persian Gulf. (In October 1983 the Thatcher government also dispatched a carrier to the Indian Ocean.) There was also considerable opposition in the alliance to heavy U.S. support of Israel's aggressive actions in Lebanon, as well as the occupied territories, and Washington's inability to bring about a comprehensive Middle East peace. Finally, there was resentment, particularly among European socialist parties, against U.S. policies in the Caribbean and Central America, which the United States considers to be its own sphere of influence. Fundamentally, many Europeans doubted that the Reagan administration's confrontation policies toward the Soviet Union would lead to greater security either in Europe or elsewhere in the world.

Finally, an ideological gap seemed to be emerging between those NATO member states that currently have socialist or social democratic governments, and those led by conservative political parties. For conservative governments, such as Mrs. Thatcher's in Britain and Mr. Reagan's in Washington, trade with the Soviet Union and Eastern Europe ought to be linked to Soviet behavior in areas such as Afghanistan and Poland, as well as in the Third World. Since October 1982, the conservative-led German government in Bonn has generally shared this view. In the absence of Soviet moderation on these issues, it is argued, NATO defenses must be given priority over social spending at home. For socialist governments, however, in France, Greece, and Spain, East-West trade is a high priority regardless of Soviet behavior because it helps business and employment at home. For the socialist government of Greece, U.S. bases on its soil appear unnecessary; the socialist government of Spain questions Spain's membership in

NATO, although not U.S. bases.[4] These doubts about NATO defense policy are based not on illusions about the Soviet threat to Western Europe but rather on a different view of the threat from that held in Washington and London. This ideological divergence between the conservative governments of northern Europe and the socialist governments of southern Europe could be exacerbated if economic recovery in 1984-85 does not result in a substantial reduction in unemployment—which remains considerably higher than in the United States and Canada. European socialist parties are also likely to resist greater spending on defense, which will be required if NATO decides to increase its conventional forces.

U.S. Interests in Western Europe

Figure 7 shows how four principal West European countries appear on the matrix of U.S. national interests. Although there has been a convergence of interests between Western Europe and North America for thirty years, serious questioning has arisen in the United States about the importance of the alliance in terms of U.S. worldwide commitments, especially the economic and political costs of keeping roughly 330,000 American forces based in Western Europe. The United States has a vital world order and a vital ideological interest in keeping Western Europe from succumbing to Soviet intimidation, but it is questionable whether Europe today is a vital economic interest of the United States. Neither West Germany nor France is as important to U.S. strategic and economic interests as is Canada or Mexico, even though the latter are smaller in terms of military power and gross national product. This is because Canada and Mexico are in North America and are also far more important as trading partners and sources of raw materials. To assert this truth is not to denigrate the vital role of the European NATO partners but rather to put their importance in perspective in terms of overall U.S. interests. The

4. In the summer of 1983, Greece concluded an agreement with the United States giving the latter the right to retain air and naval bases in Greece for another five years. Also, the Spanish government decided to put off for a year a proposed national referendum on whether Spain should remain a member of NATO. In both cases, it appeared that socialist governments found it in their countries' interests to retain a defense relationship with the United States.

Fig. 7. U.S. National Interests In Western Europe

Basic Interest at Stake	Intensity of Interest			
	Survival	Vital	Major	Peripheral
Defense of Homeland		Britain	Italy	
			France	
			West	
			Germany	
Economic Well-Being		West		
		Germany	Britain	
			France	
			Italy	
Favorable World Order		All		
Promotion of Values		All		

exception is Great Britain, whose strategic location and nuclear power status qualify it as a vital U.S. defense interest in the North Atlantic. The same may be true of West Germany's economic position, the strongest in Europe. Even though the United States is not crucially dependent on West European territory and the European Common Market for its defense and economic well-being, the European NATO area constitutes a vital world-order interest in terms of U.S. worldwide competition with the Soviet Union. Its absorption into the Soviet sphere of influence would be an intolerable blow to U.S strategic as well as ideological interests, and that is why Washington remains committed to Europe's defense. Western Europe's perception of its interests in the United States is somewhat different, however, (see figure 8). Most Europeans reluctantly agree that in regard to defense of their homelands, the United States remains a vital interest because only it can provide the military power to restrain the Soviet Union from intimidating or taking over their countries by force. Economically, the United States is also a vital interest of the Common Market countries because of the enormous influence that the U.S. economy has on their economic well-being. Regarding world-order and promotion-of-values, however, there is ambiguity in Europe's interests. Most Europeans, conservatives and social democrats, do not see their interests heavily involved with the United States *outside* Europe, and they therefore do not feel vitally involved in helping the United States protect the Persian

Gulf, Southwest Asia, Central America or the North Pacific region. In terms of ideology, most West Europeans have less in common with the Reagan administration's conservative value system than with any President since NATO was founded. This is because they see his policies as unilateralist and confrontational, based on anti-Communism and lacking in appreciation of the problems of underdeveloped countries, as well as of the poor and unemployed at home. In short, most Europeans had trouble identifying with the promotion of values interest of the U.S. government in 1983.

Fig. 8. Western Europe's Interests in the United States

Basic Interest at Stake	Intensity of Interest			
	Survival	Vital	Major	Peripheral
Defense of Homeland		U.S.		
Economic Well-Being		U.S.		
Favorable World Order			U.S.	
Promotion of Values			U.S.	

An obvious tension therefore results from this imbalance in perceptions of national interest between Western Europe and the United States. Whereas Europe vitally needs the United States to protect its homeland against the Soviet Union, the United States does not need Western Europe to an equal extent. Having American military protection may be crucial to the future of the West European countries as free societies, but the United States could survive economically and politically (albeit with difficulty) should Western Europe succumb to Soviet intimidation. That is as true today as it was in 1940 and in 1949. But the other side of the coin is that the United States needs Europe for balance-of-power reasons more than Europe needs or desires the United States. This dichotomy of interests is at the heart of U.S.–European relations. It explains the strong reaction of West Germany and other governments to Ronald Reagan's determination to scuttle ten years of detente and tighten up on trade and investments with the Soviet Union and Eastern Europe. It explains Europe's reluctance to follow the U.S. lead, under Presidents Carter and Reagan, in confronting the Soviet Union over Afghanistan and Poland, and why Europeans are cool toward accepting a military role in the Middle East except for peacekeeping forces. It also explains Europe's alarm about the possibility that the United States may send troops to Central America, just as it was alarmed about President Johnson's sending troops to Southeast Asia twenty years ago. Europe believes that the United States should not be diverted from the principal focus of international politics: namely, Europe and the need to deter the Soviet Union from launching an attack westward or intimidating Western Europe.

In sum, Europeans have never wanted the United States to be preoccupied in other parts of the world because this detracts from Washington's attention to alliance relationships. Former German Chancellor Helmut Schmidt's comments to the *Washington Post* in 1983 are indicative of the unease experienced by responsible Europeans on this question: "As chancellor I worked under four presidents, and it's quite an experience, I can tell you. I've become greatly troubled by your handling of allies and friends. . . Take the pipeline embargo. There was not the slightest consultation; we learned about it from the evening news. The grain embargo, the Olympics boycott—all these actions show enormous neglect for the alliance."[5]

The summer and fall of 1983 saw some improvement in U.S. relations with the European allies because it was clear to all that unless they showed unity on deploying Pershing II and cruise missiles, there was the possibility of serious domestic disturbances in West Germany, Britain, Belgium, and the Netherlands by the end of 1983, when U.S. missiles would begin arriving. The election victory of the German Conservative Party, led by Chancellor Helmut Kohl, in March 1983 contributed to alliance unity on defense matters; but the economic troubles of the French Socialist government, headed by President François Mitterrand, and his tendency to blame the United States for these difficulties was a source of continuing tension in the alliance. The Reagan administration appeared satisfied that even though it was forced late in 1982 to accept defeat in its efforts to curtail the building of the Siberian gas pipeline into Western Europe, it had won concessions from the West European governments that they would tighten credit to Eastern Europe and restrict the sale of advanced technology to Moscow. The renewed solidarity of the alliance was

5. *Washington Post*, 22 May 1983, p. A20.

demonstrated at the Williamsburg summit conference in May 1983, when the leaders of seven industrial nations pledged their support to the position of the United States on arms reductions.

Potential Crises in the Alliance

There are six contingencies or crises that could lead to the fracture of NATO during the next few years; four of them would be inspired by actions of West European governments and two by actions of the U.S. government. They are (1) a decision by European NATO countries to reject U.S. cruise or Pershing II missiles on their soil; (2) a decision by one or more NATO countries (Greece, Spain, Turkey, for example) to dismantle U.S. naval and air bases; (3) a significant reduction in defense expenditures by several key NATO countries; (4) refusal by NATO members to grant the United States landing and/or overflight rights in case of a new Middle East war threatening Persian Gulf oil; (5) a decision by the U.S. government to cut significantly its troop strength in Europe, or its naval presence in the Mediterranean; (6) a U.S.–U.S.S.R. agreement to withdraw from East and West Germany, leaving the two German states neutralized.[6]

A West German government decision in 1983 not to accept Pershing II missles would have produced a serious rupture in Bonn-Washington relations and might have resulted in action by Congress to withdraw a substantial number of American troops from Germany. This potential crisis passed in December 1983 when the Bundestag voted decisively to accept the American missiles, but Chancellor Helmut Kohl might nevertheless insist that President Reagan modify American nuclear policy in order to allay the growing fear of war among Germans. A Belgian or Dutch decision not to accept cruise missiles would be disappointing to the United States, but would not produce the sharp reaction that a German or Italian reversal of policy would bring. Britain under a Thatcher government will continue with the emplacement of U.S. cruise missiles.

Another threat to the NATO alliance would be posed if any

---

6. These six contingencies were first discussed in my article which appeared in *The World Today* entitled "Convergence and Divergence in the North Atlantic Relationship" [London, May 1983], pp. 164-170.

country asked for the withdrawal of U.S. military forces. When France asked the United States to withdraw its forces in 1966, there was serious questioning in Washington whether the alliance was viable without French military participation. In the current political climate, a request by the Greek or Spanish government, for example, for the removal of U.S. military bases would undoubtedly produce calls in Congress for the withdrawal of alliance protection from these countries. The same would be true of Turkey, Portugal, or Iceland.

At present, NATO governments are pledged to increase their defense budgets by 3 percent per year after inflation, but most are not making a serious effort to meet that target. If one or more decided to reduce their military budgets, in the name of economy or otherwise, it could lead to serious questioning by other NATO members about whether these states should remain under the alliance's protection, and could produce a public reaction in the United States demanding the withdrawal of substantial American forces from Europe.

During the 1973 Arab-Israeli war, U.S. Air Force planes were denied landing rights and overflight rights by NATO countries, thus impeding the flow of military equipment to Israel, which was then fighting for its survival against Egypt and Syria. If a new Middle East conflict occurs, particularly if it involves a threat to Middle East oil, the denial of landing and overflight rights would be a serious blow to the alliance and might lead to the early withdrawal of U.S. protection and military assistance from the countries denying these rights.

A unilateral decision by the United States to withdraw military forces from Europe would also have serious consequences. The danger is that a U.S. move to reduce defense expenditures by withdrawing military units from NATO would boost the political support of those elements in Western Europe that believe their security would be best served if the American military presence were reduced and eventually eliminated. Rather than forcing the European allies to do more to defend their homelands, a unilateral U.S. troop reduction would probably result in their spending less on defense and gradually accommodating the Warsaw Pact countries in some disarmament agreement. In a word, a U.S. threat to withdraw troops from Europe is not a credible political move.

Finally, the age-old fear of Europeans that the superpowers will get together and make a deal at Europe's expense is an ever present threat to the alliance. Although this fear seems completely unwarranted at the present time, given Washington's and Moscow's Cold War rhetoric, the two superpowers might decide that it is in their mutual interest to pull back forces from Central Europe and thus reduce the risk of nuclear war between them. Even the hint that such a deal might be made between Washington and Moscow would threaten the NATO alliance because West Europeans would be more fearful of each other, particularly of West Germany, without the presence of U. S. forces.

What is the likelihood that any of these six contingencies will occur?

As in 1949 when the NATO alliance was formed, the key to its continued cohesiveness is a clearly perceived Soviet military threat to Western Europe. That view of the Soviet Union's policies is not universally shared today within the alliance; indeed, there is a significant body of opinion, mostly on the left of the political spectrum, that views the Soviet Union as a political but not a military menace to Western Europe's well-being. Thus, detente is seen as a means of reducing Soviet political pressure on the West by offering trade and financial credits to Moscow and Eastern Europe. Critics branded this attitude as "appeasement." By the late 1970s, this view was challenged in Britain and the United States. First the Thatcher government and then the Reagan administration argued that offering Moscow and its satellites trade and financial assistance produced not only a larger Soviet military buildup in Eastern Europe but also the repression of free trade unions in Poland, the tightening of Soviet control over Warsaw Pact governments and the Soviet invasion of Afghanistan.

However, what would be the result if the Soviet leadership were to adopt a conciliatory line toward the West, particularly if it made some concrete concessions on arms reductions and gave evidence of lifting its heavy hand in Poland? If Moscow should decide to accept more free-market activity in Warsaw Pact countries and permit more individual freedom in Eastern Europe, the Reagan Administration would find it more difficult to persuade NATO countries to restrict trade and credits with Eastern Europe. Similarly, if Moscow should unilaterally reduce or withdraw its

SS-20 missiles in the East, there would be less justification for the United States to keep cruise missiles and Pershing IIs in Western Europe. A Soviet offer on mutual troop reductions in East and West Germany would surely increase pressure in the United States for significant troop withdrawals. In terms of extra-European affairs, a Soviet decision to reduce troop strength in Afghanistan and a declaration that it intended eventually to withdraw all its forces would negate much of the basis for the buildup of American forces in the Indian Ocean and the Persian Gulf area. Such moves on Moscow's part would undoubtedly result in political pressure within the United States, as well as in Western Europe, to cut defense and re-open trade with Eastern Europe. On the other hand, in the absence of significant change in Soviet policy in 1984-85, NATO countries will reluctantly move closer together on military and economic strategy toward Eastern Europe, even though protectionist policies between the European Economic Community and the United States may increase. A trend toward convergence on defense policy does not insure that Spain under a Socialist government will remain in NATO, or that a Greek socialist government will forsake its eventual goal to remove U.S. naval and air facilities, but it does increase the likelihood that Germany, Italy, and Britain will retain U.S. medium-range missiles and that France will quietly coordinate its military plans with other NATO countries.

In sum, the issue of convergence or divergence in the North Atlantic alliance rests on the perception of West Europeans about the intentions and policies of the two superpowers. If the Soviet leadership appears to be genuinely conciliatory toward Western Europe while President Reagan appears to be inflexible in East-West relations, divergence between Europe and North America will increase. If Moscow pursues hard-line policies on Soviet arms and on Soviet control in Eastern Europe and Afghanistan while Ronald Reagan appears more reasonable about East-West relations and arms reductions, Western Europe will accept continued U. S. leadership of the alliance. A third possibility, that both the Soviet Union and the United States will pursue tough, uncompromising policies on nuclear weapons and continue their intense rivalry in the Third World, raises the likelihood that West Germany, Greece, Denmark, and others may move away from other NATO countries—such as Britain, France and Italy—and seek some kind of non-aligned status. This is not imminent, but it would be foolish for Washington and other NATO capitals to dismiss the possibility.[7]

U.S. Long-term Interests in Western Europe

Although the United States has had vital world-order and ideological interests in the preservation of friendly, democratic regimes in Western Europe since 1940, the means by which these interests have been promoted have varied with time and circumstances. There is a serious question among West Europeans today, and a growing questioning also within the United States, as to whether the U.S. government needs to station forces totaling over 300,000 in Central and Southern Europe. At issue is whether the presence of so large an American force is required to deter the Soviet Union from launching an attack on West Germany and other NATO countries, and whether a large force is necessary to reassure Europeans that the United States will indeed defend them if the Soviet Union tries to intimidate their countries. No doubt both points are valid: the presence of credible American military power on the continent of Europe is needed to insure that the United States will be immediately engaged in case of armed aggression from the East. But how large a force is necessary to accomplish this largely political objective? Would it not be feasible to provide the nuclear umbrella for NATO defense without having to station personnel numbering more than a quarter of a million in Central Europe? The argument on the other side is that the preponderance of conventional force possessed by Warsaw Pact members necessitates a large American contribution to NATO. Futhermore, under authority of the American President, only American commanders can release U. S. nuclear weapons in time of war. The storage and control of these weapons requires a sizable number of American personnel.

7. The freeze in U.S.-Soviet relations resulting from the destruction of a Korean airliner by a Soviet fighter plane in September 1983 had the immediate effect of drawing the alliance together. The longer-term effect on the alliance rested to a large extent on whether the superpowers resumed arms control talks in Geneva and on perceived U.S. flexibility in conducting these negotiations.

In the mid-1980s, the United States faces the question of where to place its increasingly expensive military power to cover its worldwide political commitments; hard choices therefore will have to be made. President Reagan's escalating defense budgets caused much controversy in Congress and among American interest groups because of simultaneous cuts in domestic programs and because of huge budget deficits. Assuming that Congress does not cut domestic spending further, because of public resistance, ways will have to be found to limit defense expenditures without curtailing needed modernization of U.S. equipment. The size of the military forces, particularly ground forces, will be a target for budget cutters, and the most likely place for these cuts to be made is in U.S. forces stationed in Europe.

Another factor that will increase the pressure for cuts in U.S. forces in Europe is the growing requirements of the Rapid Deployment Force, renamed the Central Command in 1983. Already some forces currently in Europe are earmarked for transfer to the Central Command in case of emergency in the Persian Gulf, or elsewhere in the Middle East. Unless Congress is willing to expand the total size of the armed forces, the number committed to the defense of Europe will diminish if there is a serious military situation in the Middle East or the Indian Ocean.

Europeans, especially West Germans, have become more critical of the large presence of American troops in their midst, particularly with the drug-related crime that existed among them in the 1970s and early 1980s. Although this situation is being remedied, as the Army is able to enlist a higher quality of personnel in the 1980s, German nationalistic instincts were brought to the fore during the election campaign of March 1983, in which the neutralist/anti-nuclear Green Party obtained enough votes to get representation in the Bundestag. This anti-American party constantly whipped up resentment against the United States for its nuclear policies and against American servicemen because they were too visible to Germans. The fact that the West German electorate gave the Conservative Party a somewhat larger mandate in that election largely overshadowed the growing nationalistic sentiments that lay below the surface of German public opinion—particularly among younger voters.

The real issue for American policy-makers during the remainder of the 1980s, however, is not the level of U.S. troops in Europe but how important Europe remains in terms of world-wide U.S. interests and commitments. The events of 1983 showed that a significant shift was taking place in both official (Reagan administration) and public opinion in the direction of according greater priority to Central America and the Caribbean—the area that Americans were coming to realize had long been neglected. The White House was nudging Congress and the public toward giving a high priority to U.S. interests and resources in the Caribbean—even at the expense of resources to other areas. The interesting question is whether the new focus on Central America will be of lasting duration—thus signaling a significant change in U.S. worldwide interests—or whether Central America will be of momentary importance until Washington is able either to topple the Sandinista government of Nicaragua or strike a bargain with it to refrain from destabilizing its neighbors. If the new concentration on North America is of short duration and the problems of the Caribbean and Central America are reduced in a year or two, nothing much is likely to change in interests and military resources committed to NATO defenses. If, however, the problems of Central America prove to be fundamental and cannot easily be resolved by military and economic aid and covert operations, there is a strong possibility that some U.S. forces now assigned to Europe will be redeployed to deal with contingencies arising south of the border. For example, if the U.S. government decides on a confrontation with Castro's Cuba over its attempted export of revolution, in violation of the 1962 understanding between President Kennedy and Chairman Khrushchev that settled the Cuban missile crisis, this will require a much greater concentration of U.S. naval forces than currently exists in the Caribbean. It will require ground forces as well if revolution begins to sweep through Central America and into Mexico. The flow of hundreds of thousands of refugees northward would strain the ability of the United States to protect its borders. In short, growing U.S. concerns about the security of North America will require larger military resources and may affect the level of troop commitments in Europe, just as they did in the late 1960s when President Johnson built up American forces in Southeast Asia by redeploying troops from Europe.

The West German Issue in NATO

In the longer term, the United States and other NATO countries will be obliged to deal with the so-called "German problem" which has lain dormant for more than a decade. The issue is the reunification of the two Germanies; there is sentiment among Germans living on both sides of the current demarcation line that the division of their country is not natural and must one day be ended. The Soviet Union has tried since the end of World War II to construct a united Germany under a form of government that is compatible with Soviet national interests. A major reason why West Germany was brought into NATO in 1955 was to prevent the Soviet plan from succeeding and also to tie West Germany militarily and economically to the West. That objective was achieved, and the Bonn government has been a loyal ally for nearly thirty years. But the detente decade of the 1970s and, especially, the Helsinki Treaties of 1975 opened up the possibility for Germans that their two peoples could resume economic and cultural links while deferring political reunification to some future time. By the end of the 1970s, when it became clear to many Europeans and Americans that detente had provided greater benefits to Eastern Europe and the Soviet Union than it did to the West, the Bonn government emerged as the most reluctant of the NATO partners to give up the benefits of detente. Indeed, the social democratic government headed by Helmut Schmidt could not reconcile the dilemma between West Germany's longing for trade and cultural links to the East with the growing power and willingness of the Soviet Union to deny the political fruits of detente to Poland and other East European states. As a result, Schmidt's government resigned in October 1982 to make way for a Conservative-led coalition which shared the new direction in East-West relations held by other NATO countries. Yet no German political leader can close the door completely on the desire of West German people for improved relations with East Germany and trade with Eastern Europe; and the door to those areas lies through Moscow. The desire for accommodation with the U.S.S.R. therefore remains strong.

Is a compromise solution to the German problem and to the military confrontation between NATO and the Warsaw Pact in

Central Europe possible? To what extent is it in the U.S. national interest to promote a compromise?

In the short term, until 1986 or 1987, the political climate in Europe and the United States will not be favorable to such a solution. Movement on the German question clearly must result from, not be the cause of, an agreement between Washington and Moscow to put a cap on nuclear weapons in Europe and begin reducing conventional forces there. If Moscow finds it in its interest to reduce Soviet forces in East Germany, no doubt the American Congress would welcome the opportunity to withdraw some American forces as well, regardless of hesitation by the President. But it would have to be a significant Soviet redeployment of troops, not just to Poland or Rumania, but to the Soviet Union itself; and it would have to involve an agreement that these troops would not return except in case of emergency. Such a Soviet offer might persuade NATO governments that a significant number of Americans could also be withdrawn to the United States, or possibly to Spain, Portugal, and Great Britain. If detente between the two Germanies were accompanied by large Soviet and American troop reductions—on the order of 150,000 men each—this would set in motion renewed efforts by East and West Germany to reach a political accommodation that eventually could lead to reunification under international guarantees.

No movement toward troop reductions and an easing of political tensions will be possible, however, so long as Moscow believes it can woo West Europeans—particularly West Germans—away from their dependence on the United States for protection; and Moscow will not give up trying to split NATO so long as neutralist and anti-American political parties and groups seem to be gaining in public support. If NATO's European governments hold together on a common stance toward the East for the next several years, Moscow may conclude that the "correlation of forces" is not in its favor in the mid-1980s, as it had thought, and that a temporary accommodation with the West is desirable. A precedent for this was the 1954-55 "Spirit of Geneva," when the Kremlin decided to abandon confrontation with NATO and seek agreements in Europe. The Austrian Peace Treaty was one of the fruits of that new mood. Thirty years later, as another Kremlin leadership struggles to cement its control of the reins of power, it too may decide it is time to compromise with the West and seek significant troop reductions in Central Europe.

The Nuclear Deterrence Debate

The military strategy for defending Western Europe has been increasingly challenged in the 1980s by former U.S. officials who believe that the postwar policy of threatening the Soviet Union with nuclear retaliation is no longer credible. In an article in *Foreign Affairs* in 1982, four former high officials of the U.S. Government—McGeorge Bundy, George Kennan, Robert McNamara, and Gerard Smith—argued that any use of nuclear weapons by NATO against an invading Soviet force in Europe would quickly escalate and could lead directly to strategic nuclear war. They argued in favor of a "no first use" policy on nuclear weapons as a means of deescalating tensions that could lead to a preemptive war. They urged the NATO countries to build up their onventional forces so that a nuclear response to a conventional attack in Europe—if one should occur—would not be a President's sole option except defeat:

> What we dare to hope for is the kind of new and widespread consideration of the policy we have outlined that helped us 15 years ago toward SALT I, 25 years ago toward the Limited Test Ban, and 35 years ago toward the Alliance itself. Such consideration can be made all the more earnest and hopeful by keeping in mind one simple and frequently neglected reality: there has been no first use of nuclear weapons since 1945, and no one in any country regrets that fact. The right way to maintain this record is to recognize that in the age of massive thermonuclear overkill it no longer makes sense—if it ever did—to hold these weapons for any other purpose than the prevention of their use.[8]

In a subsequent issue of the same journal, General Bernard W. Rogers, Supreme Allied Commander in Europe and one of the

8. "Nuclear Weapons and the Atlantic Alliance," *Foreign Affairs*, Spring 1982, pp. 767-68.

most respected U.S. military thinkers, advocated a "no early use of nuclear weapons" to counter a Soviet conventional attack in Europe. General Rogers argued that NATO's conventional forces could become capable of rebuffing a massive Soviet attack on Western Europe if NATO governments increased their defense budgets about 4 percent each year rather than the 3 percent they had pledged to increase. Rogers's view, shared by many other military commanders both in Europe and the United States, was that technological improvements in conventional weapons made it possible, at modest increases in defense budgets, to stop Soviet armies without having to use tactical nuclear weapons, at least not at an early stage.[9]

Robert McNamara published a follow-up article in 1983 to the one he had coauthored the year before and concluded that there was no rational way to justify the use of any nuclear weapons except in retaliation to a nuclear attack. McNamara had this to say: "Having spent seven years as Secretary of Defense dealing with the problems unleashed by the initial nuclear chain reaction 40 years ago, I do not believe we can avoid serious and unacceptable risk of nuclear war until we recognize—and until we base all our military plans, defense budgets, weapon deployments, and arms negotiations on the recognition—*that nuclear weapons serve no military purpose whatsoever. They are totally useless—except only to deter one's opponent from using them.*" The former U.S. defense secretary went on to say:

> If we are to reach a consensus within the Alliance on the military role of nuclear weapons—an issue that is funda-mental to the peace and security of both the West and the East—we must face squarely and answer the following questions: Can we conceive of ways to utilize nuclear weap-ons, in response to Soviet aggression with conventional forces, which would be beneficial to NATO? Would any U.S. President be likely to authorize such use of nuclear weapons? If we cannot conceive of a beneficial use of nu-clear weapons and if we believe it unlikely that a U.S. President would authorize their use in such a situation,

9. "The Atlantic Alliance: Prescriptions for a Difficult Decade," *Foreign Affairs*, Summer 1982, pp. 1145-56.

should we continue to accept the risks associated with basing NATO's strategy, war plans and nuclear warhead deployment on the assumption that the weapons would be used in the early hours of an East-West conflict?

McNamara clearly believed that the answer to these questions was no.[10]

The debate about the defense of Western Europe and the usefulness of nuclear weapons has also been growing on the other side of the Atlantic. During 1983, *Foreign Affairs* carried articles by two of Britain's leading scholars on foreign and defense policy, Professor Michael Howard and Professor Hedley Bull, both of Oxford University. Michael Howard, in an article entitled, "Reassurance and Deterrence: Western Defense in the 1980s," raised many of the arguments against nuclear deterrence made by Robert McNamara but went further to propose that European members of NATO stop being so dependent on the U.S. nuclear deterrent and instead provide most of their own defense. Howard wrote:

There has been for many years what I can only describe as a morally debilitating tendency among European defense specialists to argue that if the reassurance provided by the American nuclear guarantee were to be in any way diminished, European morale would collapse. This has always seemed to me one of those unfortunate self-fulfilling prophecies, and one that American defense analysts have taken altogether too seriously. . . .What is needed today is a reversal of that process whereby European governments have sought greater security by demanding an ever greater intensification of the American nuclear commitment; demands that are as divisive within their own countries as they are irritating for the people of the United States. Instead, we should be doing all that we can to reduce our dependence on American nuclear weapons by enhancing, so far as is militarily, socially and economically possible, our capacity to defend ourselves.[11]

10. "The Military Role of Nuclear Weapons: Perceptions and Misperceptions," *Foreign Affairs*, Fall 1983, pp. 79-80.

11. "Reassurance and Deterrence: Western Defense in the 1980s," *Foreign Affairs*, Winter 1982-83, pp. 321-22.

Howard, a strong supporter of NATO and of the U.S. commitment, reflected the growing feeling among European political thinkers that Europe needed to stop its near-total reliance for defense on American strategic power.

Hedley Bull carried the argument a step further, calling for a "Europeanist alternative" to the "Atlanticist" view. "Underlying the peace movement in the West European countries," he wrote, "is the correct perception that the risks of alliance with the United States on present terms have grown to such an extent that they threaten to outweigh the gains. This points to the conclusion that the West European countries should seek to assume greater control of their own security, not by leaving the Atlantic Alliance but at least by seeking to change its structure." Bull urged Europe to develop, within the context of NATO, "a distinct European strategic pillar of the Alliance that will reduce the old dependence on the United States without creating a new dependence on the Soviet Union, and sustain the distinct interests and objectives of which West European countries are increasingly conscious in world affairs."[12]

If Howard's and Bull's thinking about the future of NATO's defense structure is a reasonably accurate reflection of moderate conservative intellectual thought in Europe, it is time for American policy makers to recognize that U.S. dominance of the Alliance may not continue in the old way and that changes are called for in the way NATO is run. The key question is whether European governments will accept this challenge and be willing to pay for the more independent defense role called for by these scholars. Announcement that the near-defunct Western European Union would meet in October 1984 to discuss Europe's defense needs was an encouraging sign.

Summing Up

Thirty-five years after the formation of the North Atlantic Alliance, Western Europe remains a vital world-order and ideological interest of the United States; and the latter remains a vital defense of homeland and economic interest for Europeans. This

12. "European Self-Reliance and The Reform of NATO," *Foreign Affairs*, Spring 1983, p. 879.

convergence of interests represents perhaps the most enduring multinational alliance in history. Nevertheless, the alliance is changing, as the United States remains committed to being a world power and as Europeans think more narrowly in terms of continental interests. How to deal with the continuing Soviet security threat in Europe is the nub of the issue for Europeans.

President Reagan's hard-line policies toward the Soviet Union caused serious strains in the Atlantic Alliance during 1981-1982 and gave impetus to the European peace movement and neutralist sentiment. In 1983, U.S. foreign policy under the direction of Secretary of State George Shultz appeared to reassure West European governments and policy elites that Washington was not determined to act unilaterally in its worldwide competition with the Soviet Union and that President Reagan was following prudent policies even though his conservative rhetoric sounded menacing. The remarkable convergence among the U.S., British, French, and West German governments on defense planning during the third year of Mr. Reagan's presidency was indicative of his success in healing the wounds that had been caused by his policies toward Eastern Europe—highlighted by the Siberian gas pipeline controversy. The relationship among French, Italian, British, and American peacekeeping forces in Lebanon in September 1983, under very difficult conditions, was further evidence of cooperation among these allies in an important area *outside* the European theater. However, the growing convergence of interests was a momentary phenomenon resulting from the current makeup of the governments that were in power. The real question was whether the NATO governments could devise a new alliance strategy—in security and economic affairs—that would persuade their opposition parties to continue the strong alliance policies that guided them when they were in power. This is particularly crucial in the cases of the German Social Democratic Party and the British Labour Party, both of which adopted anti-nuclear policies and tended toward neutralist points of view during 1983-84. In the United States, the problem will be to keep a frustrated public and Congress believing strongly that a large U.S. military presence is necessary in Europe at a time when the European peace movements would have Americans believe that a U.S. military presence is no longer needed or wanted.

Whoever the American President turns out to be in 1985, it will be one of his most important tasks to establish a new relationship with the West European allies, one that provides them with reassurance that they have a real voice in American strategy on how best to protect Western Europe, and at the same time enables them to enjoy the economic and political gains that Europeans have achieved during the last thirty-five years. There is no reason why North Americans and West Europeans should not continue to be each other's most important friends and allies. But it will require of the President a special effort to coordinate the interests and policies of the United States with those of its major European partners.

5. Eastern Mediterranean and Persian Gulf: Containment of U.S.S.R.

The U.S. interest in the eastern Mediterranean dates from President Truman's decision in 1947 to provide military and economic aid to Greece and Turkey to help them resist the Soviet Union's pressures to expand southward. The President's proposal was made before a joint session of Congress on March 12, 1947, and it soon became known as the "Truman Doctrine." In it President Truman went beyond a request for aid to Greece and Turkey and declared that "it must be the policy of the United States to support free peoples who are resisting attempted subjugation by armed minorities or by outside pressures." The President later wrote, "This was, I believe, the turning point in America's foreign policy, which now declared that wherever aggression, direct or indirect, threatened the peace, the security of the United States was involved."[1] Thus, the United States decided early in 1947, following Britain's decision to terminate its aid program in Greece, not only to put United States prestige on the line in Greece and Turkey, but to go further and announce that the United States would oppose Soviet expansionist efforts *wherever* they were manifested. It is noteworthy that Truman's declaration preceded by a few months the famous "Mr. X" article written by George Kennan in *Foreign Affairs*, which many observers saw as the intellectual basis for subsequent U.S. containment policy toward the Soviet Union.

1. Harry S. Truman, *Memoirs: Years of Trial and Hope* (Garden City, N.J., 1956), 2:105, 106.

In 1947 the issue of security in the eastern Mediterranean was related to the economic recovery and military security of Western Europe. Those issues were raised again when the Marshall Plan was unveiled and in subsequent years when the North Atlantic Pact was concluded. Although Greece and Turkey were not original members of the North Atlantic Pact, they were admitted to membership in 1951 and the U.S. bilateral defense commitment thus was expanded into a multilateral one.

It is clear that U.S. national interests in Greece and Turkey were from the beginning based on world-order considerations, not on defense of the U.S. homeland, or on economic benefits to the United States, or even on ideological grounds, although preventing Communist insurgents from taking control of the Greek government was an objective advanced by President Truman. The issue in 1947 was fundamentally an expansion of U.S. world-order interests to include two countries close to Soviet borders where the United States previously had not perceived a deep interest. This area had been a British sphere of influence after World War I; when a nearly bankrupt Britain decided early in 1946 that it could no longer carry the economic and military burden of defending this area, the United States decided it must do so in order to contain Soviet expansionist designs. The impulse giving rise to the Truman Doctrine was applied in other parts of Asia during the 1950s when the Eisenhower administration made defense agreements with Iraq, Iran and Pakistan—in addition to Turkey—to build a network of friendly states around the periphery of the Soviet Union in furtherance of the containment policy. Unlike Western Europe, where the United States had deep historical, ideological, and cultural ties, these Asian states had little in common with the United States except their willingness to resist Soviet efforts to expand its influence in the direction of the Indian Ocean and the Mediterranean.

The Persian Gulf was a key area for the United States and Britain because of its oil reserves and the growing need of Western economies for its low-cost oil. Although Persian Gulf oil had not yet assumed the crucial importance it acquired during the 1970s (because the United States was an oil exporter and could supply Europe with its oil needs if necessary, as it did during the Suez crisis of 1956 and the Arab-Israeli war in June 1967), the Eisenhower administration nevertheless helped to topple the

Mossadegh government in Iran in 1953 and restore the Shah to power.

The question today is, does the United States have vital interests in the eastern Mediterranean and the Persian Gulf that require it to go to war, if necessary, to defend those areas? Greece and Turkey are covered by the North Atlantic Treaty and the United States is pledged to come to their aid if either is attacked by the Soviet Union. Other than these two countries, however, there are no treaties by which the United States is bound to any country in the Middle East or South Asia.[2]

Another state in the eastern Mediterranean that obviously deserves to be called a vital U.S. interest is Israel. The Jewish state came into being in 1948 with the help of the United States, and every American President since then has affirmed his support for its survival and well-being. Strong U.S. backing for Israel cost Washington the support of many Arab countries in the period after 1948, most notably Egypt under Gamal Abdel Nasser during the 1950s and 1960s, Syria, and Iraq (after a revolution there in 1958). Following Nasser's death in 1970, his successor, Anwar Sadat, decided to oust the Soviet advisers and make peace with Israel at Camp David in 1979. Since then, the United States has become the primary supplier of Egypt's economic and military aid, and Egypt has become a vital world-order interest of the United States. Unlike Egypt, however, Israel is a vital *ideological* as well as world-order interest because of its democratic institutions, the strong cultural attachment that many Americans feel for the Jewish people, and its support of the U.S. ideological point of view on most international issues. This is true despite the serious policy differences that existed between the government of Prime Minister Menachem Begin and two American presidents, Jimmy Carter and Ronald Reagan, over disposition of Israeli-occupied territories and Israel's aggressive policies in Lebanon in 1979 and 1982.

In sum, in 1983, there were four countries in the eastern Mediterranean that could reasonably be called U.S. vital interests: Greece and Turkey, where the U.S. interest dated from 1947;

2. Pakistan withdrew from the Southeast Asia Treaty Organization early in the 1970s, and the United States never had a formal defense treaty with Iran, even though it maintained a close military relationship with the Shah's government until his ouster in 1979.

Israel, where it was a major interest in 1948 but became a vital one following Israel's successful war against Egypt, Jordan, and Syria in 1967; and Egypt, which moved from the peripheral to the major level in the 1950s and became a vital world-order interest in the late 1970s when President Sadat made peace with Israel and entered into a defense agreement with the United States. Although Sadat was assassinated in 1981, his successor, Hosni Mubarak, has continued the policy of collaboration with the United States. His attitude toward Israel remained cool, however, because of the Begin government's unwillingness to deal seriously with the Palestinian homeland issue, also covered by the Camp David Accords of 1979. Evidence that the United States now considers these four eastern Mediterranean countries vital interests is the fact that the preponderance of U.S. military and economic aid goes to them in the form of grants and loans on concessional terms. U.S. military units are based in Greece and Turkey, as part of the NATO commitment, and the United States has access to facilities in Israel and Egypt, although it does not currently have military bases in either.

Israel's Invasion of Lebanon
and U.S. Interests

The Lebanon war of 1982, precipitated by an Israeli invasion in June, was a momentous event in recent Middle East history. It had the effect of bringing U.S. peacekeeping troops into Lebanon for the second time in twenty-four years, and it set the stage for a potential partition of that state between Israel and Syria. The war greatly strained U.S.-Israeli relations and called into question how deep the U.S. commitment to Israel should be. Since President Reagan was personally involved in seeking a settlement that would deal with the Palestinian homeland issue as well as the withdrawal of foreign troops from Lebanon, a more detailed discussion of events and the U.S. reaction from June to September 1982 is in order.

The timing of Israel's invasion of Lebanon was remarkable. President Reagan and Secretary of State Alexander Haig were in Paris for an economic summit conference with six other heads of government. News of the Israeli invasion, which arrived during the meeting at Versailles, annoyed the President because he had

hoped to achieve a diplomatic success on this, his first, visit to
Europe as the President. While still in Washington and before the
invasion commenced, Mr. Reagan had sent Prime Minister Begin
several messages urging him not to overreact to the attempted
assassination of the Israeli ambassador to Britain, which Israel
blamed (mistakenly) on the Palestine Liberation Organization.
However, since Israel had been preparing for months to invade
southern Lebanon in order to rout PLO forces, which had ter-
rorized the northern border of Israel, Mr. Begin was not to be
dissuaded from launching the drive into Lebanon—which he
dubbed "peace for Galilee." The invasion started on June 6, and
President Reagan immediately summoned his Middle East en-
voy, Philip Habib, to Paris for consultation. He then dispatched
Habib to the Middle East to try to arrange a cease-fire.

Israel's military advance into Lebanon was so swift that by the
time the first cease-fire became effective in mid-June, its forces
were approaching Lebanon's capital, Beirut. This was in contra-
diction to assurances that Israel's ambassador to the United
States, Moshe Arens, had given publicly in Washington: namely,
that Israel intended to clear out PLO forces in a 25-mile area of
southern Lebanon and that it had no plan to remain in Lebanon
and no claim to "one single square inch of Lebanese territory."
Meanwhile, President Reagan was visiting several other European capitals, and the Israeli advance into Lebanon undercut his
efforts to be seen as a world leader—causing European leaders to
question whether he had any influence over the Begin government's use of American military equipment. Israel's use of U.S.
"cluster bombs" in Lebanon became known early in the war. One
reason for White House reticence in speaking out strongly
against Israel was its misunderstanding of Israel's military objectives. The President was told that Israel would advance only
twenty-five miles into Lebanon in order to oust the PLO from
areas within artillery range of Israeli territory. However, Israeli
Defense Minister Ariel Sharon had no such limitation in mind.
His forces bombed Syrian positions well beyond this line, and he
sent armored columns up the coast to the outskirts of Beirut.
When the White House became aware of Israel's real objectives, it
tried to exert diplomatic pressure on the Begin government but
met with only limited success.

During the President's European trip, Secretary of State Haig became embroiled in conflict with other members of the Reagan administration, and he resigned on June 25. Haig was a strong supporter of Israel's position and had instructed the U.S. permanent representative to the United Nations to vote against a Security Council resolution on June 8 calling for sanctions against Israel. The United States was opposed by all other Security Council members and incurred criticism in Europe and elsewhere for its unyielding support of the Begin government. At the end of June the President replaced Haig as Secretary of State with George P. Shultz, a former cabinet officer in the Nixon administration who reportedly was less sympathetic than Haig to Israel's Middle East objectives. The dramatic change in leadership at the State Department was interpreted by many observers as a shift in U.S. Middle East policy—away from unquestioning support of Israel and toward a more evenhanded policy with regard to the Arab states.

In his news conference on June 30, the first after Israel's invasion of Lebanon, the President was asked this question: "Mr. President, there are some who say that by failing to condemn the Israeli invasion of Lebanon and refusing to cut off arms to the invading armies, the United States and Israeli policies have become—and the goals have become—identical. If there's a difference, what is it?" President Reagan responded: "There's no question but that we had hoped for a diplomatic settlement in the Middle East, in that situation. We were not warned or notified of the invasion that was going to take place. On the other hand, there had been a breaking of the cease-fire, which had held for about 11 months in that area . . . We have a situation in Lebanon in which there was a force, the PLO, literally a government within a government and with its own army. And they had pursued aggression themselves across a border by way of rocket firing and artillery barrages." The President listed three U.S. goals in Lebanon: (1) to get the various factions together to form a central government and "control their own country and have a single Lebanese army;" (2) to guarantee Lebanon's southern border with Israel so that the PLO could no longer "create acts of terror across that border;" and (3) "to get all the foreign forces—Syrians, Israelis, and the armed PLO—out of Lebanon."[3] In response to a

3. *Presidential Documents* 18, no. 26 (5 July 1982): 850-51.

subsequent question about displaced Palestinians in Lebanon, the President added another: "It's been our goal for quite some time—and that is, once and for all, when these other things are accomplished—once and for all, to deal with the problem of the Palestinians and settle that problem within the proposals and the suggestions that were made in the Camp David accords."[4] This goal set the stage for the President's subsequent policy regarding the disposition of the West Bank and Gaza Strip.

During July and August 1982, the United States sought to implement the first three of these presidential goals in Lebanon, with only partial success. The Begin government seemed intent on occupying all of Beirut and physically ousting the PLO from its strongholds in the western sector of that city. President Reagan advised Prime Minister Begin that if the Israelis did so, there would be serious repercussions in terms of U.S. economic and perhaps military aid. In late August the President agreed to send 800 Marines to Beirut as part of an international peacekeeping force to supervise the evacuation of seven thousand PLO guerrillas, with the understanding that their families who remained in West Beirut would not be attacked. The President suspended the shipment of cluster bombs to Israel after he received evidence that these antipersonnel weapons had been used against civilian targets in violation of U.S. law. Israel's massive bombing of West Beirut in August brought outrage from the U.S. allies in Europe, from segments of Congress, and from much of the American press. The President then wrote a stern letter to Begin reminding him that U.S. weapons given to Israel were to be used only for defensive purposes. The implicit warning of a weapons cutoff did not escape the Israeli prime minister, who reportedly exploded: "Nobody, nobody is going to bring Israel to her knees. You must have forgotten that Jews do not kneel but to God. . . . Nobody is going to preach to us humanitarianism."[5]

The sending of 800 Marines to Beirut in a peacekeeping role was part of Mr. Reagan's strategy to prevent Israel from using force against the PLO trapped in West Beirut and to encourage PLO leader Yasser Arafat to agree to the evacuation of his forces. The larger goal was to arrange a political settlement within

---

4. Ibid., 851.
5. *Time*, 16 Aug. 1982, p. 12.

Lebanon that would encourage the Syrians and Israelis to leave the country and permit the Lebanese the opportunity, for the first time since 1976, to govern themselves without foreign interference. But that goal was inextricably tied up with another goal that President Reagan had expressed in his June 30 press conference: to reach a solution of the Palestinian problem in accordance with the Camp David Accords, negotiated by President Carter in 1979. The President was persuaded by his advisers, reportedly including Secretary of State George Shultz, that no lasting solution to the Lebanon fighting was likely without a solution of the Palestinian homeland issue, which had plagued both the Carter and Reagan administrations. There were strong hints that the Israeli government's objective in Lebanon was to annihilate the PLO so that it would no longer be a threat to Begin's plan to annex the West Bank and Gaza Strip after settling a large number of Israeli citizens there. Defense Minister Sharon made no secret that he thought the Palestinians should set up their homeland in Jordan, with or without King Hussein's agreement, and that Israel should forever control "Samaria and Judea." The Begin government knew it could not get the Carter administration to acquiesce in this bold plan to scrap the Camp David Accords and United Nations Resolution 242, which called for Israel's withdrawal from occupied lands. But Ronald Reagan had campaigned as a staunch advocate of Israel's strategic importance to the United States, and he had asserted that Israeli settlements on the West Bank were not illegal, as claimed by most other countries and the Carter administration. By agreeing to completely evacuate the Sinai Peninsula in April 1982, Mr. Begin thought he had shown his good faith and that the Reagan White House should not stand in Israel's way if it gradually extended its sovereignty over the West Bank—as it had already done in East Jerusalem and the Golan Heights. Washington's mild reaction in December 1981 when Israel annexed the Golan area may have led Mr. Begin to conclude that President Reagan could be induced to trade Israel's withdrawal from Lebanon for tacit support of Israel's "creeping annexation" of the West Bank and Gaza. If Israel's government had such hopes, they were dashed on September 1, 1982, by a major U.S. policy statement made by President Reagan.

The setting for Mr. Reagan's television address to the nation was unusual. He was at his ranch in California instead of at the

White House, where he had expected to make the address later in the week after Arab leaders and the Begin government had been briefed on its contents. However, the initial reaction in Jerusalem was so negative that White House aides feared Begin would leak the contents and try to embarrass the President before he could announce his new Middle East peace plan. The address was therefore made from a Hollywood film studio. His remarks are quoted in some detail here because they laid out in reasonably clear terms the President's view of U.S. interests in the Arab-Israeli controversy over occupied territories and of U.S. objectives for peace in the Middle East.

In his introduction, President Reagan outlined the extent of U.S. national interests in the Middle East: "Our involvement in the search for Mideast peace is not a matter of preference; it's a moral imperative. The strategic importance of the region to the United States is well known, but our policy is motivated by more than strategic interests. We also have an irreversible commitment to the survival and territorial integrity of friendly states. Nor can we ignore the fact that the well-being of much of the world's economy is tied to stability in the strife-torn Middle East. Finally, our traditional humanitarian concerns dictate a continuing effort to peacefully resolve conflicts." The President said he fully supported the Camp David Accords, and complimented Egypt and Israel for completing the withdrawal of Israeli forces from the Sinai. But he called attention to the "unfinished business" of arranging for autonomy talks for Palestinians living on the West Bank and Gaza Strip—which also were agreed to at Camp David. Observing that the Lebanon war, though tragic, had left the United States with a new opportunity for Middle East peace, the President asserted that "we must seize it [the opportunity] now and bring peace to this troubled area so vital to world stability while there is still time." Mr. Reagan asserted that the question was how to reconcile Israel's legitimate security concerns with the legitimate rights of the Palestinians and concluded that this could be done only if both sides were willing to compromise. He called on Israel to "make clear that the security for which she yearns can only be achieved through genuine peace, a peace requiring magnanimity, vision and courage." The Palestinians, he said, should "recognize that their own political aspirations are inextricably bound to recognition of Israel's right to a secure future." As for the Arab States, the President asked them "to accept the reality of Israel—and the reality that peace and justice are to be gained only through hard, fair, direct negotiations."[6]

Recalling that the United States had not been willing to offer its own peace plan because it had hoped the parties themselves would see it to be in their own interests to negotiate a settlement, he now concluded that there needed to be a clearer sense of the U.S. position in order "to encourage wider support for the peace process." He then reaffirmed the Camp David call for a five-year period of local autonomy for the Palestinians to run their own affairs, and he called for the cessation of new Israeli settlements on the West Bank. The President voiced his opposition to the creation of an independent Palestinian state at the end of the five-year transitional period, but he also made clear that he would oppose Israel's annexation or control of the West Bank and Gaza. He asserted: "It is the firm view of the United States that self-government by the Palestinians of the West Bank and Gaza in association with Jordan offers the best chance for a durable, just and lasting peace. We base our approach squarely on the principle that the Arab-Israeli conflict should be resolved through negotiations involving an exchange of territory for peace." Mr. Reagan also said the United States believed that Jerusalem must remain an undivided city but that its final status should be decided through negotiation. In case American Jews or Israelis had any doubt that he had diminished his support of Israel's security, the President added that "America's commitment to the security of Israel is ironclad and, I might add, so is mine."[7]

The Begin government, as expected, totally rejected Mr. Reagan's plan and expressed displeasure that he had launched it so dramatically and without consultation. The Arab countries did not reject it but began a round of talks among their leaders to determine whether and under what conditions they might be prepared to support part of the U.S. initiative. Although it was clear to U.S. policy-makers that a breakthrough on the Palestinian autonomy question was some time off—perhaps after Menachem Begin had given up power in Israel—it was also clear that the Reagan administration had made a significant break with its own

6. *Presidential Documents* 18, no. 35 (6 Sept. 1982): 1082.
7. Ibid., 1085.

past views and had decided that true peace in the Middle East could not be achieved unless Israel withdrew from occupied territories. It was a major affirmation of U.S. national interests in the eastern Mediterranean area.

Events since September 1, 1982, show that President Reagan's effort to deal not only with the issue of troop withdrawal from Lebanon but also the larger issue of the future of the West Bank and Gaza territories has not been successful in bringing the key parties into agreement. The Begin government dismissed the President's plan and showed its disdain by refusing to enter serious negotiations about troop withdrawal from Lebanon until early in 1983. Meanwhile, the State Department sought to bring King Hussein of Jordan into negotiations with Israel and Washington on the Palestinian issue, but the king failed in April 1983 to persuade PLO leader Yasser Arafat to give him authority to negotiate for the Palestinians. With the PLO as well as Israel rejecting President Reagan's peace plan, his bold September 1 initiative seemed all but dead. What remained was the other U.S. goal, to get a troop withdrawal agreement on Lebanon. For this Secretary of State Shultz used shuttle diplomacy in April and May 1983 and finally achieved an agreement between the Israeli government and the Lebanese government of Amin Gemayel. Israel was to evacuate all its troops as part of a similar withdrawal of Syrian and PLO forces from eastern and northern Lebanon. However, Syria refused to accept the Israeli-Lebanon deal and vowed to resist withdrawal of its troops from Lebanon until Israel had made further concessions. By mid-1983, therefore, Lebanon remained occupied by Israeli and Syrian troops while the United States, Italy, France, and Great Britain kept peacekeeping troops in and around Beirut to prevent a resumption of Lebanon's civil war. The likelihood of de facto partition of Lebanon between Israel and Syria loomed large, unless the United States could persuade Syria to change its policy.

U.S. involvement as peacemaker between Israel and Lebanon and the reinforcement of the Marine battalion in Beirut as a peacekeeping force showed that Lebanon had become a very important U.S. interest in 1982-83. But was the U.S. interest *vital*, requiring it to remain in Lebanon indefinitely? Although the United States could not compel Syria to withdraw its roughly 40,000 troops from Lebanon or prevent it from inviting Soviet technicians to help defend its territory, the United States and its European allies had the capability to prevent the disintegration of the Lebanese state and/or its absorption into a Syrian and perhaps Soviet sphere of influence. So long as U.S. troops remained in Beirut and U.S. diplomacy supported the weak Gemayel government in its effort to assert authority over the country, U.S. interest and influence in Lebanon were considerable.

Secretary of State George Shultz, in testimony before the Senate and House Foreign Affairs committees in September 1983, summed up the Reagan administration's view of U.S. interests in Lebanon at that time: "The crisis in Lebanon cannot be isolated from the larger Middle East crisis. It involves many of the same issues of Middle East peace. It involves similar questions of security, respect for sovereignty, and peaceful settlement of disputes." He ended his presentation with this assertion: "At stake also are some concerns that affect our national interest and the security of our friends and allies. If American efforts for peaceful solutions are overwhelmed by brute force, our role is that much weakened everywhere. Friends who rely on us will be disheartened. Moderates in the Arab World whom we are encouraging to take risks for peace will feel it far from safe. The Soviet Union's efforts to disrupt our diplomacy will have scored a victory; radical and rejectionist elements will be strengthened. The cause of peace and justice will have suffered a setback."[8] Shultz believed that Lebanon was a key test of U.S. prestige in the Middle East, but his view was not shared by Congress, whose members brought increasing pressure on the Reagan administration to withdraw U.S. Marines. Early in 1984, the chaotic political situation in Lebanon persuaded President Reagan that a further peacekeeping role was impossible, and he withdrew the Marines. It may therefore be concluded that the U.S. interest in Lebanon never went above the *major* level. If it had done so in 1983- 84, the President should have sent combat troops to Lebanon and forced the Syrians and their Lebanese allies to stop their attacks on the Gemayel government.

Conclusions about U.S. national interests in the eastern Mediterranean may be summarized on the interest matrix as seen in

8. "Excerpts from a Statement by George P. Shultz," *New York Times*, 22 Sept. 1983, p. A12.

Fig. 9. U.S. National Interests in the Eastern Mediterranean

Basic Interest at Stake	Intensity of Interest			
	Survival	Vital	Major	Peripheral
Defense of Homeland			Israel Egypt	Lebanon
Economic Well-Being			Israel	Egypt Lebanon
Favorable World Order		Israel Egypt	Lebanon	
Promotion of Values		Israel	Egypt	Lebanon

Figure 9. This shows that neither the defense of the United States nor its economic well-being is vitally affected by what happens to Egypt, Israel, or Lebanon; nor, in fact, are U.S. ideological interests (values), except in the case of Israel. But the U.S. world-order interest in this area would be vitally affected were Israel or Egypt to be subverted from within or attacked by a hostile power. Dealing with internal subversion is a more difficult problem than a foreign attack; for example, defending a military government in Egypt against internal subversion would be difficult for an American government to justify. Nevertheless, this arc of countries along the eastern Mediterranean constitutes a vital part of U.S. containment strategy, and a President would be justified in using U.S. forces, if necessary, to defend all of them against a Soviet or Soviet-supported attack. This would apply also to Lebanon if it were threatened with a Soviet takeover.

The question of U.S. obligations to Israel is more complex. The key question is whether the United States has a vital interest in defending Israel *regardless* of the policies that country's government pursues toward its neighbors. Should the United States be committed to the security of Israel if its policies are so extreme that they turn the Arab world against Israel and the United States? I think not. The U.S. interest in Israel, even though it is deeper because of the ideological aspect than in any other country in the eastern Mediterranean, is not absolute: the level of interest ought to be contingent on Israel's being reasonable about dealing with its neighbors, including more than one million Palestinians who live under Israeli occupation. This means that Israel should not assume that an extreme view of *its* national aspirations will be supported by the United States. Even though President Reagan's peace proposals of September 1, 1982, were not accepted either by the Arabs or by Israel, they nevertheless set forth a reasonable resolution to the Palestinian problem, one which Israel will continue to ignore at the risk of further difficulties with the United States. In this respect, President Reagan's public definition of U.S. national interests in the region was an important step in defining U.S. goals for the future, goals that ought to become bipartisan in the U.S. political context.

U.S. Interests in Turkey and Greece

Turkey is the most important U.S. ally, from a strategic point of view, in the entire Mediterranean area. It controls the gateway for Soviet shipping between the Black Sea and the Mediterranean, and it has a long border with the Soviet Union. As one of the two countries directly affected by the Truman Doctrine of 1947, successive Turkish governments provided the United States with extremely valuable military and intelligence facilities from which to monitor Soviet weapons tests and gather other sensitive information. Since joining NATO in 1951, Turkey has been among the staunchest members of the alliance and has maintained strong defense forces. After the fall of the Shah in Iran in 1979 and the revolutionary regime's decision to close U.S. military facilities there, Turkey has become even more important to the United States as a monitoring post of Soviet missile testing. For this reason, Turkey is the only country in the Middle East that is near the vital level of U.S. defense-of-homeland interest. The loss of U.S. military and intelligence facilities in Turkey would directly affect the defense of North America, and Turkey is therefore an extremely important asset for United States defenses. Although Turkey is a member of NATO and a key factor in helping to protect NATO's southern flank, it constitutes a special case because it is the only member of NATO that is not Christian in religion and Western in culture; furthermore, it is not a fully democratic country. Severe security problems occurred in the late 1970s and caused the military to step into the government in order to prevent a civil war. The United States probably has only a peripheral ideological interest in Turkey.

Fig. 10. U.S. National Interests in Turkey and Greece

Basic Interest at Stake	Intensity of Interest			
	Survival	Vital	Major	Peripheral
Defense of Homeland			Turkey	Greece
Economic Well-Being			Greece	Turkey
Favorable World Order		Turkey Greece		
Promotion of Values			Greece	Turkey

The national interest matrix applied to Turkey and Greece is seen in Figure 10. The difficulty for American foreign policy in assigning Turkey so high a priority is that this conflicts with U.S. interests in Greece, another NATO ally, but one which believes that Turkey is a greater threat to its security than is the Soviet Union. Greece's antipathy for Turkey is rooted in a long history and need not concern us here; it is enough to say that all Greek governments, particularly the one headed by Dr. Andreas Papandreou in 1983, have found it politically prudent to protest large amounts of U.S. military and economic assistance to Turkey, even though both Turkey and the other NATO countries understand that this assistance is to bolster Turkish defenses against the Soviet Union. What gives Greek governments a powerful voice in Washington, particularly in Congress, is the same factor that gives Israel so much respect there: Greece can count on a powerful lobby of Greek Americans to argue against military aid to Turkey, in spite of the fact that such aid is essential in persuading Turkey to give the U.S. government permission to use its soil for vital operations related to U.S. defense interests.

This competition is nowhere better illustrated than in the congressional reaction to Turkey's decision in 1974 to send an invasion force to protect the Turkish minority population living in Cyprus. Since the majority of Cypriots are Greek by nationality, the Cyprus government coordinated its foreign policies closely with those of Athens and some Cypriot elements pressed for union with Greece—a totally unacceptable idea to Turkey, whose southern coast could then be threatened by a potentially hostile government in Athens. Finally, the Turkish population in Cyprus was being persecuted in 1974 to the point where the situation was intolerable for the Turkish government, that is, it became a *vital* interest.

The near-disaster for U.S. defense interests arose from the decision of Congress in 1975 to bar military aid to Turkey until it withdrew its troops from Cyprus—something Turkey flatly refused to do. As a result, the Turkish government closed U.S. military facilities in that country, and the state of readiness of its armed forces deteriorated measurably in the absence of U.S. aid; not even spare parts for previously purchased equipment were made available. Other NATO allies, notably West Germany, stepped in partially to fill the assistance gap. Yet the Congressional ban on aid to Turkey constituted a far more significant blow to U.S. interests in the eastern Mediterranean than another congressional prohibition on all aid to Angola which occurred the same year. In both cases, Congress prevailed in imposing its view of the national interest on the President. By 1979, with Iran eliminated as a strategic U.S. outpost on the Soviet border, Congress changed its view and again voted for military assistance to Turkey. However, the amount of aid is still subject to sharp debate in Congress because the Greek government protests regularly that an imbalance is developing in its military readiness, given Turkey's growing strength. The issue of aid to Greece in 1983 was closely tied to that government's decision on whether to permit the continuation of four U.S. air and naval facilities in the country, and on what conditions. The United States felt a greater obligation to provide large-scale aid to Turkey in return for use of its strategic territory than it did to a leftist Greek government, whose declared policy was to terminate U.S. military operations on its soil. In the summer of 1983, however, Greece agreed to an extension of U.S. base rights for another five years.

The Persian Gulf Region in U.S. National Interests

The Persian Gulf, in my view, is not as important to U.S. national interests as the eastern Mediterranean; and it is clearly not as important as Western Europe. The declarations of President Jimmy Carter in 1980 and of President Ronald Reagan in 1981 that the Persian Gulf is a *vital* area of interest to the United States are open to serious challenge when the basis of that claim is assessed against the national interest framework.

The U.S. interest arose originally during World War II when some 30,000 American troops were stationed in western Iran. Their purpose was to protect the Lend-Lease lifeline from the United States to the Soviet Union and thus to help the latter remain in the war against Nazi Germany. Similarly, the United States had forces stationed in Saudi Arabia to protect the Persian Gulf region against the Axis powers. A large airbase at Daharan was built by the U.S. Army as a communications link to British forces in India as well as U.S. forces in Iran. President Roosevelt met with King Ibn Saud in 1945, as part of his journey to the summit conference in Yalta with Prime Minister Churchill and Soviet Party Secretary Josef Stalin. After the war the United States established cordial relations with both the Saudi and the Iranian monarchies, and the Shah of Iran became one of the region's best friends to the U.S., remaining so until he was deposed in 1979. The United States was instrumental in saving the Shah's throne in 1953 when it helped to oust Mossadegh from power after he declared Iran's intention to nationalize its oil resources. Iraq, the third important Persian Gulf state, was friendly with the United States until a violent revolution took place in 1958, overturning the monarchy in favor of a leftist government. The new regime was anti-American, and it established close relations with the Soviet Union.

The Eisenhower administration believed that the Persian Gulf region was important to the United States as part of the world-wide containment policy established by President Truman. Eisenhower and Dulles supported a British-sponsored Middle East defense arrangement called the Baghdad Pact, linking Turkey, Iraq, Iran, and Pakistan with Britain and the United States in a security chain designed to enable them to resist Soviet political and military pressure. The United States never formally joined this pact because Secretary of State John Foster Dulles ascertained that he could not obtain Senate ratification of a treaty. Therefore, the United States accepted associate membership status and provided considerable military and economic assistance to the members, as well as political support to the pact's objectives. In 1958, as a result of the revolution in Iraq and Baghdad's withdrawal from the pact, the organization changed its name to the Central Treaty Organization (CENTO). It then continued to function into the 1970s, when it ceased to exist because of Pakistan's withdrawal and Turkey's disenchantment with U.S. policy. Syria and Egypt, however, formed an alliance and accepted arms from the Soviet Union. Iraq also accepted Soviet aid after 1958. CENTO therefore became the umbrella under which the United States provided military assistance to Iran and Pakistan—both of which continued to support U.S. containment objectives in the Middle East. Pakistan's unsuccessful war with India in 1971, during which Washington stopped military aid, caused its government to review relations with the United States; it came to the conclusion that a military pact with Washington was no longer in its interest. It then withdrew from the Southeast Asia Treaty Organization as well as from CENTO.

In sum, the military containment policy started in the Truman administration and broadened in the Eisenhower administration was not successful in uniting the Arab countries, Iran, and Pakistan into a bloc of Middle East states, actively working in concert to resist Soviet political influence. By 1979, when Iran underwent a revolution, the United States had lost the support of all the Asian members of the original Baghdad Pact—Iraq, Iran, Pakistan, and even Turkey. By any measurement, this represented a serious reversal of twenty-five years of American diplomacy in the Middle East. The decision of Iran's Revolutionary Government to hold fifty-two American diplomatic personnel as hostages for fifteen months in 1979 and 1980 was a dramatic demonstration that the United States had seriously miscalculated its ability to pursue ambitious policies in this area of the world, or even to protect its own citizens. It was the nadir for U.S. postwar policy in the Middle East.

Current U.S. policy to defend the Persian Gulf region with U.S. forces is not based on any treaty commitments but rather on a declaration made by President Carter in his State of the Union address to Congress in January 1980, and reiterated by President Ronald Reagan early in 1981. The basis for Mr. Carter's astonishing extension of U.S. vital interests into the Persian Gulf region was his fear that the Soviet Union, which had sent an invasion force into Afghanistan only three weeks earlier, was then positioning itself for military moves into Iran and Pakistan. "The invasion of Afghanistan," the former President wrote in his memoirs, "was direct aggression by the Soviet armed forces against a freedom-loving people, whose leaders had been struggling to retain a modicum of independence from their huge neighbor. . . . The brutality of the act was bad enough, but the threat of this Soviet invasion to the rest of the region was very clear—and had grim consequences. A successful take-over of Afghanistan would give the Soviets a deep penetration between Iran and Pakistan, and pose a threat to the rich oil fields of the Persian Gulf area and to the crucial waterways through which so much of the world's energy supplies had to pass." Mr. Carter recalled that "I sent Brezhnev on the hot line the sharpest message of my Presidency, telling him that the invasion of Afghanistan was 'a clear threat to the peace' and could mark a fundamental and long-lasting turning point in our relations."[9]

The bold statement on the Persian Gulf that President Carter included in his State of the Union message on January 23, 1980, read as follows: "Let our position be absolutely clear: An attempt by any outside force to gain control of the Persian Gulf region will be regarded as an assault on the vital interests of the United States of America, and such an assault will be repelled by any means necessary, including military force." The President explained later that "this statement was not lightly made, and I was resolved to use the full power of the United States to back it up. . . The fact was that mine was a carefully considered statement, which would have been backed by concerted action, not necessarily confined to any small invaded area or to tactics or terrain of the Soviets' choosing. We simply could not afford to let them extend their domination to adjacent areas around the Persian Gulf which were so important to us and to other nations of the world."[10]

The astonishing aspect of this declaration of U.S. willingness to engage in war in the Persian Gulf region was that it was not given sanction in any congressional resolution, such as the Tonkin Gulf Resolution which President Lyndon Johnson obtained in August 1964 when he decided that American military force might have to be used in Southeast Asia. Indeed, there was widespread skepticism in the U.S. press and congressional cir-

9. Jimmy Carter, *Keeping Faith* (New York, 1982), 471-72.
10. Ibid., 472.

cles in 1980 that this so-called "Carter Doctrine" was an empty
threat because the United States clearly did not have the military
forces available to repel a Soviet attack on Iran, or any other
country in the region. While it is true that the Carter administration proceeded immediately to strengthen the newly created
Rapid Deployment Force for use in the Gulf area, it was obvious
in 1980 that there was little the United States could do to repel a
sustained Soviet military thrust into Iran if Moscow chose to take
that course. The important fact is, however, that an American
president for the first time declared that the Persian Gulf region is
a *vital* interest of the United States and that it would be defended
by American military forces. That declaration remains the official
view of the U.S. Government, but it has not been approved by a
specific act of Congress—which leaves open to doubt the U.S.
national commitment to the Persian Gulf as a vital interest.

In his annual report to Congress for fiscal year 1984 Secretary of
Defense Caspar Weinberger, stated: "It is our policy to support
the independence and territorial integrity of the countries in this
politically unstable region, and to prevent a further spread of
Soviet domination. Furthermore, one-third of the free world's oil
supply is produced in SWA [Southwest Asia] making it vital to
the interests of the U.S. and especially to those of our allies." The
Secretary went on to describe the threats that he saw to U.S.
interests: "The continuing Soviet occupation of Afghanistan, the
Iran-Iraq war, and the lower level interregional disputes, such as
those between North and South Yemen, exemplify the range of
regional instabilities that complicate our policy and strategy. . . An overt Soviet invasion would of course represent a far
more demanding requirement for a military response. Such an
invasion would lead to the establishment of Soviet control in vital
areas if the U.S., together with our allies and regional friends,
were unprepared to respond rapidly with sufficient force."[11]

An excellent short report issued by the Congressional Budget
Office early in 1983, entitled *Rapid Deployment Forces: Policy and
Budgetary Implications*, was more explicit as to why the Reagan
administration was planning for a military force of 440,000 men
for quick deployment to the Persian Gulf: "The configuration of

---

11. Caspar W. Weinberger, *Annual Report to the Congress, Fiscal Year 1984*
(Washington, D.C.: Government Printing Office, 1983), 192.

this force is designed primarily to counter what the Administration believes is the most serious threat to Southwest Asia: a Soviet invasion of Iran. Inherent in this thinking is the belief that all contingencies of a lesser nature could be handled using only part of the larger RDF. Thus, if the United States could defeat a Soviet invasion of Iran, it could carry out the Carter Doctrine that commits the United States to repel any outside attempt to gain control of another nation in the Persian Gulf region."[12]

The CBO study assessed the amount of oil flowing to the West from the Persian Gulf to be 20 percent, rather than the 33 percent used by the Secretary of Defense in his report to Congress, but agreed that "a successful invasion of Iran could cut off these oil supplies and exert severe economic pressures on the West." The study went on to question whether even an enlarged Rapid Deployment Force could stop a Soviet invasion of Iran, in view of the fact that no Middle Eastern country had thus far given the United States permission to use its territory as a staging area for the RDF. It also doubted that any Iranian government would welcome another U.S. military presence on its soil. The CBO study said the Soviets would have considerable difficulty trying to take over Iran and that a more likely scenario, if Moscow moved at all, would be "a limited attack to secure the northwest region of Iran. Such an action would be motivated by logistic concerns similar to those underlying the Soviets' aggression against Afghanistan." The report concluded that "a Soviet invasion of Iran appears to most military analysts to be a highly implausible prospect. The Administration agrees that limited regional conflicts or subversion are in fact far more likely. Yet it has decided that RDF sizing and planning should be based on the worst possible threat."[13]

There are only two grounds on which the United States might have a vital interest in the Persian Gulf or Southwest Asia region: (1) to insure the continued flow of Persian Gulf oil to world markets, unimpeded either by outside interference in the region or by conflicts among states within it—such as the Iran-Iraq war: and (2) to prevent the Soviet Union from expanding its influence

12. *The Rapid Deployment Force and Budgetary Implications* (Washignton, D.C.: Congressional Budget Office, 1983), 11-12.
13. Ibid., 14-15.

or domination in the Middle East and challenging the world balance of power. The latter is the U.S. world-order interest, and the former is its economic well-being interest. Let us examine these two bases of a vital interest.

A decade ago, in 1973, the Western world was confronted by an embargo of Persian Gulf oil by the Arab States. Europe, Japan, and the United States all suffered serious economic dislocations as a result—including a four-fold increase in the price of oil. Yet despite this clear threat to U.S. economic well-being, President Nixon decided that the U.S. economic interest was *major*, not vital, and concluded that the country could live with the consequences of his decision even though the gas lines in the United States and the increased prices of energy were painful. The idea of using force, as some commentators proposed at the time, was not a wise course of action for many reasons, not least because the American public and Congress were in no mood to be involved militarily in the Persian Gulf six months after the last American forces had been withdrawn from Vietnam. Much has happened in the last ten years to make Persian Gulf oil less important to the economic well-being of the U.S. American dependence on this area's oil has declined significantly as Mexican and Alaskan oil has become available in significant quantities; as Britain has become self-sufficient in oil; as energy consumption in the United States, Japan, and Western Europe has declined dramatically; and as alternative sources of energy have been developed. For example, the U.S. import of Arab oil in the first quarter of 1983 was 60 percent below what it had been a year earlier. In 1984 only 3 percent of U.S. oil imports came from the Persian Gulf. In sum, the United States, Western Europe, and Japan had all cut their dependence on Persian Gulf oil dramatically, and in early 1983 OPEC was forced to reduce oil prices. Saudi Arabia, in particular, decided to reduce its production from about ten million barrels a day in 1979 to about half that amount in 1983 in order to maintain the world price at $28 per barrel.

By most standards, it cannot be argued effectively that the United States and Europe in 1984 are heavily dependent on Persian Gulf oil; therefore, oil from this region should not be viewed as a *vital* U.S. interest. Admittedly, Japan continues to be heavily dependent on Iranian oil, but Japan too is aware of the danger to its economy and is finding alternative sources of oil, as well as developing its nuclear power capacity. Indonesia and Mexico are increasingly important as Japanese sources of oil.

A second possible basis for declaring a U.S. vital interest in the Persian Gulf—the one that clearly motivated President Carter to make his January 1980 assertion—is potential Soviet encroachment on its southern neighbors' territory and use of this strategic position to dominate the politics of the Persian Gulf and Southwest Asian states. The Soviet thirst for influence and control in the direction of the Indian Ocean goes back to Czarist times and was reaffirmed at the time of Stalin's pact with Hitler in 1939, when the two countries divided Poland and sought to carve out spheres of influence. The Shah's Iran and the British Navy effectively checked this Soviet ambition after World War II, but the fall of the Pahlavi dynasty in Iran in 1979, the power vacuum left in the Indian Ocean by the British military withdrawal east of Suez in 1971, and the perceived weakness of the Carter administration in dealing with the political situation in Iran may have led the Kremlin to conclude that it could safely undermine the government of Afghanistan, make that country another client state, and position itself for a strike into Iran when the opportunity arose. The Soviet desire, or interest, to extend its influence southward toward the Indian Ocean is not questioned by most experts on the Soviet Union; what is in dispute is what risks Moscow is willing to take, how strongly the small Persian Gulf states would resist Soviet pressures, and whether it is a U.S. *vital* interest—entailing the potential use of force—to prevent the Soviet Union from increasing its influence in this region. In short, has the containment of Soviet influence outside Iran, Iraq, Kuwait, and Saudi Arabia become so important to the United States that the President should ask Congress for authorization to engage in warfare with the Soviet Union? This question is particularly pertinent when nearly all experts agree that such a war could not be fought in Iran, or elsewhere in the region, without diverting U.S. troops and aircraft from the European theater and depriving NATO of U.S. reinforcements in time of crisis.[14]

The near-term issue in the Persian Gulf, insofar as U.S. interests are concerned, is Iran. In the longer term, the issue is Saudi

14. Ibid., ch. 3, "The Effects of an RDF Mobilization on the U.S. Commitment to NATO."

Arabia. Both have large oil reserves and both are capable of larger production. Both would like to exercise the primary influence among other Persian Gulf states, and both consider the Soviet Union to be an undesirable influence in the region. However, the Saudi government has been, and remains, friendly to the United States and to Western involvement in the security of the region. The revolutionary government instituted by the Ayatollah Khomeini in Iran after his elevation to power in 1979 is adamantly opposed to both Western and Soviet influence. It is hard to imagine that the American people and Congress would accept Iran as a vital or even major American interest in the foreseeable future, after the humiliation the Ayatollah's regime inflicted on American diplomats in 1979-80 and its unremitting propaganda blasts against "the Great Satan." Therefore, if the U.S. Defense Department believes that Iran is a strategically vital interest, this view must be weighed against the fact that Iran is hostile to the United States and that the American people would not be prepared to protect Iran in case the Soviet Union decided to invade or subvert it. In sum, Iran like Iraq (after it changed governments in 1958 and turned against the West) is not likely to gain the support of any Western country if it asks for help to resist Soviet intimidation or a Soviet-sponsored insurgency designed to topple the revolutionary regime. Most Americans would more likely say that Iran and the U.S.S.R. deserve each other.

Saudi Arabia is a different case, a country that has shared U.S. interests in the region since World War II and which could seriously affect the West's economic well-being if it succumbed to Soviet or Iranian influence, or to the accession to power of a deeply nationalist, anti-Western government. Yet the Saudi government today is unwilling to have U.S. forces stationed on its soil, and it refuses to make peace with Israel until the latter agrees to provide the Palestinian people with a homeland. Although Saudi Arabia is certainly important to the United States, it is difficult to make the case that Saudi Arabia is so crucial, either for economic or world-order reasons, that U.S. troops should be used to defend it—particularly if the Saudis do not want U.S. military facilities on their soil. In my view, the only scenario that would justify treating Saudi Arabia as a *vital* interest would be an attack on it by the Soviet Union, either from the north through Iraq or from the east through Iran. U.S. military action would

Fig. 11. U.S. National Interests in the Persian Gulf

Basic Interest at Stake	Intensity of Interest			
	Survival	Vital	Major	Peripheral
Defense of Homeland			Saudi Arabia	Iran Iraq
Economic Well-Being			Saudi Arabia	Iran Iraq
Favorable World Order		Saudi Arabia	Iran Iraq	
Promotion of Values				Saudi Arabia Iran Iraq

have to be contingent on the Saudi government's willingness to grant the United States the bases necessary to handle Air Force planes and the logistical facilities necessary to support the Rapid Deployment Force. Under no circumstances should the United States use its forces to intervene in a Saudi civil war, or a threatened coup d'état.

The level of U.S. interest in the Persian Gulf may be summarized as shown on the interest matrix in Figure 11. It is assumed here that the promotion of values interest does not include trying to institute Western-type governments or Christian values in the Muslim countries, and that guaranteeing individual freedoms is not a primary objective of U.S. foreign policy in this area. The U.S. economic interest is major because of oil; its world-order interest is vital only in the case of Saudi Arabia because of that country's central location and great influence on other Persian Gulf states.

Summing Up

The United States has had a vital world-order interest in the Mediterranean area since 1947 when President Truman, with congressional support, declared that Greece and Turkey were vital U.S. interests. Following the 1967 Arab-Israeli war, Israel became a vital interest because of its military power and the growing ideological interest of the American people in Israel's security. Egypt became a vital U.S. interest when President Anwar Sadat reversed Egyptian policies in the 1970s by ousting Soviet military advisers, by making peace with Israel, and by linking Egypt's defense efforts with those of the United States. Even though his successor, President Mubarak, has not agreed to the permanent stationing of U.S. forces in his country, military cooperation between Egypt and the United States is growing, and Egypt has shown through joint military exercises that it would be allied to the United States in time of war. President Reagan's decision to send U.S. Marines to Beirut as peacekeepers in 1982 suggested that Lebanon might be added to the list of eastern Mediterranean states that are vital world-order interests of the United States, but this was denied in February 1984 by U.S. reluctance to become more involved in that country's internal problems and President Reagan's decision to withdraw the Marines.

Conversely, there is no country in the Persian Gulf region, or in Southwest Asia, that can realistically be considered a vital U.S. interest even though two Presidents have said that region is vital. The possible exception is Saudi Arabia, whose oil reserves remain sufficiently important to the Western world and whose government is so cooperative that the United States probably could not tolerate letting it come under Soviet influence through intimidation or armed conflict. Neither Iran nor Pakistan can today be viewed as a vital U.S. interest, but Pakistan does qualify as a high major interest in terms of world-order. The United States would be justified in using economic and military assistance and a modest amount of covert actions to support its interests in the Southwest Asia/Persian Gulf area; but it would be unwise to acquire military bases there or contemplate using U.S. forces to defend any country in that region—except Saudi Arabia—if the Soviet Union makes additional military moves similar to its 1979 action in Afghanistan. The United States has no interest in Iran that would warrant the use of American forces there.

In the longer term, as part of a general accommodation of U.S. and Soviet interests in the Middle East and a reduction of military threats and tensions, the United States, Western Europe, and Japan may be forced into a situation where they will have to settle for a division of Iran into spheres of influence. Such accommodation would acknowledge that the Soviet Union has a key political role in northern Iran, with which it shares a long border, while the United States, Europe, and Japan have large interests in the southwestern part. A political division of responsibility in Iran occurred during World War II when the Soviet Union, the United States, and Britain were allied against Nazi Germany. Although it is doubtful that any American President or Congress could formally agree to such an understanding in the 1980s, it is conceivable that a tacit arrangement could be reached in the future to prevent Iran from becoming the trigger for a war between the United States and the Soviet Union—one which could spread to Europe and North America. If neither the United States nor the Soviet Union has an interest in controlling *all* of Iran, a deal to neutralize or occupy it might be a logical alternative to war between the superpowers.

6. East Asia: Area of American Ambivalence

The Far East, as it was officially known until the 1960s, was an important economic area for the United States before World War II but was never considered a vital interest. This was so even after the United States gained control of the Philippines, following the Spanish-American War, and established military bases there. Acquiring these islands gave the United States a major stake in what happened in the western Pacific, but it did not imply that the United States was prepared to take a leading role in the international relations of Northeast Asia (Japan, Korea, Soviet Union) or in Southeast Asia which, with the exception of Thailand, was under the colonial control of the British, French, and Dutch. The Open Door policy toward China never signaled more than a major U.S. interest in that country.

Japan's rise as a major power during the early part of the twentieth century was not seen by U.S. policy-makers as a serious threat to U.S. interests in the western Pacific so long as Imperial Japan confined its ambitions to Northeast Asia and to China. Consequently, Washington acquiesced in Japan's invasions of China in 1931 and 1937 and its occupation of French-controlled North Vietnam in 1940. Even though the United States carried on extensive trade in China before the war, American policy-makers did not view China as a vital interest and were not prepared during the 1930s to challenge Japan's drive to control the whole of mainland China. After Hitler's armies attacked the Soviet Union in June 1941, Japan took advantage of Russia's preoccupation to invade South Vietnam and Cambodia (then part of French Indochina) and impose its own control. Only then, in July 1941, did

President Franklin Roosevelt heed British Prime Minister Winston Churchill's warning that the Japanese were preparing to attack southward into Malaya, Singapore, and the Dutch East Indies.[1]

President Roosevelt's decision in July 1941 to freeze Japanese assets in the United States and ban oil shipments was a frontal challenge to the Japanese government and signaled that U.S. world-order interests in East Asia had risen from the major to the vital level. This sudden action struck at the vital economic interests of Japan: it could not continue its military buildup in Asia without oil from the United States, and it could not achieve its dream of a Japanese-dominated Southeast Asia if the U.S. Navy were used to block its movement southward. In the fall of 1941, therefore, Japan had a choice between accommodation with the new U.S. vital interest in Southeast Asia or war with the United States. If Tokyo chose the latter course, it needed quickly to seize control of the oil fields of Sumatra and protect the sea-lanes from there to Japan. The United States was the only power that stood in the way of Imperial Japan's reaching its goal of dominant power in East Asia, because all the European powers with interests in Asia (Britain, France, the U.S.S.R., the Netherlands) were by then absorbed in the European war.

It is clear from a comparison of U.S. and Japanese interests in the fall of 1941 that Japan's were of higher intensity than those of the United States and that Tokyo might therefore start hostilities at any time. The Roosevelt administration was aware after July 1941 that the two countries were on a collision course and that war probably would ensue. Having broken Japan's secret codes, the U.S. government expected the Japanese Navy to attack somewhere in the Pacific, the Philippines being considered the most likely place. It may have been a surprise that the attack was on Hawaii, but Japan's decision to go to war was not. Roosevelt, deciding that vital U.S. interests were at stake, gave the Imperial Government its choice: to capitulate to U.S. demands that it withdraw from Indochina and stop the invasion of China, or to go to war.

1. The Netherlands, the colonial power in the Dutch East Indies, and France, which controlled the three Indochina states, were defeated and occupied by Hitler's armies in the spring of 1940. Britain continued to resist Hitler's attacks and retained control of Malaya, Singapore, and North Borneo until December 1941.

U.S. world-order interests in East Asia moved from the major to the vital level in 1941 for balance-of-power reasons—not economic, ideological, or even defense-of-homeland reasons. The United States could not tolerate having all of East Asia and the western Pacific being controlled by one great power, just as it could not tolerate a similar situation in Europe. The Japanese declaration of war on the United States on December 7, 1941, solved a potentially serious dilemma for Roosevelt on two continents: Japan's attack on Pearl Harbor mobilized American public opinion to defeat its ambitions in Asia, and Japan's declaration of war caused Hitler's Germany to declare war on the United States a few days later. The United States was suddenly a united country in the struggle against both Axis powers.

After World War II and the defeat of Japan, the United States again decided that it had no vital interests at stake on the mainland of East Asia. Even though strong political forces in the country and in Congress thought the United States should have a vital interest in preventing the Chinese Communists from winning their revolution and establishing a Marxist-Leninist regime in China, President Harry Truman decided early in his tenure that the United States had only a major interest in the outcome of the Chinese civil war. He therefore put a ceiling on the amount of military assistance he would grant to the Nationalist government, and he ruled out using U.S. military forces in an attempt to influence the outcome of the war. Similarly, Truman decided to withdraw U.S. military occupation forces from South Korea in 1949, as part of an effort to defuse tensions on that peninsula. This was done because the Truman administration did not believe that U.S. vital interests were involved in Korea and because U.S. forces worldwide were stretched too thin. In Southeast Asia, although the United States could have played an important security role there after World War II, the U.S. Government decided that only peripheral U.S. interests were at stake and that the British, French, and Dutch should provide security in that region. Had Franklin Roosevelt lived, there is a strong likelihood that he might have opposed the return of French and Dutch colonial rule to Indochina and the East Indies, respectively; but Truman, who assumed office in April 1945, believed U.S. interests in Europe were far more important than those in the Far East, and he therefore limited the U.S. presence in Southeast Asia to the

Philippines. Independence was given to the Philippine people in 1946, as scheduled, and the United States concluded a defense treaty that gave it the right to maintain military bases and large military forces in the country. The Philippines, for historical and strategic reasons, was reestablished as a vital world-order interest of the United States in 1946 and has remained so ever since. Australia and New Zealand, which had been protected by the United States during World War II and contributed enormously in manpower to the Allied war effort, remained a vital world-order interest of the United States after 1945. This was confirmed by conclusion of the ANZUS Pact in 1951. Japan was an occupied country after August 1945, under the complete dominance of the United States, which set about to remake Japanese society. It eventually became a vital interest of the United States for three reasons: economic well-being of the United States, balance of power in Asia, and promotion of democratic values and government in Asia.

In sum, from 1945 to 1950, U.S. interests in East Asia remained at the major level except for the island chain off the mainland: Japan, Okinawa (later returned to Japan), the Philippines, Australia, and New Zealand. The United States also administered, under United Nations supervision, the Pacific Trust Territories, groups of former Japanese-controlled islands in the western Pacific. This large area of the Pacific was assigned to the United States as a strategic trust. The United States has maintained military facilities there since World War II, and the Pacific islands remain a vital world-order interest of this country today.

Truman's Shift in View of U.S. National Interests

Secretary of State Dean Acheson, with President Truman's endorsement, gave a major speech at the National Press Club in Washington on January 12, 1950, in which he laid out his assessment of U.S. interests in East Asia. This was delivered in a highly charged political atmosphere, due to the fact that the Communist Party of China had established a new government there only three months earlier and General Chiang Kai-shek had fled with his remaining Nationalist forces to Formosa (Taiwan). Congressional Republicans had mounted a vigorous campaign around the theme of "Who lost China?" and called for Acheson's resignation. In the Press Club address, Acheson defended the administration's decision to end U.S. support of Chiang's corrupt regime, and he asserted a limited view of U.S. vital security interests in the Western Pacific. In his memoirs Acheson relates why he made this controversial speech: "Its purpose was to bring home what the United States Government had done to defend vital interests in the Pacific, not to speculate on what it would do in the event of various exigencies in Asia. Our defense stations beyond the western hemisphere and our island possessions were the Philippines and the defeated, disarmed and occupied Japan. These were our inescapable responsibilities. We had moved our line of defense, a line fortified and manned by our own ground, sea, and air forces, to the very edges of the Western Pacific." Acheson pointed out that General Douglas MacArthur had stated a year earlier in Tokyo that the U.S. defense line in the Pacific started in the Philippines and continued through the Ryukyu Archipelago and then bent back to include Japan and the Aleutian Island chain to Alaska. Acheson asserted that *his* defense line followed MacArthur's but went from northeast to southwest: "This defensive perimeter runs along the Aleutians to Japan and then goes to the Ryukyus. . . . The defensive perimeter runs from the Ryukyus to the Philippine Islands."[2] Acheson was attacked later by Republican critics who held him responsible for signaling to North Korea that his defense line did not include South Korea.

Two events that occurred during the first six months of 1950 shattered Acheson and Truman's view of U.S. security interests in Asia and forced them to extend the U.S. vital interest line to include South Korea: the Sino-Soviet Defense Treaty of February 14, 1950, and North Korea's attack on South Korea on June 24, 1950. These actions sharply altered the U.S. government's perception of its interests in East Asia and led to the U.S. military intervention in Korea in 1950 and in Vietnam fifteen years later. In both cases the United States intervened in civil wars on the Asian mainland in the belief that the "Sino-Soviet Bloc" was determined to accomplish what Japan had been prevented from achieving in World War II: the political domination of all of East Asia. The historical and political differences between the Soviet Union and

2. Dean Acheson, *Present at the Creation* (New York, 1969), 356-57.

Communist China were not taken seriously by American policy-makers in 1950, or in 1965; what mattered was that after the Sino-Soviet Pact of February 1950, the United States under both Democratic and Republican presidents concluded that Moscow and Peking were acting in tandem in the Far East and that U.S. world-order interests were threatened just as severely in 1950 and 1965 by the Communist powers as they had been in 1941 by Imperial Japan. It was no longer sufficient, U.S. policy-makers concluded, for the United States to base its Pacific defense on the offshore islands along the periphery of the Asian mainland. In view of the Communist threat, President Truman concluded that it was imperative for the United States to make defense agreements with Chiang Kai-shek's government in Taiwan, with the South Korean government of Syngman Rhee, and with the military government of Thailand to contain the expansionist power of China and the Soviet Union. It was also necessary, after June 1950, for the United States to reverse its hands-off policy toward French colonialism in Indochina and give the French the necessary military and economic aid to participate in this containment effort in Asia. Britain was already fighting a Communist insurgency in Malaya and could be counted on to endorse the containment policy, but few Asian countries were interested in an Asian anti-Communist pact. Indonesia, the largest East Asian country after China, had achieved independence from Holland in 1949 and was opposed to joining either of the great power blocs. President Sukarno instead joined with India's Nehru in forming the nonaligned group of nations. Burma too followed a nonaligned course. In short, everything changed in 1950 in the U.S. perception of the stakes in East Asia when North Korea with Soviet support attacked South Korea and China entered that war a few months later. The realization in Washington that Japan would be severely threatened by Sino-Soviet domination of the Korean Peninsula caused President Truman to conclude that Korea as well as Japan was a vital world-order interest. Therefore, he immediately dispatched U.S. troops to defend this expanded interest, and U.S. forces have remained in South Korea ever since. Truman took special care, however, to insure that U.S. military moves were part of a United Nations effort, not a unilateral American intervention.

In Indochina, the U.S. interest escalated from a peripheral one prior to 1950 into a major one as a result of China's and the Soviet

Union's support of Vietnamese Communist forces led by Ho Chi Minh. In 1954, when France was on the verge of abandoning its position in Indochina, President Eisenhower made an agonizing decision about whether to support French forces with American air power, and possibly ground forces as well; he decided against it—despite strong recommendations from Secretary of State John Foster Dulles and Admiral Arthur Radford, Chairman of the Joint Chiefs of Staff. In effect, Eisenhower concluded that although preventing a Communist takeover in Indochina was a major U.S. concern, it was not a vital one and did not therefore warrant the use of American military force. He believed that a Communist victory over French forces would be painful but not intolerable for the United States, and he therefore instructed Secretary Dulles to seek a negotiated settlement of the conflict. This resulted in the Geneva Accords of 1954, which divided Vietnam into two administrative parts: the North controlled by the Viet Minh Communists, and the South controlled by non-Communist political groups which eventually supported a government headed by Ngo Dinh Diem. Laos and Cambodia were given independence and were to remain unaligned.

The Vietnam War and U.S. Interests

In 1961, when John F. Kennedy became President, the security situation in Laos and South Vietnam was deteriorating. The new President had to decide whether the U.S. interest should remain at the major level, meaning economic and military aid only, or whether a Communist takeover of South Vietnam and probably Laos and Cambodia would be an intolerable blow to U.S. world-order interests and thus require stronger action. After about six months of intensive debate within his administration, President Kennedy and his National Security Council decided late in 1961 that the U.S. interest in preventing a Communist takeover of South Vietnam was a vital one and that American combat forces should be used, if necessary, to defend South Vietnam if its government proved incapable of doing so. From 1962 until 1965, the U.S. military involvement in Vietnam rose steadily, with helicopter crews, Green Beret units, and thousands of military advisers being sent there.

When Lyndon Johnson became President in November 1963,

the security situation in South Vietnam was nearly hopeless. In August 1964, he asked Congress for a joint declaration, known as the Tonkin Gulf Resolution, which declared that the defense of Southeast Asia against Communist aggression was a vital interest of the United States and would warrant the use of U.S. forces. This resolution, which gave what critics later called a "blank check" to the President to use U.S. forces in Vietnam, was passed by overwhelming majorities in both the Senate and the House of Representatives. After Mr. Johnson's landslide election victory in November 1964, he had the choice of deciding whether to accept President Kennedy's view that Vietnam was *vital*, or reverse the 1961 decision and go back to Dwight Eisenhower's view that Indochina constituted only a major interest. Lyndon Johnson, who had urged President Kennedy in 1961 to take a military stand in Vietnam, predictably decided not only to increase the U.S. commitment, but to do so massively in the expectation that the Hanoi government would recognize that it could not win a war in South Vietnam and would then negotiate a permanent division of the country into two sovereign states. When extensive aerial bombing of North Vietnam early in 1965 did not achieve this result, President Johnson sent a large number of Army, Navy, and Air Force units to Vietnam, which eventually numbered more than half a million men. When even this massive use of U.S. power did not cause North Vietnam to end its intervention in South Vietnam, President Johnson decided in March 1968 to deescalate the war and seek a negotiated settlement. In effect, the President decided that "winning" in Vietnam was not a vital U.S. interest after all, and that the U.S. military force there should be reduced. It was left to his successor, Richard Nixon, who took office in January 1969, to find a way to extricate the United States from a dangerous overcommitment of arms and prestige in Southeast Asia. In 1973 a negotiated settlement was finally arranged whereby all U.S. military forces were removed from Vietnam. Two years later the North launched a final, massive attack and took over South Vietnam.

Historians and pundits will argue for many years about whether the United States should ever have been involved in the armed struggle for Vietnam and, if it had vital interests there, why it did not invade the North and win a military victory. In my view, the United States had a vital interest in preventing Soviet and Chinese influence from taking over all of the area known as Southeast Asia, but it did not have a vital interest—at least not one requiring the deployment of half a million U.S. combat forces—in protecting the government of South Vietnam if the latter could not deal effectively with the Viet Cong insurgency by using U.S. aid. In 1963, President Kennedy realized that the South Vietnamese government was incapable of winning a victory over the Viet Cong, and he decided to replace the Diem government with what proved to be a series of military rulers—none of whom could command the full loyalty of the South Vietnamese people. The fateful decision about U.S. intervention was made by President Lyndon Johnson in the summer of 1965, and it soon became clear that the American public and Congress would not support a long war, particularly if it entailed high casualties. After three years of ever increasing U.S. involvement, the President decided to negotiate. In effect, what the Johnson administration had found *intolerable* in 1965 became more tolerable by 1968.

If the U.S. interest in Southeast Asia was a *vital* one in 1965, the disaster that befell U.S. policy in Vietnam must be balanced against what occurred in the rest of Southeast Asia at that time, particularly in Thailand (which had joined with the United States in the Manila Pact of September 1954), in Indonesia, and in Malaysia/Singapore. In retrospect, it may be concluded that unless the United States had made some kind of stand against Communist-supported revolutions in the area, Indonesia under President Sukarno's tutelage probably would have become a Communist-dominated state in the autumn of 1965. That is when the PKI (Indonesian Communist Party) staged a revolt against the army and came close to taking over the government with Sukarno's approval. However, the army rallied, after most of its top command had been murdered, under the direction of a senior officer, General Suharto. It was important to the future direction of this army-led government that the United States was seen as prepared to resist the southward thrust of Asian Communism into Southeast Asia. Earlier, in 1963-64, British, Australian, and New Zealand forces might not have been willing to prevent Sukarno from taking over Malaysia had the Commonwealth governments believed that the United States would restrict its vital interests to the Philippines and permit areas to the west to be subdued by pro-

Communist forces. Similarly, the history of Thailand in playing off the colonial powers in the nineteenth century and accommodating to Japan during World War II suggests that had the country's rulers concluded in 1964-65 that Communism was the wave of the future, they would have reached an accommodation with Hanoi and Peking.

What is suggested here is that while the Johnson Administration may have believed the U.S. had a vital interest in preventing the Communization of Southeast Asia—as it did in 1941 in preventing "Japanization"—this did not necessarily mean engaging in a large and risky U.S. military effort to "save" South Vietnam. As in 1954, when Dwight Eisenhower decided that negotiation rather than intervention was the wiser course for the United States in Indochina, so in 1963 or 1964 John Kennedy or Lyndon Johnson might have decided that negotiations with Hanoi were desirable. Even if that had meant allowing South Vietnam eventually to fall under Hanoi's control, there was still a possibility in 1964-65 of negotiating an agreement that Laos and Cambodia would remain neutral, independent buffer states *not* under Hanoi's control. Historically, their role had been that of a buffer between Vietnam and Thailand. By risking U.S. power and prestige in a vain effort to save South Vietnam without invading the North, the Johnson administration not only failed to prevent the Communization of South Vietnam but also opened the way for Hanoi to extend its control over Laos amd Cambodia. American prestige and credibility in Asia have improved somewhat from the low point of 1975, but it would be unwise for an American President again to send U.S. troops to any country in that area to help it resist a Communist insurgency. Southeast Asia remains a *major* U.S. world-order interest, not a vital one.

U.S. Interests in East Asia and the Western Pacific

The countries in the East Asian and Pacific area that are most important to the United States are Japan, South Korea, China (including Taiwan), the Philippines, Australia, New Zealand, Indonesia, Thailand, Singapore, and—stretching the area a bit—India. The key question is which of these are vital U.S. interests in the 1980s, and for what reasons. To distinguish U.S. interests in this great arc of nations, three sub-areas are used in the matrix in Figure 12.[3] The importance of these areas and countries to the United States is heavily influenced by their economic and military relationships with Washington and their capacity for influencing a favorable world-order in the East Asian and Pacific areas. Each country is briefly discussed here.

Japan. Japan is the most important U.S. national interest in Asia, and it will undoubtedly remain so for the indefinite future. In defense-of-homeland terms, Japan constitutes a major U.S. interest because of its proximity to Alaska and Canada and because the Japanese Self-Defense Force is closely tied to the United States through military purchase arrangements and through joint intelligence and training operations. Similarly, as the third most powerful economy in the world and growing rapidly, Japan is the second largest trading partner of this country (after Canada) and thus a high major U.S. economic interest. It is not at the vital economic level, however, because a severe drop in U.S.-Japanese trade would not be a shattering blow to the American economy. For Japan, however, the U.S. market is a vital economic interest because its loss would probably cripple the Japanese economic system. In ideological terms (promotion of values), Japan is the only truly democratic country in East Asia today (not including Australia and New Zealand), and the United States therefore has a major stake in helping Japan to reinforce the free institutions that Washington imposed upon it after 1945.

It is in the world-order category, however, that Japan assumes a truly vital interest for the United States. This is because Japan exercises great political and economic influence on all the countries of East Asia, and because it has the potential of exercising a large security influence in the western Pacific and the South China Sea in the future. Like Australia, Japan has the capacity to be a full alliance partner of the United States, one that can contribute to the economic and political security of Asia as well as provide the United States with military facilities. No other Asian

3. For purposes of identifying countries on the matrix, *N.E. Asia* includes Japan and South Korea; *S.W. Pacific* includes the Philippines, Australia, and New Zealand; *S.E. Asia* includes Indonesia, Malaysia, Thailand, and Singapore. China is a separate entity. India, also discussed in this chapter, is not considered part of East Asia.

Fig. 12. U.S. National Interests in East Asia and the Pacific

Basic Interest at Stake	Intensity of Interest			
	Survival	Vital	Major	Peripheral
Defense of Homeland			N.E. Asia S.W. Pacific China	S.E. Asia
Economic Well-Being			N.E. Asia	S.W. Pacific S.E. Asia China
Favorable World Order		N.E. Asia S.W. Pacific	S.E. Asia China	
Promotion of Values		S.W. Pacific	N.E. Asia	S.E. Asia China

country, with the possible exception of China, currently has that capability.

The problem in U.S. relations with Japan lies not in defining U.S. interests but in persuading Japan that it must contribute more to the mutual security of the East Asian region. Washington has sought for a decade to persuade Japan that it should accept a defense role commensurate with its economic capability and that it must, after thirty years of protecting domestic industries, open up the home market to U.S. products as the U.S. market is open to Japanese goods. The rise to power in 1982 of Takeo Nakasone as Japan's prime minister signaled some modest expansion in Japan's defense forces and policies, permitting the Japanese Navy and Air Force eventually to patrol to a distance of 1,000 miles from the homeland. Japan will also spend somewhat more on its defense forces, but projections show that total defense outlays will be only about 1 percent of Japan's GNP, compared with about 7 percent for the United States. In 1983 the Reagan administration finally convinced Japanese leaders that Japan cannot only be concerned about defense of its homeland and economic well-being, but must also be prepared to defend a world-order interest in East Asia, to an extent commensurate with Japan's economic capabilities. Acceptance of an expanded world-order role by Japan will be a gradual process because many Asian countries remember the results of an Imperial Japanese thrust into China and Southeast Asia in the 1930s and 1940s and want no repetition now. European countries, which have similar suspicions of a resurgent Germany, long ago agreed to permit a large German army and air force to be established and recently agreed to an enlarged patrolling function for the German Navy in the Atlantic. It will be a challenge to U.S. diplomacy to convince China, South Korea, the Philippines, Thailand, and Indonesia that they must recognize the Japanese contribution to the security of East Asia, and that the United States will not continue to fill this role unilaterally.

The economic problem for Japan is that its government must find ways to constrain successful Japanese businesses and industries, which have penetrated the American market in a large way and are not concerned about unemployment in the American auto, electronic, and other industries. As the U.S. recession deepened in the early 1980s and large numbers of U.S. auto and steel workers were laid off, the Reagan administration applied considerable pressure on Tokyo both to limit the number of cars exported to the United States and to open Japanese markets to more American products, particularly agricultural ones. The U.S. trade imbalance in Japan's favor, projected at $24 billion in 1983, became a source of controversy in Congress and in American business circles. Several Democratic presidential aspirants began to speak of permanent import quotas. Japan reluctantly agreed to limit its export of cars to 1.6 million per year, in order to help U.S. car manufacturers recover from the recession and bring out competitive small cars. But in June 1983, the Japanese government announced that it would not renew this auto export limitation agreement when it expired in 1984. This caused further agitation in Congress for restrictions on Japanese auto imports, with the most serious proposal being that cars sold in the United States must contain a certain percentage of parts made in the United States (domestic content). Protectionism was clearly on the rise in the United States in 1983, and it was questionable whether the recesson's end would reduce the pressure from industries such as auto and steel for protection against "unfair" Japanese business practices.

The argument is made by some American political leaders and scholars that since Japan is a vital world-order interest of the United States, this country should not pressure the Japanese government to show restraint in its export/import policies with the United States because the current huge trade imbalance will work itself out as American technology catches up with Japan in cars, steel, and electronics, and as American labor costs moderate following the recession of the early 1980s. Some argue that as Japan expands its defense forces, this effort will absorb the energies of many Japanese manufacturers and lessen their penetration of the U.S. market. The opposite view is that as Japan expands its armaments industry, it will compete more aggressively with American aircraft manufacturers and the U.S. computer industry—both of which held a lead over Japanese firms during the 1970s and early 1980s.

Judging by the intensity of feeling in the U.S. auto industry and auto unions, it is probably inevitable that some form of protectionist legislation will emerge from Congress, making it more difficult for Japan to export cars and other industrial products to the United States—unless it opens more plants in the United States and employs American labor. However, President Reagan stated in 1983 that he would veto domestic content legislation if Congress passed it. I believe that although Japan remains a vital world-order interest of the United States, U.S. leaders have valid reasons to insist on "fairness in trade" and make openness to the U.S. market conditional on reciprocal opportunities for American exporters to sell their products in Japan—without the multitude of restrictions that have blocked such expanded trade for many years. Japan needs to behave like a responsible great economic power and to give up much of the protectionism that it has practiced since its economic recovery in the 1960s. President Reagan's announcement on July 5, 1983, that the United States would impose restrictions on high-quality steel into the United States from Europe, Japan, and Canada was further evidence that domestic pressures were having their effect, despite the administration's general commitment to free trade, and that economic relations with Japan will continue to be strained.

Philippines. The Philippines, like Japan, is a vital U.S. interest for world-order reasons. This interest has historical roots for the United States, going baack to the turn of the twentieth century when President McKinley decided to annex the Philippines. The Philippines is also a major defense-of-homeland interest because it is the westernmost outpost of U.S. naval and air power in the

Pacific. The Naval Base at Subic Bay and the Air Force Base at Clark Field are among the most important U.S. bases in the world, and their loss would be a serious detriment to U.S. ability to project power not only in the Pacific but also in the increasingly important Indian Ocean area. This fact was underlined in the spring of 1983 when the Reagan administration agreed to a substantial increase in U.S. military and economic assistance to the Philippine government as part of a new base agreement.

The United States also has a major ideological stake in the Philippines because it brought that country to independence in 1946 after a long period of educating its people in democratic institutions. By the late 1960s, however, Philippine democracy was fraught with so much corruption and tampering with the electoral process that President Ferdinand Marcos suspended the constitution in 1971 and remained in power, creating what his critics charged was corrupt authoritarian rule. During the Carter administration, the U.S. government publicly criticized the Marcos administration for a poor human rights record, but it kept this criticism within bounds in order not to jeopardize the vital U.S. military bases. The Reagan administration muted public criticism of the Marcos government, preferring to make its comments about the lack of democracy in private. However, President Reagan's decision in October 1983 to postpone a state visit to the Philippines following the assassination of a major opposition leader, Benigno Aquino, was indicative of growing U.S. sensitivity to the decline of democratic government in this former colony and fear that Marcos may be leading his country into revolution. The Philippines is an excellent example of the tradeoff between U.S. world-order and ideological interests.

Australia and New Zealand. These two South Pacific countries, especially Australia with its large land mass and rich resources, are vital interests of the United States, dating from the Second World War when General Douglas MacArthur made Australia his base of operations prior to retaking the Japanese-occupied Pacific islands. In 1951, after the outbreak of war in Korea, President Truman concluded the ANZUS Pact with these Commonwealth countries, thus providing the basis for U.S. use of important military installations in Australia. Since several of these are strategic facilities, Australia has become a major defense-of-homeland interest of the United States as well as a vital world-order interest. The United States has major ideological interests in Australia and New Zealand because both have modern democratic systems. Australia and (to a lesser extent) New Zealand have been military partners with the United States in the Korean and Vietnamese wars, and both participated with Britain in defense of Malaysia in the early 1960s. Today, Australia maintains a modest naval presence in the Indian Ocean, and it sent an aircraft carrier to the waters off the Persian Gulf in 1980 at the time of Washington's concern that the Iranian revolution and the subsequent Soviet invasion of Afghanistan might result in a restriction of Persian Gulf oil to world markets.

South Korea. South Korea has been a vital interest of the United States since President Truman decided in June 1950 that it would be intolerable for the United States to see North Korea, with Soviet and Chinese support, control all of the Korean peninsula and threaten the security of Japan. President Carter decided in 1977 to withdraw U.S. ground forces from South Korea, but he was persuaded by Japan and by U.S. military commanders that it would be an unwise move. South Korea's poor record on human rights was a factor in President Carter's view that the United States should not be closely identified with its authoritarian regime, but he reluctantly decided to retain approximately 40,000 U.S. military personnel in Korea to help defend it against the North. The United States has limited economic interests in Korea, and the country is not important insofar as defense of North America is concerned. The real U.S. interest there is a derivative one: South Korea is vital to the defense and economic well-being of Japan. If Japan is a vital world interest of the United States, the reasoning goes, then Korea must also be at the vital level. This is tenuous reasoning.

Even if this premise is valid, should it be a U.S. responsibility to supply the majority of foreign forces in South Korea? Why should not Japan and China be the principal guarantors of South Korean security and provide whatever deterrence is required to insure that North Korea does not again invade the South? It should be remembered that when U.S. forces went to Korea in 1950, China had just concluded an alliance with the Soviet Union and both supported North Korea's thrust into the South. That situation is different today. China is an antagonist of the Soviet Union; it has established friendly relations with the United States; and Japan and China have normalized their trade and political relationships. It should not be necessary in this changed political climate for the United States to continue in the primary role of defending South Korea. South Korea has a formidable army that fought well during the Vietnam War, and it has received excellent U.S. equipment. Why should it not be able, particularly since it has a considerably larger population than North Korea, to provide the ground forces required to defend its territory and permit Japan and the United States to supply the air and naval presence to deter North Korea and the Soviet Union from attacking the South? China has diplomatic relations with North Korea, but not yet with South Korea; the Peking government should find it in its interest to establish relations with the South and take more responsibility for security in that area. During 1983 the beginnings of such a relationship began to emerge.

The U.S. interest in South Korea in 1984 is at the *major*, not vital level, and it is time the United States reduced its ground forces there to a modest level. Korea's position in Northeast Asia is similar to that of Saudi Arabia in the Middle East: both are important to the United States for world-order reasons (Saudi Arabia is also important for economic reasons), but neither is so crucially essential that the United States should be obliged to maintain large military forces there. A *major* world-order interest in South Korea means that the United States should continue to provide large amounts of military assistance and use its political influence to support South Korea's position in Asia; the United States should also encourage trade and investment in South Korea. But a major interest does not justify 40,000 American combat personnel being stationed on the Korean peninsula indefinitely. The U.S. government should therefore gradually phase out its ground forces from Korea and withdraw them all by the end of the 1980s. U.S. Air Force and Navy units in Japan can serve as a continuing deterrent to North Korea.

China and Taiwan. China was an enemy of the United States for twenty-one years—from 1950, when it entered the war in Korea, until 1971, when Dr. Henry Kissinger, President Nixon's National Security Adviser, made the first soundings about establishing official contacts with the People's Republic. The Nixon visit to China in 1972 and the Shanghai Communique issued at the end of his visit moved China into the major world-order interest of the United States. Later in the 1970s, the Carter administration sought to go beyond simply normalizing relations and conclude a strategic understanding with Peking. This was rejected by many U.S. Republican Party leaders who were unwilling to sacrifice U.S. interests in, and responsibility for, the security of Taiwan in order to achieve harmony with Peking. Candidate, and then President, Ronald Reagan shared this view. There was also a serious question about whether "playing the China card," as it was called, was consonant with U.S. relations with the Soviet Union. In the 1970s some American business interests believed that China offered vast economic opportunities for trade and investment and that the U.S. economic interest should be at the *major* level. This proved illusory because China did not, and will not for some time, have the economic resources to pay for the large amount of foreign technology and goods that are required to bring China to great-power status. In short, China's economic needs were a major hindrance to its ability to serve as a key player in superpower rivalry.

When Ronald Reagan became president in 1981, the movement toward a strategic relationship with China, which President Carter and Secretary of State Cyrus Vance envisioned, came to an abrupt stop. The Reagan administration believed strongly that Taiwan should continue to receive U.S. protection against any effort by Peking to establish political control over the island by force. Nevertheless, Republicans were not willing to reject Richard Nixon's declaration that there was only one China and that Taiwan was part of it. After two years in office, and after strong protests by Peking that relations with the United States would suffer if the United States persisted in treating Taiwan as a protectorate, the Reagan administration announced in 1983 that it would not provide the government of Taiwan with modern aircraft and would eventually phase out military assistance to the island. This action, plus a decision to grant China trade concessions, particularly an enlarged textile quota, led to more harmonious relations. Secretary of Defense Caspar Weinberger's visit to China in September 1983 moved the two countries closer to a strategic relationship.

Nevertheless, China is not, and should not be, viewed in the foreseeable future as a vital interest of the United States, even though its animosity toward the Soviet Union is beneficial to U.S. strategic interests. China today is a peripheral economic interest of the United States, and its totalitarian system makes it no more than a peripheral ideological interest even though it is adopting a more nearly free-market economy. China should be viewed as a major defense-of-homeland interest for the United States because its large standing army serves as a brake on Soviet ambitions in the Middle East as well as East Asia and thus contributes to the security of North America. But because of its stabilizing influence on the Asian continent, it is in the world-order category that China serves the most useful role for U.S. interests. China's fear of Soviet imperialism in the late 1960s caused it to view rapprochement with the United States as desirable, despite the ideological gap between the two countries. China since then has been a restraining influence on Vietnam and has provided greater security in Northeast Asia by restraining North Korea and opening a dialogue in 1983 with the South Korean government. China is an important political force in dramatizing Soviet occupation of Afghanistan, and it carries a significant voice in the United Nations as a critic of Soviet imperialism. This is useful to U.S. interests; but there is risk to the United States in entering into a military collaboration with China, as the Carter administration and some members of Congress advocated, for two reasons: first, a military relationship between Washington and Peking, even if it were not formalized, would make it less likely for the United States and Soviet Union to work toward accommodation of their worldwide differences; second, since China is a Communist country with a previous strong defense relationship with the Soviet Union, it is conceivable that a new radical leadership could reemerge in Peking, reverse the current anti-Soviet policies, and again seek accommodation with Moscow. If, in the meantime, the United States substantially assists China to become a formidable military and industrial power, that could eventually work to the detriment of the United States. Unlike the NATO countries and Japan, China does not share a democratic value system, and its long-term policies are therefore less likely to be convergent with those of the United States.

In sum, China is a strong *major* interest of the United States, but not a vital one. This suggests that the United States should provide China with a moderate amount of assistance to build its economy and to improve its defense capability, and grant it trade concessions. But Washington should not for the reasons stated above, give China advanced military equipment and technology, or guarantee China's defense. Good political relations and expanded trade are in the U.S. interest, but a strategic relationship at this time is not. In time, as China's Communist system evolves into something more compatible with American values, perhaps the political relationship will deepen.

Thailand and Indonesia. Neither of these two Southeast Asian countries is a vital interest of the United States in the 1980s, even though Thailand has an indirect defense relationship with Washington stemming from the Manila Pact of 1954.[4] The Southeast Asia Treaty Organization (SEATO) no longer exists, having been terminated after the end of the Vietnam War. The U.S. security tie to Thailand is therefore somewhat tenuous because no bilateral treaty links the two countries, as is the case with the Philippines and Japan. Neither Thailand nor Indonesia is a major economic interest to the United States, although Indonesia's oil and mineral exports are important to the world economy, especially to Japan. Ideologically, Thailand and Indonesia are ruled by military-led governments, and they have not had much success with democratic experiments. As with China, it is the world-order category that makes them *major* interests for the United States: Thailand is a front-line state bordering Communist-dominated Laos and Cambodia and, behind them, a united Vietnam; and Indonesia, the largest and most richly endowed Southeast Asian state, is stratgically situated on the water routes between the South China Sea and the Indian Ocean. Seventy percent of Japan's oil comes from the Persian Gulf and passes through the Strait of Malacca between Sumatra and Singapore. U.S. Navy ships moving from the Pacific to the Indian Ocean use the same channel when deployed near the Persian Gulf. Thailand and Indonesia are two of six nations (others are Malaysia, Singapore, Brunei, and the Philippines) making up the regional group known as the Associa-

4. The original members of the Manila Pact were Thailand, the Philippines, Pakistan, Britain, France, the United States, Australia, and New Zealand.

tion of Southeast Asian Nations (ASEAN), which is important in determining the political and economic policies of that region.[5] The United States has provided substantial amounts of military aid to Thailand and Indonesia, and in the spring of 1983 it airlifted military equipment to Thailand when Vietnamese forces were harassing Cambodian refugee settlements inside Thailand. During the Vietnam war, from 1965 to 1975, Thailand made numerous military facilities available to the U.S. Air Force, for bombing operations and reconnaissance in Laos and Vietnam. After the U.S. evacuation from Vietnam in 1975, Thailand asked that these facilities be removed, and the United States today has only a modest military assistance mission in that country. Indonesia has never permitted the United States to use its soil for military operations but has accepted a military assistance group to administer an aid program. Unlike Thailand, Indonesia refused to join the Southeast Asia Treaty Organization in 1954 and, under Sukarno's leadership, became increasingly hostile to U.S. policy in Southeast Asia. The government of General Suharto, which came to power in 1966, has followed a friendly but nonaligned policy toward the United States and other Western countires. Both the Thai and Indonesian governments are strongly anti-Communist.

Although the Reagan administration reaffirmed the U.S. commitment to defend Thailand, in case it is attacked by a Communist power, that country should not today be considered a *vital* national interest of the United States. As with South Korea, Thailand may have been a vital world-order interest of the United States while China was a hostile power cooperating actively with Moscow. When China and the Soviet Union became antagonists in the 1960s, however, and China moved toward detente with the United States, Thailand was less threatened. With China now on friendly terms with the United States and Japan, it is desirable

5. ASEAN was formed in the mid-1960s, following the overthrow of Sukarno's government in Indonesia, as a means of creating a nonmilitary forum for consultations among five western-oriented states of Southeast Asia. Burma and Cambodia were offered membership but declined. South Vietnam sought admission to ASEAN, but some members believed this would embroil the association too heavily in the Vietnamese war. Indonesia pressed for a declaration that ASEAN should work for the elimination of foreign bases in the ASEAN area, but this was resisted by the Philippines and Singapore, which relied on U.S. and Commonwealth protection.

that these two Asian powers take the primary responsibility for protecting Thailand against united Vietnam and its clients, Laos and Cambodia. China has increasingly filled that role since the end of the Vietnam War; as Vietnam extended its control over Cambodia in 1978, China aided the Cambodian insurgents and gave Thailand political and some material support in its efforts to protect its border. China even fought skirmishes against Vietnam as a warning to Hanoi. Japan is Thailand's largest trading partner today, and Tokyo has an important interest in seeing that Thailand remains an independent, non-Communist state. The United States should, therefore, refrain from reestablishing a close military relationship with Thailand and should encourage Bangkok to improve its security ties with China and Japan as well as with the ASEAN countries.

India. India is neither an East Asian nor a Middle Eastern state and therefore does not fall neatly into a consideration of U.S. interests in those areas. However, India has been an important political (world-order) and ideological (promotion-of-values) interest of the United States since it gained independence from Great Britain in 1948. As the country with the second largest population in the world and also as the largest democratically governed state, India was supported by the United States from 1950 until the 1970s with large amounts of economic aid because it was considered by American leaders to be a counterweight to the growing power and hostility of Communist China. Under Prime Minister Nehru, India resisted U.S. efforts to bring the country into a Western military arrangement in Asia, preferring to be a leader of a nonaligned Third World—along with Indonesia's Sukarno, Egypt's Nasser and Yugoslavia's Tito. Because Pakistan joined SEATO as well as the Baghdad Pact (later CENTO), U.S. interests in the Indian subcontinent were difficult to sustain when India and Pakistan went to war in 1971. Pakistan lost its Eastern segment, which became Bangladesh, and it blamed the United States for failing to restrain India. India had concluded an agreement to buy military equipment from the Soviet Union and maintained warm relations with Moscow; as a result, U.S. aid to India was phased out during the 1970s. Following the Soviet Union's invasion of Afghanistan in December 1979, India decided to improve its relations with the United States and it also established a detente with Pakistan. India opposes the naval buildup by both superpowers that has taken place in the Indian Ocean since 1978. In 1983, U.S. relations with India improved considerably, and the Reagan Administration then decided to revise U.S. policy and sell India fuel for its nuclear power plants, a move that caused considerable criticism in Congress and in the American press.

In sum, India is a major world-order interest of the United States because of its location, size, and democratic institutions. It will become more important as a power as it develops into an economically strong country in Asia, one with which Washington hopes to build a friendly, lasting relationship based on a shared belief in democratic government.

Summing Up

U.S. national interests in East Asia moved from the major to the vital level in the 1950s, following the Communist conquest of China, its subsequent alliance with Moscow, and its intervention in the Korean War. So long as China remained hostile to U.S. interests in Asia, successive governments in Washington concluded that all the countries bordering China were vital to the U.S. objective of containing China's aggressive policies. The disastrous Vietnam War caused President Nixon to seek accommodation with Peking in order to permit the United States to withdraw "with honor" from Vietnam. Although a new relationship with Peking resulted in the 1970s, it did not prevent the United States from suffering a humiliating defeat in Vietnam in 1975. The U.S. military withdrawal from the Asian mainland and the new relationship with China convinced Presidents Nixon, Ford, and Carter that the U.S. interest in Southeast Asia should in the future be at the *major,* not vital, level. While the Reagan administration's public statements suggest that Thailand may be in the vital category, it is unlikely that U.S. forces would again be sent to fight in that country, because China has replaced the United States as the principal protector of Thailand against Vietnam. Indonesia and India are *major* U.S. world-order interests, and both countries prefer that designation because it avoids suggestions that they should accept U.S. military protection and a large military assistance mission. South Korea, by virtue of the fact that 40,000 American troops are stationed there, is on the borderline between a major and a vital interest; yet that country's value to the United States is based on Japan's concerns rather than directly on the U.S. stake in Korea. It is therefore desirable that American ground forces gradually be withdrawn from Korea and that U.S. air power become the major deterrent to any North Korean attack. If foreign ground forces are required to protect South Korea, Japan should form a rapid deployment force and make it ready for transfer to Korea if war should erupt there. China should be prepared to use its influence with North Korea to restrain its pressure on the South. In the 1980s and onward, the primary responsibility for defending South Korea should be Asian, not American.

Finally, the United States should press Japan to take greater responsibility for the security of Northeast and Southeast Asia. Forty years after the Second World War, Japan and the other Asian countries must realize that the United States should not be expected to carry this responsibility alone—particularly as the U.S. assumes new burdens in the Indian Ocean and takes care of the growing security problems closer to its homeland in the Caribbean and Central America. As for the Philippines, the United States should expect its former colony to do a better job of living up to the democratic traditions that the United States taught it early in this century. A return to democratic government is in the vital interest of the American as well as the Philippine people, and Washington should use its vast influence there to make that possible.

7. South America and Southern Africa: Secondary U.S. Interests

Traditional thinking in the United States about U.S. interests in and policies toward South America has been blurred by the Monroe Doctrine legacy, which assumed that everything in the Western Hemisphere was a vital national interest. This view was reinforced by the Rio Pact in 1947, which treated the security of all parts of Latin America as equally important to the security of the United States. The assumption is not valid, however, either in strategic or economic terms, and certainly not in ideological terms. Looking realistically at U.S. national interests in a broader context, the term "Latin America" should not be the controlling geographical concept. The division of the Western Hemisphere into North America (discussed in Chapter 3) and South America is much more appropriate in defining the basic national interests of the United States. Even then, the continental division is not precise, because two South American countries bordering on the Caribbean—Venezuela and Columbia—are more appropriately part of the North American sphere, as their economic, cultural, and security interests all flow northward.

A similar division exists on the continent of Africa. The North African states—Morocco, Algeria, Tunisia, Libya, and Egypt—border on the Mediterranean and are a part of the NATO defense area, even though none of the five countries is a member of the European military pact. By race, trade, and political ties, North Africa is closer to Spain, France, Italy, and Greece than to the countries of southern Africa. In terms of U.S. national interests, it is easier to deal conceptually with the division of Africa between north and south than it is to divide South America, because the term "Africa south of the Sahara" is widely used in government and in academia. No similar term separates the northern part of South America (Venezuela and Colombia) from the rest of the continent.

U.S. Interests in South America

South America is one of the fastest developing areas of the world, and it constitutes an important area of U.S. trade and investment. Brazil, for example, has the potential of being an economic power of the first magnitude by the year 2000. Argentina and Chile are economically advanced and have a moderate amount of military power. All three countries have important trade links with the United States, but none of them today can be considered a U.S. vital interest—in economic, defense, or ideological terms. All three states have a history of repressive political leaderships, resulting from the polarization of politics among important segments of their societies. In 1983 Argentina held elections and abandoned its military dictatorship, however. Brazil has recently shown promise of a relaxation of military rule and renewed interest in democracy, but the social and economic tensions within the vast country are so great that any movement toward democracy is likely to be a slow process. Chile remains firmly under military control.

It is U.S. world-order interests in South America that make the continent important. As a rapidly developing area with an exceedingly high population growth rate, any significant part of South America would become a serious problem for the United States and Western Europe if it turned hostile to the North Atlantic countries. This would be particularly so if any of the large countries—Brazil, Argentina, Chile, Peru—were to adopt a Communist system and align itself with the Soviet Union. The Nixon administration viewed the threat of a Marxist government in Chile, under Salvadore Allende, to be intolerable to U.S. world-order interests and used heavy U.S. economic and political pressure to bring about its downfall. This suggests that Chile may have been a vital interest to President Nixon and his National Security Advisor, Dr. Henry Kissinger, yet it is debatable whether

Chile matters so much to U.S. world-order interests in South America. Argentina is a similar case: although it is an important South American state and has the potential of being a strong economic and political power on that continent if it can solve its deep internal political problems, Argentina cannot now be considered more than a major interest of the United States; it is not in a position today to vitally affect U.S. security or economic well-being.

Brazil is in a somewhat different category; it is larger, more strategically located, and has greater political stability than Argentina. Brazil is potentially an economic superpower, with a GNP in 1983 of $250 billion. Its economy grew at a fast rate during the 1970s, a result of very high foreign investment and government borrowing, and this overspending caused a serious economic crunch early in 1983 when the country owed foreign banks and other creditors about $80 billion and could not pay the interest without additional loans. Seventeen percent of Brazil's exports go to the United States, and 17 percent of its imports are from the United States. Brazil is by far the most influential political entity in South America, and its military forces maintain close links with the U.S. armed forces. Brazil's strategic location in the South Atlantic was important to the Allies during World War II because it provided the route by which U.S. planes bound for Europe and the Middle East were ferried to West Africa and the war theaters. Were Brazil to be attacked by a hostile outside power, there is little doubt that the United States would aid its government under terms of the Rio Pact. However, it is questionable whether the United States should or could stop a leftist revolution that might try to overthrow the current military government—if economic conditions, for example, should become intolerable there. This does not mean that the United States should deny the Brazilian government military aid if it comes under severe internal political pressure; but it is difficult to imagine a situation in which U.S. military forces should be used to prevent a Brazilian government from being overthrown, even if insurgents were being supplied by a neighboring country. In short, the U.S. interest in Brazil is at the *major*, not vital level.

U.S. interests in South America are summarized by placing three important countries—Brazil, Argentina, and Chile—on the national interest matrix, as seen in Figure 13. This elaboration of

Fig. 13. U.S. National Interests in South America

Basic Interest at Stake	Intensity of Interest			
	Survival	Vital	Major	Peripheral
Defense of Homeland			Brazil	Argentina Chile
Economic Well-Being			Brazil Argentina	Chile
Favorable World Order			Brazil Argentina Chile	
Promotion of Values			Brazil Argentina Chile	

interests suggests that Brazil is a high major interest of the United States. It might under some circumstances become a vital interest—depending on the situation that would threaten Brazil's security. Neither Argentina nor Chile ranks as high as a defense interest, but they share with Brazil the major category under world order. This is because they have long coastlines and are in a strategic position regarding commercial ocean traffic in the Southern Henisphere. Brazil's and Argentina's navies are important to the security of the South Atlantic; however, they are of only major national interest to the United States at present because the South Atlantic is not a primary theater of superpower rivalry. The U.S. Navy may sense a vital interest at stake in the South Atlantic because of the important sea routes around the Cape of Good Hope and Cape Horn; yet, the vital interests of neither the United States nor the Soviet Union are tied up in the South Atlantic today. This is the principal reason that Brazil and Argentina continue to be major U.S world-order interests.

The Falkland Islands Crisis and the U.S. Response

The relative importance to United States interests of South America and the South Atlantic area was highlighted by the short war between Great Britain and Argentina in the Falkland Islands (Islas Malvinas) during the spring of 1982. Here was a case where the Reagan administration was obliged to make a difficult

choice between two countries with which it had good relations—
Argentina and Great Britain—as they clashed over several small
islands near the southern tip of South America. The decision-
making of the Reagan administration in this episode is indicative
of the dilemmas that policy-makers face in deciding tradeoffs in
national interests. A brief analysis of this crisis illustrates how the
national interest matrix may be used to determine which interests
take priority when they are in conflict.

When Argentina invaded the Falklands on April 2, 1982, it was
inevitable that the Reagan administration would have to choose
between two allies and that it stood to lose prestige no matter
what it decided. Once the British decided to retake the islands by
force, President Reagan and Secretary of State Alexander Haig
had only one possibility of averting a diplomatic firestorm: con-
vincing the Argentine government that it should withdraw its
9,000 troops from the Falklands and permit the United States to
negotiate the sovereignty issue with Britain. Otherwise, an
armed clash was inevitable as soon as the British fleet and troops
arrived in the South Atlantic. Secretary of State Haig left no doubt
where the U.S. government stood: according to an authoritative
account published by the Sunday *Times* of London, the State
Department sent a strong message to the Galtieri government
advising that unless it called off its imminent invasion of the
Falklands, the warm relationship with the United States would be
in jeopardy. The Buenos Aires government did not take the
warning seriously, however. On April 1, President Reagan tele-
phoned President Galtieri and spent nearly an hour trying to
convince him that American public opinion would not accept the
use of force and that the invasion should be called off. The
President's personal intervention had little effect.

The U.S. position was clarified in a White House statement
issued on April 2: "We have made clear to the Government of
Argentina that we deplore use of force to resolve this dispute. We
have called on Argentina to cease, immediately, hostilities and to
withdraw its military forces from the Falkland Islands."[1] The
following day the United States voted with the majority of the
United Nations Security Council in a resolution demanding the
immediate withdrawal of all Argentine forces from the Falkland

1. *Department of State Bulletin* (DSB), June 1982, p. 81.

Islands and calling on the governments of Argentina and the United Kingdom to seek a diplomatic solution to their differences.

From the beginning of the Falklands crisis, U.S. policy supported Britain against Argentina on the latter's use of force to settle a longstanding territorial dispute with Britain. In order to persuade Argentina to withdraw its forces before Britain used force to retake the islands, President Reagan sent Secretary Haig on a mediation mission between London and Buenos Aires to see whether an agreement could be reached that would enable the Argentine government to withdraw its troops before the British were in position to attack—a period of about four weeks. The dilemma faced by the United States in trying to avert war between two friendly states was illustrated in President Reagan's press conference statements on April 5. He said: "It's a very difficult situation for the United States, because we're friends with both of the countries engaged in this dispute, and we stand ready to do anything we can to help them. And what we hope for and would like to help in doing is have a peaceful resolution of this with no forceful action or no bloodshed." Answering another question, the President asserted that "we're friends of both sides in this, and we're going to try, strive for—and I think that they will be willing to meet in the idea of a peaceful resolution [*sic*]." In response to the question as to what the United States would do if diplomacy failed to resolve the crisis before fighting erupted, the President said, "I hope I never am faced with that."[2]

Haig's shuttle diplomacy brought no results in Argentina because all his efforts foundered on one central point: Argentina insisted that it had sovereignty over the Falklands, while Mrs. Thatcher's government insisted that the will of the Falkland Islanders had to be a decisive element in the final determination about the islands' sovereignty. The U.S. negotiating position was made more difficult when the Council of the Organization of American States (OAS) requested Britain to "cease the hostilities it is carrying on within the security region" covered by the Inter-American Treaty of Reciprocal Assistance (Rio Pact) and "refrain from any act that may affect inter-American peace and security." The resolution called on both sides to resume negotiations aimed

2. *Presidential Documents* 18, no. 14 (12 April 1982): 441.

at a peaceful settlement of the conflict by "taking into account the rights of sovereignty of the Republic of Argentina over the Malvinas (Falkland) Islands and the interests of the islanders."[3] This OAS resolution was adopted by a vote of 17 to 0, with four abstentions—including the United States. The OAS thus affirmed its belief that Argentina was entitled to sovereignty and that Britain had no right to use force to dislodge the Argentine forces then in control of the islands. It also put the United States squarely at odds with most of the Latin American countries. Although Secretary Haig, in his statement at the OAS meeting, sought to focus on the initial use of force by Argentina, the OAS resolution implicitly gave Argentina the right to retain troops in the Falklands while negotiations on the sovereignty question took place. At a time when it needed hemispheric support in Central America to isolate the Marxist government of Nicaragua, the United States found itself in a difficult diplomatic position because of its failure to support the claims of a Latin American country against an outside power.

On April 30, 1982, as British forces launched their first air strike on Argentine forces in the Falklands, Secretary Haig defined the Reagan administration's policy in the crisis by announcing economic sanctions against Argentina. The Secretary said that the United States was guided by the principles of rule of law and peaceful settlement of disputes. The collapse of this principle, he argued, would result in chaos and suffering. Haig took account of the U.S. stake in the dispute by saying: "We made this effort because the crisis raised the vital issue of hemispheric solidarity at a time when the Communist adversaries seek positions of influence on the mainland of the Americas." Haig reported that Argentina had turned down his proposal for a joint U.S.-U.K.-Argentine interim authority in the Falklands because it did not recognize Argentine sovereignty. He asserted: "Now, however, in light of Argentina's failure to accept a compromise, we must take concrete steps to underscore that the United States cannot and will not condone the use of unlawful force to resolve disputes." The Secretary said the President had ordered economic sanctions and a halt in military assistance to Argentina, and that the United States would provide material support for British forces—with-

3. *DSB*, June 1982, p. 87.

out, however, the direct involvement of U.S. military personnel. Finally, Haig reiterated a U.S. readiness to help the parties reach a mutually acceptable settlement of their dispute: "In the end, there will have to be a negotiated outcome acceptable to the interested parties. Otherwise, we will all face unending hostility and insecurity in the South Atlantic."[4]

The President's decision to support Britain was reinforced by a Senate resolution on April 29 declaring that the United States "cannot stand neutral" and must help Britain to "achieve full withdrawal of Argentine forces" from the Falklands. The vote was an overwhelming 79 to 1 in favor of support for Britain. Only Senator Jesse Helms of North Carolina voted against, arguing that Argentina had sovereignty over the Falklands predating the British takeover in the 1830s. Helms felt strongly that the United States needed Argentina's help in combating Communism in the Western Hemisphere and that a U.S. decision to support Britain in this dispute would alienate U.S. friends in Latin America at a time when Washington needed their support for its foreign policy goals.

The U.S. decision to support Britain in retaking the Falkland Islands and to impose sanctions against Argentina did not end the debate within the U.S. government over how to limit the damage to U.S. relations with Latin America. Led by the U.S. Permanent Representative to the United Nations, Jeane Kirkpatrick, and to a lesser extent by the Assistant Secretary of State for Inter-American Affairs, Thomas Enders, the pro–Latin America group argued that the United States had deep political, economic, and security interests in Latin America and that strong efforts should be made through diplomatic channels to initiate negotiations between Britain and Argentina. Meanwhile, the OAS became a forum for anti-American sentiment. On May 29, for example, the 20th Meeting of OAS Foreign Ministers voted 17-0, with four abstentions (including the United States) in favor of a resolution "to condemn most vigorously the unjustified and disproportionate armed attack perpetrated by the United Kingdom, and its decision, which affects the security of the entire American hemisphere, of arbitrarily declaring an extensive area of up to 12 miles from the American coast as a zone of hostilities." It blamed

4. Ibid., pp. 87-88.

the United Kingdom for not being willing to negotiate its differences with Argentina and for refusing to accept a cease-fire.
The OAS urged the United States to order the immediate lifting of
sanctions against Argentina and to stop giving material assistance to Britain, "in observance of the principle of hemispheric
solidarity recognized in the Inter-American Treaty of Reciprocal
Assistance." The OAS requested members to give Argentina "the
support that each judges appropriate to assist it in this serious
situation."[5] The United States was thus isolated diplomatically in
Latin America because of its support for Britain.

The U.S. dilemma in trying to walk a thin line between support
for Britain and preservation of its ties with Latin America was
illustrated by President Reagan's informal session with reporters
on May 28. When asked about the impending OAS vote against
U.S. sanctions on Argentina and against U.S. support for Britain,
the President said: "The only thing that we have to face here is the
issue . . . whether we can allow armed aggression to succeed
with regard to such territorial claims. There are 50 places in the
world right now where, if this succeeds, that could be opened to
the same thing happening. And the armed aggression, I'm sorry,
did start by the action of one of our neighbors here in the Americas. That principle must not be allowed to fail."[6]

Early in June, while the President and Secretary of State were
in Europe attending several summit conferences with European
leaders, the administration found itself in a deeply embarrassing
situation at the United Nations when Ambassador Jeane
Kirkpatrick voted with the British government against a Security
Council resolution calling for an immediate cease-fire in the
Falkland Islands. A few minutes later, after receiving new instructions from Secretary Haig, she informed the Council that the U.S.
position should have been "abstention." The blunder was com-
pounded when Secretary Haig, asked by a reporter why he had
not called Kirkpatrick on the phone instead of sending instructions through the State Department bureaucracy, said that a field
commander does not deal directly with a company commander.
The Haig-Kirkpatrick blowup over U.S. policy on the Falklands
issue was the most visible manifestation of a growing split within

5. *DSB*, July 1982, p. 90.
6. *Presidential Documents* 18, no. 22 (7 June 1982): 726.

the State Department over U.S. national interests in Latin America.

The swift and decisive British military victory in the Falklands was a godsend for an increasingly divided U.S. government. The British success relieved the political pressure on Washington to show more concern for the Argentine position because, with British forces in full possession of the islands and Argentine troops defeated, the calls for a cease-fire and a U.N. peacekeeping force were outdated. Thus, President Reagan could state in a news conference on June 30, in response to a question about when he would remove sanctions on Argentina: "I can't give you an answer on that, what is going on right now. We did our best, as I said before, to try to bring about a peaceful settlement. It didn't happen. And there was armed conflict, and there has been a victor and a vanquished, and now it's hardly the place for us to intervene in that. We'll stand by ready to help if our help is asked for."[7]

Comparing U.S. Interests in the North Atlantic and South Atlantic

The public wrangling between the Secretary of State and the U.S. Ambassador to the United Nations during June 1982 illustrated Washington's difficulty in deciding on, and adhering to, a clear assessment of its national interests in two sectors of the Atlantic Ocean. In brief, the issue could be stated like this: did the United States have vital interests at stake in South America and the South Atlantic equivalent to its interests in the North Atlantic area?

Looking at U.S. actions and the public statements of its top political leaders from April through June 1982, it is clear that the Reagan administration decided early that if Argentina invaded the Falklands, the United States would uphold the principle that disputes should not be settled by military force and that Argentina would not be supported. However, the United States was not prepared to agree that Britain had a clear legal right to the Falklands, despite the fact that it had been in possession of them for 150 years. This was the U.S. official position. yet the question

7. *DSB*, August 1982, p. 38.

that was actually at issue in Washington was whether Britain or Argentina was a greater political asset to the broader national interests of the United States. Secretary Haig and Ambassador Kirkpatrick obviously disagreed on this point, and the State Department found itself divided when it was clear that Argentina would not withdraw its troops from the Falklands without a prior commitment regarding its sovereignty.

The relative importance of British, Argentinian, and U.S. interests in the Falklands crisis is illustrated in Figure 14. What this suggests is that both Argentina and Britain had vital interests at stake—particularly world-order interests—but that the United States had only peripheral and major ones in this conflict. The U.S. interest was strongest in the world- order category, and that was to support its ally, Great Britain, when the Thatcher government decided to retake the Falklands if Argentina refused to accept a reasonable compromise. But the United States also had a major interest in keeping the lines of communication open to Argentina, for two reasons: (1) the Galtieri government had given President Reagan strong support for his efforts in 1981 and 1982 to stem the growth of Communist influence in Central America; and (2) Argentina had the moral support of most Latin American countries in its dispute with Britain over sovereignty in the Falklands. Even though Argentina's government and political system were antithetical to the values of the American people (promotion-of-values), the authoritarian government in Buenos Aires had cooperated with the United States in many of its international policies (world-order). The basic miscalculation made by the Galtieri government was in thinking that its ties with Washington had become so important to the Reagan administration that Washington would not join with Britain if Mrs. Thatcher decided to use force. Argentina assumed that its strong support would be viewed as vital to U.S. world-order interests when, in fact, it never was. It may be recalled that Great Britain made an equally serious error in judgment in 1956 when the Eden government assumed that it could invade Egypt and retake the Suez Canal without incurring the wrath of President Eisenhower.

A footnote to the Falkland Islands war and the British victory was a United Nations General Assembly resolution on November 4, 1982. The resolution, jointly sponsored by twenty Latin American countries, called on Argentina and Britain "to resume nego-

Fig. 14. Interests at Stake in the Falkland Islands, 1982

Basic Interest at Stake	Intensity of Interest			
	Survival	Vital	Major	Peripheral
Defense of Homeland		Argentina	U.K.	U.S.
Economic Well-Being				U.S.
				U.K.
				Argentina
Favorable World Order		U.K.	U.S.	
		Argentina		
Promotion of Values		U.K.	U.S.	
		Argentina		

tiations in order to find as soon as possible a peaceful solution to the sovereignty dispute relating to the question of the Falkland Islands (Malvinas)." After getting the original resolution modified so that the question of sovereignty was not prejudged and force would not again be employed in this dispute, the United States joined 89 other nations in voting for it; 52 nations abstained, including most West European countries and many Commonwealth nations. The British press and government expressed dismay that the United States had voted for the resolution rather than abstaining, and calls of betrayal were heard in London. However, cooler British heads understood the reasons for the U.S. decision, particularly as the resolution was not binding on either Britain or Argentina.

Kenneth Adelman, U.S. Representative to the General Assembly's 37th Session, summed up the U.S. dilemma: "For the United States, the Falkland crisis has been and still is a particularly agonizing, tragic event. As the whole world knows we have a longstanding alliance and, beyond that, the closest relations of friendship with Great Britain, the country from which our political institutions, law and language derive. But we have not forgotten for a moment our close geographical, economic and political relations with our Latin neighbors. We do not only care about this hemisphere, we are part of this hemisphere, and we share many of the aspirations, goals and dreams of all nations of the Americas." Adelman emphasized that the resolution expressly reaffirmed the principle of nonuse of force in international relations and said the United States welcomed its references that the parties should not renew the threat of force. He expressed hope that the resolution would "serve as a basis for negotiation to close this unhappy chapter and move forward again toward peace, understanding and development in this hemisphere."[8]

The Falkland Islands crisis underlined the fact that U.S. national interests in South America are not as crucial as U.S. interests in the North Atlantic region. This is not to say that the South Atlantic is not important to the United States, but only that its *relative* importance is lower than that of Great Britain and Europe. Nor does the Falklands crisis suggest that U.S. interests in Central America and the Caribbean region were downgraded; on the contrary, the episode showed more clearly than before that the United States does not view Latin America as one general interest but distinguishes between those parts that are in close proximity to the United States and those that are not.

U.S. Interests in Africa

North Africa. The five countries of this region (Morocco, Algeria, Tunisia, Libya, and Egypt), all bordering on the Mediterranean, are of considerably greater importance to U.S. national interests than the numerous states of Central and Southern Africa. This results from their geographical proximity to Europe and to NATO's bases in Spain, Italy, Greece and Turkey. It also results from growing U.S. interests in the eastern Mediterranean area. Egypt became a vital world-order interest of the United States after it made peace with Israel in 1979 and decided to cooperate with the United States in defense planning for the Middle East area. Three of the other four North African states are friendly to the United States (Morocco, Tunisia, and Algeria); the fourth (Libya) is hostile. The United States has a major world-order interest in insuring that the three friendly countries remain favorable to U.S. interests in the Mediterranean, and a major interest in preventing Libya from upsetting the political stability of its

---

8. United States Mission to the United Nations, press release 122-82, 4 Nov. 1982.

neighbors to the south or hindering U.S. military operations in the Mediterranean. The Reagan administration underlined this fact in 1981 when it sent a carrier task force into the Gulf of Sidra, to demonstrate its intention to uphold the principle of "freedom of the seas." The administration also sent planes to Egypt in 1982 when Libya reportedly sought to aid guerrillas it had trained to overthrow the government of Sudan. U.S. interests in several other East African countries, notably Kenya and Somalia, increased from the peripheral to the major level in the early 1980s as a result of the buildup of U.S. forces in the Indian Ocean near the Persian Gulf. Both countries granted the United States facilities of considerable importance to U.S. naval operations in the Indian Ocean. They are not American bases, however.

A minor crisis for U.S. interests in North Africa occurred in August 1983 when Libya intervened with its own forces in a civil war in neighboring Chad. Although the Reagan administration believed that France, as the former colonial power in Chad, had the primary national interest there, Washington nevertheless sent a carrier task force to waters off Libya and early warning planes (AWACS) to Sudan to monitor Libyan air attacks in Chad. U.S. interests in Chad normally would not be considered higher than peripheral, but President Reagan apparently believed that U.S. interests in Egypt and Sudan (on which Egypt depends for water resources and political support) would be severely affected if Libya, with its pro-Soviet government, succeeded in replacing the Chad government with another pro-Soviet regime. The apparent U.S. interest in this remote African civil war was expressed by White House spokesman Larry Speakes, who asserted on August 5, 1983, that "the United States has a strong strategic interest in assuring that Qaddafi [Libya's leader] is not able to upset governments or to intervene militarily in other countries as is currently happening in Chad. If Libya or Libyan-supported forces were to gain control of Chad, close U.S. allies such as Egypt and Sudan would be seriously concerned about their own security. Other states in the region would also be deeply worried."[9]

This was a classic case of the U.S. government's trying to convince its friends as well as the American public that it had a high stake in a remote part of Africa when, in fact, most Amer-

9. *Washington Post*, 6 Aug. 1983, p. 1.

icans would conclude that the interest was at the *major* level at best. The threat of Libyan-backed revolutions in Africa may indeed be of vital importance to Egypt and Sudan, and perhaps to France; but the Reagan administration was stretching credibility in trying to persuade the world and the American public that U.S. interests were being so severely tested by Libya that the White House should contemplate using U.S. forces to restrain Libya.

Southern Africa. Historically, U.S. interests in the southern part of Africa have been peripheral. Most of the countries there were part of European colonial empires until the 1960s and early 1970s, and the United States was content to permit France, Britain, Belgium, and Portugal to exercise the primary political influence in these poor, extremely backward countries. South Africa, a white minority dominated country, held a higher place in U.S. interests for two reasons: (1) it occupies an important location on the sea routes between the South Atlantic and Indian Oceans and has excellent port facilities for naval as well as commercial vessels; and (2) the country is one of the world's major sources of precious minerals, among them diamonds and gold. Thus, South Africa during the early postwar period was a major economic and world-order interest of the United States. By the 1970s, however, these factors were increasingly outweighed by a strong U.S. ideological bias against the South African government's blatantly repressive apartheid policies. South Africa's condemnation by the United Nations for its racist laws against the black majority and its subsequent withdrawal from the British-led Commonwealth caused the United States to downgrade relations with that country. A contributing factor was the growing demand of the American black community for tougher U.S. policies against South Africa's racist regime.

A significant change occurred in the U.S. Government's view of world-order interests in 1974, following Portugal's decision to withdraw from colonial rule in Angola and Mozambique and to grant those countries independence. A Marxist faction quickly gained political control in Mozambique and established warm relations with the Soviet Union and other Communist countries. In Angola, a civil war ensued among three factions, two of pro-Western orientation and the other a Marxist, pro-Soviet group. At the urging of Secretary of State Henry Kissinger, the United States provided covert military aid to the non-Communist forces in Angola until Congress decided late in 1975, as a legacy of anti-Vietnam sentiment in the United States, to prohibit all military and covert assistance to any group in Angola. Almost immediately, Soviet arms and 15,000 Cuban troops were introduced into Angola, and within a few months the Marxist faction had control of the government. Cuban troops with strong Soviet support remain there today. The Marxist government recently has sought better relations with the United States and has encouraged private American firms, particularly oil companies, to operate in the country; but it has been unwilling thus far to ask Cuba to withdraw its forces, a condition set by the Reagan administration for normalizing relations. In 1975 Angola was a test case between the President and the Congress in determining the level of U.S. interest in Southern Africa. Congress mandated that the level of U.S. interest should be *major*, not vital, and it was one of Dr. Kissinger's rare political defeats as chief architect of U.S. foreign policy.

The mid-1970s witnessed another serious setback to U.S. interests in Africa, on the East coast of that continent. Ethiopia, which had been pro-West as long as Emperor Haile Selassie remained in control, underwent a profound change of direction when a military coup overthrew the monarchy in 1975. The leftist military group that seized control vowed to establish a Marxist-socialist state, and it turned to the Soviet Union and Cuba for help. Within a short space of time, Ethiopia became a base of Soviet and East European power in East Africa, and about 20,000 Cuban troops were dispatched there to help the new regime maintain order and build the armed forces. Neighboring Somalia, which had been pro-Soviet and had granted Moscow a naval base on the Gulf of Aden, then became alarmed over Soviet support of its traditional enemy, Ethiopia, and asked the United States for political and military support. The Carter administration wrestled with the issue of U.S. interests in the "Horn of Africa" and decided that they were at best *major*.

In Southern Africa, President Carter strongly emphasized human rights (ideology) as a major component of U.S. interest and policy. His administration put great pressure on both the white minority Rhodesian government to relinquish control to the majority blacks, and on the South African government to give up control of Namibia (Southwest Africa) in accordance with United Nations resolutions. After Prime Minister Margaret Thatcher came to power in Britain in 1979, her government negotiated a peaceful transition of power in Rhodesia (now Zimbabwe) to the black majority. The United States strongly endorsed this action. In Namibia, however, U.S. policy on that country's independence remains tied to the withdrawal of Cuban forces from Angola.

In the mid-1980s, the United States has major national interests at stake in Southern Africa, but not vital ones. This is true for all four basic U.S. interests. In terms of defense-of-homeland, the west coast of Africa is a major U.S. defense interest because of its proximity to oil supply lines from the Middle East. In economic terms, the need of U.S. industry for scarce minerals from the African states is growing, and some of these countries will become important U.S. trading partners. Nigeria, with its large population and significant export of oil, is the most important black African country, both economically and politically. South Africa remains a major economic interest of the United States and could become a major political one as well if it makes peace with its neighbors. In ideological terms, black Africa looms increasingly important to U.S. interests for two reasons: (1) these newly independent countries make up a large voting block in the United Nations, and they are well disposed toward the United States so long as U.S. policy is opposed to racist regimes; and (2) American blacks, increasingly conscious of their roots, have taken a much greater interest in U.S. relations with African countries and exert growing influence on U.S. policy there. Just as American Jews give enormous political support to Israel and American Greeks lobby Congress on behalf of Greece, so do American blacks feel a responsibility to press for greater attention by U.S. policy-makers to the needs and concerns of the black African nations.

U.S. world-order interests are an ambiguous area, however, as was the case in 1975 when Henry Kissinger pressed for large-scale military assistance to Angola and Zaire to help stem growing Soviet and Cuban influence in Africa. Specifically, the issue is whether U.S. interests in Southern Africa are so crucial (vital) that it would be intolerable for Washington to consider sharing influence on that continent with the Soviet Union and its satellites. For example, the Reagan administration has refused to give its blessing to independence for Namibia until neighboring Angola asks Cuban troops to withdraw. Washington's reasoning is that Namibia would quickly fall into civil war and succumb to Marxist insurgents if Cuban forces across the border in Angola provided them help. The issue is not whether Namibia should be free of South African control (South Africa agreed in 1982 to give up control if there were guarantees for Namibian security); it is whether the Soviet Union and its client states should continue to have a foothold on the west coast of Africa and, possibly, expand their influence there. The Reagan administration's policy was to give military and economic assistance to Zaire in Central Africa—despite its government's poor record on human rights and its corruption—because Zaire is strategically located, is pro-West, and forms a bulwark against further Soviet expansion in West Africa. In East Africa, the United States has concluded agreements with Kenya and Somalia for naval facilities, and in 1983 it carried out military maneuvers on Somalian soil. In Nigeria, the richest African state, the United States is giving political support to a new military government established in 1983 even though it would prefer to deal with a democratically elected one. The previous government had led the country to near economic ruin, and Nigeria is now in need of financial assistance despite its great oil wealth.

Figure 15 indicates which of the southern African countries currently qualify as *major* national interests of the United States. This listing of countries on the matrix suggests that the United States has major interests (but no vital ones) in Southern Africa. There is a strong rationale therefore to supply these and other selected countries in the region with economic and military assistance and political support where these are required to maintain good relations and to prevent anti-Western forces from gaining control. In the mid-1980s, however, there is no country in southern Africa that qualifies at the vital U.S. level; the United States should therefore refrain from concluding defense agreements and deploying U.S. military forces there. In relations with South Africa, which is by far the most developed country and the

Fig. 15. U.S. National Interests in Southern Africa

Basic Interest at Stake	Intensity of Interest			
	Survival	Vital	Major	Peripheral
Defense of Homeland			South Africa	
			Nigeria	
Economic Well-Being			South Africa	
			Nigeria	
			Zaire	
Favorable World Order			South Africa	
			Nigeria	
			Zaire	
			Kenya	
			Somalia	
			Angola	
Promotion of Values			South Africa	
			Nigeria	
			Zaire	

most pro-West in its political leanings, U.S. policy should encourage that government to modify its apartheid policies, broaden its political base, and adopt a cooperative attitude toward the black African countries. Such cooperation is possible if the Nationalist government moves away from repression of its majority population and includes blacks and coloreds in the political process. If South Africa is willing to make such concessions, it might one day be considered a vital U.S. interest and be worthy of a close military relationship. For the time being, however, U.S. ideological interests preclude a defense relationship with the Pretoria regime.

Summing Up

North Africa and Southern Africa are important areas in terms of U.S. economic and world-order interests, but they do not qualify as vital U.S. concerns today. North Africa, because of its importance to Western Europe and to the eastern Mediterranean, has several countries—notably Egypt and possibly Morocco—that may be in the vital interest category for world-order reasons. If the South Atlantic region becomes strategically important in world affairs, as the Falkland Islands crisis suggested, it is conceivable that other African countries—Nigeria, Zaire, and Angola—may one day be viewed as vital U.S. interests. In the mid-1980s, however, there is little if anything south of the equator, either in Africa or in South America, that should cause the United States to go to war.

8. The Soviet Empire: An Enduring Competitor

The Soviet Union is the only serious competitor of the United States for power and prestige on a worldwide scale. Despite the earlier speculation of academics and journalists about the emergence of a "multi-polar world," there are only two powers today that can justifiably be called superpowers. Neither Britain nor France, two European powers with modest nuclear military capability and interests outside Europe, is a competitor of the Soviet Union and the United States. Japan and Germany are world economic powers, and they exert regional political influence as well, but neither is willing at this time to reach for the kind of great power role that their previous regimes played in the 1930s and 1940s.

The Soviet Union and the United States not only emerged from World War II with their military power and prestige enhanced; they also exhibited the political *will* to extend their influence into areas that they were not willing to exploit prior to World War II. The American prewar sphere of influence was limited primarily to the Western Hemisphere and the Pacific islands—including the Philippines. The Soviet prewar area of influence was the Soviet Union itself plus the Baltic states and, after August 1939, half of Poland. By virtue of their military victory over Nazi Germany, both the United States and the Soviet Union extended their influence into Central Europe. Their troops remain there forty years after the cessation of hostilities to reinforce that postwar reality of European politics.

In Asia, it appeared for a while after World War II that the Soviet Union, in alliance with the People's Republic of China, would extend Communist influence into Southeast Asia and over the entire Korean peninsula. However, the falling out between Moscow and Peking in the 1960s had the effect of limiting Moscow's reach in East Asia. Since December 1979, the Soviet Union has extended its power into Afghanistan, which poses a threat to Pakistan, Iran, and the Persian Gulf. The United States retained exclusive military and political influence in Japan following World War II and concluded defense ties with South Korea, Taiwan, Thailand, and the Philippines. After Great Britain withdrew its military presence from the Indian Ocean and the Persian Gulf in 1971, the Soviet Union and the United States competed for position and influence in Asia with increasing intensity—particularly after the fall of the Pahlavi dynasty in Iran in 1979.

Despite their intense competition in the post–World War II period, neither country demonstrated territorial ambitions in the other's immediate sphere of influence. While Soviet and American rhetoric suggested that each side would like to replace the government of the other with a political system more compatible with its own, there is little evidence that either country seriously contemplated pursuing this objective. In the economic sphere, the Soviet Union is not a serious competitor of the United States for markets and raw materials around the world because the Soviet economy has little to offer in exports except oil and gas, certain minerals, and military equipment; few countries buy Soviet manufactured goods for hard currencies. In the ideological competition, it was clear by the 1980s that the Marxist-Leninist model of government had lost its appeal in Western societies; and only a few developing countries were attracted to it because Communism seemed to offer a shortcut to economic growth and political cohesion. The Marxist appeal seems strong only in those Third World countries that have wide disparities in wealth and where few, if any, human rights prevail. This situation exists in many Caribbean Basin countries, a traditional area of U.S. influence, and Soviet efforts are increasingly directed there in the 1980s. In terms of defense-of-homeland, economic, and ideological interests, the competition between the Soviet Union and the United States is probably not at the vital level, because neither side covets the territory or economic system of the other.

It is the world-order interests of the two superpowers that constitute the dangerous area of world competition. This embraces the struggle for influence and prestige in the large world arena, and it involves a determination by each one not to be humiliated or slighted by the other in pursuit of international objectives. In effect, the last half of the twentieth century is witnessing a classic case of two proud empires vying with each other for political influence on a global scale. It is not unlike the competition between Great Britain and France during the eighteenth and nineteenth centuries, first in North America, then in Europe, and—after the Napoleonic Wars—in Africa and Southeast Asia. When a third power, Germany, asserted itself in the twentieth century, Britain and France agreed to cooperate to put down the new threat to their colonial empires and the security of Europe. Similarly, the U.S.S.R. and the United States cooperated during World War II when Nazi Germany sought to upset the balance of power in Europe and the Middle East. Since 1945, the peace of Europe has been maintained by Soviet and U.S. forces in Germany, with the NATO and Warsaw pacts supporting the two superpowers in maintaining a new balance between the Soviet and the Euro-American spheres of influence. In Asia, the independent power of China has been informally added to that of the United States in a new balance that seeks to restrain Soviet expansionism in East and Southeast Asia.

A fundamental question in the 1980s, therefore, is this: where do the superpowers consider their vital world-order interests to lie and under what conditions are they willing to risk war to advance or defend them? If we assume that neither superpower will directly threaten the other's homeland because it would risk its own annihilation, the challenge for policy-makers in Moscow and Washington is to find ways to enhance their own country's world-order interests without threatening the vital interests of the other. That suggests an analysis of how each country views its national interests in the mid-1980s and where the ambiguities as well as flash points in the relationship probably lie.

The Soviet View of Its Interests Vis-à-Vis the U.S.

There is little ambiguity about what the current Soviet leadership views as its nation's vital defense-of-homeland interests: all of Eastern Europe; the areas along the Soviet border in Southwest Asia, including Turkey, Iran, Afghanistan, and the long border with China; and North Korea and the waters off Sakhalin and Kamchatka in the Far East. Moscow has demonstrated on several occasions that it will use force to maintain pro-Soviet regimes in Eastern Europe, the most recent being its threat in 1981-82 to intervene in Poland if the Polish government failed to crush the Solidarity free trade union movement. Whether the Soviet military intervention in Afghanistan in December 1979 was motivated by ambition to extend the Soviet sphere of influence southward or whether it was a defensive move designed to prevent that country from creating an anti-Soviet regime, the move clearly improved the Soviet Union's security situation on its southern border, particularly among the fifty to sixty million Moslems living in that part of the U.S.S.R. In East Asia, Moscow has built up Vietnam militarily—to warn China against pressing historic claims on Soviet territory along their lengthy mutual border and to enhance Soviet influence in Southeast Asia. In sum, Soviet leaders view the areas adjacent to their borders, particularly in Eastern Europe where most invasions of Russia have occurred, to be vital defense interests. The Soviet leadership apparently has no qualms about using force—even limited nuclear war—to protect its borders. The shooting-down of a Korean commercial airliner over Sakhalin in September 1983 demonstrated the acute concern felt by Soviet leaders over foreign intrusions on Soviet territory.

The Soviet Union probably has no vital international economic interests, because its economy has been largely insulated from the outside world (other than the Soviet trading bloc with Eastern Europe). Because of its highly centralized and controlled economy, the Soviet Union is less dependent on international trade and foreign sources of raw materials than any other major power. The exception is grain, and Soviet leaders have made great efforts in the past decade to insure that bad harvests at home will not result in starvation. Even when President Carter decided to put an embargo on grain sales to the Soviet Union in 1980, in retaliation for the invasion of Afghanistan, Moscow was able partially to overcome this deficit by increasing purchases from Argentina, Australia, and Canada. The Soviet leadership wishes to obtain advanced technology from the West and has gone to great lengths to steal it through clandestine means when it could not be obtained on the open market. In the early 1970s Moscow thought that detente with the United States would bring economic as well as political benefits; however, when Congress blocked plans by the Nixon administration to grant "most favored nation" treatment to the Soviet Union, Kremlin leaders viewed that move as a violation of understandings reached at the Moscow summit conference in 1972. Moscow's building of a gas pipeline from Siberia to Western Europe in the early 1980s was seen by the Reagan administration as Moscow's attempt to earn $10 billion dollars a year in hard currency from West Europeans in order to ease its dearth of hard currency to pay for grain imports as well as Western manufactured products. In sum, the Soviet Union has a major interest in trade with the United States and the West, but certainly not a vital interest. In case of an emergency or war, the Soviet Union would be self-sufficient in most essential goods. As for food, the Kremlin leadership has demonstrated on many occasions that it can force a tighter diet on its citizens, if necessary. It is unlikely that the Soviet leadership will ever permit the country to become crucially dependent on food imports from the West.

Soviet world-order and ideological interests are the areas where the risk of war may be substantial because Soviet leaders seem prepared to risk confrontations in Third World areas when they believe they will be successful or when they are committed to defend a Communist ally. The Brezhnev Doctrine, enunciated by the Soviet leader at the time of Soviet intervention in Czechoslovakia in 1968, proclaimed that once a country has adopted a Communist system of government, it can count on the Soviet Union to provide whatever support is necessary to insure that the system is not overthrown by either internal or external means. Although Czechoslovakia is within the Soviet defense-of-homeland interest, the implication of Brezhnev's 1968 statement was that Moscow would intervene *anywhere* if it believed that a true socialist government was being threatened. This doctrine clearly applies to Cuba, and it also includes Vietnam since 1978, when the two countries signed a mutual defense pact. The Brezhnev Doctrine probably also includes Angola, whose Marxist government was brought to power in 1976 with Soviet and Cuban support: it also applies to Syria, whose government, although not Communist, nevertheless welcomed a Soviet defense guarantee in 1981 as insurance against an attack by Israel. In sum, the Soviet

Union has staked out in Asia, Africa, Latin America, and the Middle East certain interests that are probably at the vital world-order level. Moscow reinforces these world-order interests with strong ideological rhetoric designed to show solidarity with "fraternal Communist governments." In return, those governments are expected to cooperate with Moscow in furthering the cause of socialism in their parts of the world and to provide the U.S.S.R. with military facilities and voting support in the United Nations.

How far is the Kremlin leadership willing to go in pressing its brand of socialism and its military power into distant areas of the world? Professor Seweryn Bialer, a leading Sovietologist from Columbia University, had this evaluation in the spring of 1983: "Soviet ambition and ideology are rarely in conflict, but rather reinforce each other, adding virulence to Soviet international ambitions and expectations. The direction of Soviet military and foreign policy is determined by these forces and the Soviet capacity to pursue them, independent of any behavior of the Western powers." Bialer argues that Soviet foreign and military policy are primarily conditioned by the extreme Soviet preoccupation with defense-of-homeland interests and that the projection of Soviet power and influence into other parts of the world is of only secondary importance. He asserts that no amount of military expenditures by the state will make Soviet elites feel fully secure: "What they are actually pursuing, therefore, is total security, which in reality is unattainable." As for Soviet objectives in the Third World, Bialer thinks they are based on "the idea that the achievement of strategic parity with the United States should be translated into visible gains in Soviet influence and power, and that the term "political equality" means that the Soviet Union will be as free as the United States to project its power and influence anywhere in the world.[1]

It is reasonable to conclude that Soviet national interests are based fundamentally on the protection of Soviet borders and institutions as well as adjoining areas in Eastern Europe and Central Asia (defense of homeland), and thereafter on projecting Soviet power and influence to other areas of the world where Soviet leaders believe they have earned the right to be consulted

1. "The Soviet Union and the West in the 1980s: Detente, Containment, or Confrontation?" *Orbis* (Spring 1983): 42-43.

about *any* international issue. Soviet ideology justifies supporting "socialist forces" everywhere in the world, particularly if this weakens the ability of the United States and Western Europe to resist Soviet pressures internationally. The risks that Soviet leaders are willing to take to advance their country's world role are based on the "correlation of forces" and their ability to gain advantage from Western weakness or indecision. Since 1970, Soviet leaders have been bolder in pushing their advantage outside the area of Soviet defense interests. This corresponds to the growing Soviet capability to project military power to other parts of the world and to take advantage of the uncertain direction of U.S. foreign policy after the failure of that policy in Vietnam. President Carter's emphasis on human rights as an important component of American foreign policy baffled Soviet leaders, as did his uncertain policies on strategic arms limitations and his indecision on dealing with Iran in 1978-79. By the end of the 1970s, Soviet leaders were contemplating the fracture of NATO over the issue of theater nuclear weapons, believing that the Soviet Union could intimidate West Europeans—especially West Germans—into accepting the presence of Soviet medium-range missiles in Eastern Europe while rejecting corresponding American missiles in Western Europe.

Moscow's decision to take greater risks in pursuing its world-order interests, dating from the early 1970s, corresponds with that country's achievement of nuclear parity with the United States. Its success in catching up with the other superpower in strategic weapons resulted from a crash program initiated after the humiliating Cuban missile crisis of 1962 when the Kremlin decided never again to be caught in an inferior military position in relation to the United States. From 1970 onward, Soviet leaders were confident of their ability to protect their borders against conventional attack on Soviet territory. Therefore, Soviet leaders could afford to be less worried about possible attacks on Soviet territory and to pay greater attention to ways in which their country could play a world role and enhance its ability to trade with the West (economic interest). They decided to increase Soviet political influence abroad by supporting governments that were friendly to Soviet objectives (world-order) and providing clandestine aid to Communist insurgent groups that were fighting "capitalist exploiters" in the underdeveloped world (ideology). By 1983, Moscow was pushing its influence not only into Africa, Southeast Asia, the Middle East, and Southwest Asia, as it had done in the 1970s; it was also risking a confrontation with the U.S. government in Central America. Whether stirring up revolutions on the U.S. doorstep was viewed by Moscow as retaliation for the Reagan administration's strong rhetorical support for free trade unions in Poland or as a response to a tempting opportunity following the overthrow of the Somoza dictatorship in Nicaragua in 1979 is not clear. What is not in doubt, however, is that the Kremlin apparently gave its client, Fidel Castro, a green light to see how far he could push in undermining all the Central American governments before getting a strong reaction from Washington. By the summer of 1983, it was clear that the Reagan administration would use force in Central America to prevent the spread of Cuban and Soviet influence; Castro then began to talk about negotiations and withdrawal of his military advisers if the United States did the same. But Soviet and Cuban influence was by then already deeply embedded in Nicaragua.

Soviet national interests relative to the United States in the mid-1980s can be illustrated on the interest matrix as seen in Figure 16. The policy implications of this analysis of interests are as follows: (1) Soviet leaders will use force whenever they think their own territory, or the territory of an adjacent friendly state, may be attacked or when the government of any neighboring friendly country might be replaced with a less friendly one; (2) Moscow is likely to use force whenever it believes the correlation of forces in areas not part of the Soviet defense area is in its favor, and it will risk confrontation with the United States unless Moscow believes that doing so could result in a nuclear war. Neither economic nor ideological interests are at the vital level of intensity for the Kremlin's leaders because they have insulated their economy from heavy outside dependence and because promotion of Marxism-Leninism, by itself, has not been seen as a vital interest to Soviet leaders. Yet, the creation of a world order that is more pro-Moscow and less pro-Washington has become a vital national interest of Soviet leaders in the past decade because Soviet military capabilities have more nearly matched Soviet world ambitions. Seweryn Bialer, cited earlier, thinks that Soviet international behavior can be explained by the ideology of its elites: "Soviet ideology should be understood not as a set of

Fig. 16. Soviet National Interests Vis-à-Vis the United States

Basic Interest at Stake	Intensity of Interest			
	Survival	Vital	Major	Peripheral
Defense of Homeland		U.S.		
Economic Well-Being			U.S.	
Favorable World Order		U.S.		
Promotion of Values			U.S.	

doctrinal dogmas that directly dictates Soviet actions, but as tendencies and patterns of thought and belief that shape the mind-set of Soviet policy-makers, and are a product of the fusion of the most general doctrinal precepts with Soviet and Russian historical experience."[2]

The U.S. View of Its Interests Vis-à-Vis the U.S.S.R.

U.S. relations with the Soviet Union have never been cordial, even during World War II when the two countries were allies against Nazi Germany. From 1917, when the Bolshevik revolution swept Lenin and his lieutenants into power, until 1933, when President Roosevelt first opened diplomatic relations with the new regime, the United States was chiefly concerned with the ideological thrust of the Soviet revolution and the determination of Soviet leaders to undermine capitalist systems in Western Europe and North America. After 1933, the United States dealt "correctly" with the Soviet government while keeping the U.S. Communist Party under close surveillance. This became a particular problem between the summer of 1939 and June of 1941, because the American Communist Party agreed with Stalin's policy of cooperation with Nazi Germany at a time when official American policy was moving toward support of Britain. This changed when Hitler attacked Russia in June 1941 and President Roosevelt initiated Lend-Lease aid for the Soviet Union. When the United States joined the war against Germany in December 1941, President Roosevelt and British Prime Minister Churchill vigorously supported Stalin's efforts to resist Hitler's armies.

2. Ibid., 41.

Stalin suspected that the Allied invasion of the continent was purposely postponed until 1944 so that the German and Russian armies would exhaust each other and permit Roosevelt and Churchill to arrange the peace terms—to Moscow's disadvantage. Despite Roosevelt's efforts at Yalta to extract commitments from Stalin to respect the independence of Eastern Europe, Stalin had no intention of permitting any East European country, particularly Poland, to adopt a government that was not friendly to the Soviet Union. The presence of Soviet troops in Eastern Europe at the war's end insured that Soviet power and influence would be supreme up to the line dividing Germany into Soviet and Western occupation zones.

In 1945, the Soviet Union was no longer just an ideological threat to the United States; it had also become a military menace whose near-term ambition was the extension of Soviet power over Western Europe. President Harry Truman had the task, from the moment he took office in April 1945, of deciding U.S. national interests in relation to the Soviet Union; it soon became clear to him that Stalin was not interested only in dominating Eastern Europe, which his armies had liberated from Germany, but that he intended also to dominate all of Germany and, through the help of the French and Italian Communist parties, to dominate Italy and France as well.

Truman's assessment of Soviet postwar interests and policies was made at the Potsdam summit conference with Stalin and Churchill in July 1945. He came away from that intensive series of meetings with a deep suspicion of Soviet objectives: "The personal meeting with Stalin and the Russians had more significance for me, because it enabled me to see at first hand what we and the West had to face in the future." The Russians were "relentless bargainers, forever pressing for every advantage for themselves," Truman wrote in his memoirs. "Yet I was not altogether disillusioned to find now that the Russians were not in earnest about peace. It was clear that the Russian foreign policy was based on the conclusion that we were heading for a major depression, and they were already planning to take advantage of our setback." Truman revealed that the only secret agreement he reached at Potsdam was that the Soviet Union reaffirmed its intention to enter the war against Japan, which it had pledged to do at the Yalta Conference earlier that year. But his experience in dealing with Stalin caused the President to conclude that he would never agree to a joint occupation of Japan: "Anxious as we were to have Russia in the war against Japan, the experience at Potsdam now made me determined that I would not allow the Russians any part in the control of Japan. Our experience with them in Germany and in Bulgaria, Rumania, Hungary, and Poland was such that I decided to take no chances in a joint setup with the Russians. . . . Force is the only thing the Russians understand. And while I was hopeful that Russia might someday be persuaded to work in co-operation for peace, I knew that the Russians should not be allowed to get into any control of Japan."[3]

From 1945 to 1953, the year Stalin died, U.S. policy was to confront the Soviet Union's expansive world-order interests head on, in Greece and Turkey, in Iran and Korea. U.S. policy also tried to slow down the absorption of Eastern Europe into the Soviet empire, even though Truman knew that this could only be a delaying action, given the Soviet army's tight grip on these countries. The one exception was Yugoslavia, which in 1948 broke with Moscow and followed an independent Communist course under its wartime leader, Marshal Tito. The Berlin Blockade, imposed by Stalin in 1948, was a different matter. This was seen as a bold move to freeze out the British, French, and Americans from their occupation rights in West Berlin. The crisis could well have involved the United States in war with the Soviet Union had not a remarkable U.S. airlift succeeded in keeping the economy of West Berlin functioning. The North Atlantic Pact in April 1949, and the subsequent U.S. decision to create a separate West German state in NATO, was part of the Cold War containment policy designed by President Truman to prevent Moscow from achieving its postwar goal of undermining West European governments. The Truman Doctrine of aid to Greece and Turkey sought to prevent Soviet domination of the straits between the Black Sea and the eastern Mediterranean. Stalin's support for the North Korean attack on South Korea in June 1950 confirmed Truman's suspicion that the Soviet Union was preparing for a military showdown with the United States in Europe, and he persuaded NATO leaders to set up a unified command under an American supreme commander, the first one being General Dwight D. Eisenhower. When Truman

3. Harry S. Truman, *Memoirs: Year of Decisions* (New York, 1955), pp. 411-12.

left office in January 1953, the Cold War was at its height, and the Korean War was stalemated. Stalin's death a few months later, however, opened an opportunity for a reassessment of U.S.-Soviet relations.

The Eisenhower administration continued Truman's hard line against Soviet expansionist policies, but because of the death of Stalin, it was able to take advantage of the new Soviet leadership's willingness to avoid confrontations and to negotiate an end to the Korean War, a truce in Indochina, a peace treaty for Austria, and begin a dialogue designed to reduce conflict over Berlin and Central Europe. The Geneva summit conference in 1955 ushered in a period of East-West detente which saw a lessening of tensions, exchange programs between U.S. and Soviet groups, and a visit to the United States by Soviet Party Secretary Nikita Khrushchev. This "spirit of Geneva" came to an end in the summer of 1960, however, on the eve of another summit conference in Paris. The Soviet government had shot down an American U-2 spy plane over its territory and sought to embarrass President Eisenhower by making public the identity of the pilot and the nature of his mission. Instead of denying the charge, as governments normally do when accused of espionage, the President admitted that the United States had been overflying Soviet territory with the U-2 plane for four years, gathering crucial intelligence information. This admission so infuriated Khrushchev that he canceled the summit meeting and began a renewal of the previous confrontation policy—in Berlin, Laos, and the Middle East.

President John Kennedy, who assumed office in January 1961, became the object of Khrushchev's determination to push the Soviet psychological advantage that resulted from having been the first country to orbit an earth satellite. Moscow had also successfully tested an intercontinental missile. Kennedy was humiliated first by the unsuccessful CIA-supported invasion of Cuba by Cuban exiles at the Bay of Pigs in April 1961, then by the subsequent erection of the Berlin Wall in August. He was also unable to persuade Khrushchev to stop Laotian Communist forces, with Soviet support, from advancing against the Laotian capital of Vientiane—defended by forces supplied by the United States. All three of these setbacks for American policy in 1961 put the Kennedy administration on the defensive in relations with the

Soviet leadership and caused the President to inaugurate a massive military buildup, with particular emphasis given to strategic forces. This period of confrontation came to an end in October 1962 when Chairman Krushchev overplayed his hand by secretly placing Soviet medium-range nuclear missiles in Cuba and bringing on the Cuban missile crisis. Because of President Kennedy's dramatic ultimatum to Moscow, the Soviets withdrew the missiles and suffered a humiliating diplomatic defeat.

In 1963 a new period in U.S.-Soviet relations ushered in the first serious efforts at control of strategic nuclear weapons. After Kennedy's death in November 1963, President Lyndon Johnson continued the attempt to reach accommodation with the Soviet Union on the arms question, but he subsequently became so preoccupied with the war in Vietnam and with Chinese pressures in East Asia that his administration was unable to complete these arms negotiations before leaving office in January 1969. President Johnson wanted to hold a summit conference with the Soviet leader, Leonid Brezhnev, in 1968; but the Soviet invasion of Czechoslovakia in September, to impose a hard-line Communist government there, precluded the presidential visit.

From the time that Richard Nixon became President in January 1969 until January 1981, when Ronald Reagan assumed the presidency, the American view of the Soviet Union vacillated between two major conflicting viewpoints, both of them based on the conclusion reached by Harry Truman in July 1945 that the U.S.S.R. was an aggressive power and would pursue relentlessly its goal of world domination. The first of these opposing views held that Soviet leaders were as anxious as American leaders to control the development and deployment of strategic nuclear weapons and that they were prepared to make real concessions to reduce the danger of nuclear war. Some American leaders, among them Dr. Henry Kissinger, President Nixon's National Security Advisor, believed that Soviet leaders would work toward a reduction of world tensions and show restraint in pursuing Soviet world- order interests in the Third World. Proponents of this view thought that the United States could encourage Soviet leaders to act "responsibly" by offering them economic incentives, such as "most favored nation" treatment in trade and financial credits to assist in the import of U.S. products. The sale of large quantities of American grain was seen as an inducement to good Kremlin behavior. This view formed the basis of the "linkage" theory, and it constituted the undergirding of Nixon's and Kissinger's approach to Moscow on arms control and on managing U.S. world-order interests.

The second view, one often associated with the late Senator Henry Jackson of Washington and shared by many Republicans (including the 1976 presidential candidate, Ronald Reagan), assumed that the Kremlin leadership was interested in arms control only to the extent that it enhanced the Soviet Union's power position. Adherents of this view argued that Moscow wanted to encourage Western Europe and the United States to reduce their defense expenditures and to expand trade and credits to the financially pressed countries of Eastern Europe while gearing its own economy to an ever expanding war machine. Proponents believed that Kissinger was wrong in his assessment of Moscow, that the Soviet Union would never modify its ambitious world-order interests in return for economic incentives or for the sake of arms reduction. Soviet and Cuban exploitation of the Angolan civil war in 1975 and their subsequent move into Ethiopia in 1977 to support a Marxist military group reinforced the hard-line criticism that Kissinger's detente policies had resulted in gains for the Soviet Union in the Third World, while the United States and Western Europe cut back on defense programs and on Third World involvements.

Although the policies espoused by the second group of policy-makers are believed to have commenced in 1981 when President Reagan took office, this hard-line actually commenced a year earlier, in January 1980, when President Carter decided that the Soviet invasion of Afghanistan proved that the Russians could not be trusted. Mr. Carter's policies then hardened considerably. They included a cancellation of American participation in the 1980 Olympic Games in Moscow, suspension of grain sales to the Soviet Union and an imposition of economic sanctions and suspension of cultural contacts. These actions were designed to show U.S. displeasure with Soviet behavior not only in Afghanistan but also in Africa, in Southeast Asia (support of Vietnam's occupation of Cambodia), and in Eastern Europe, where the Soviets began installing medium-range nuclear missiles while objecting to NATO's plan to install similar weapons. The Carter administration also shifted policy toward Nicaragua in 1980, and it began sending arms to the El Salvador government to help it cope with insurgents being armed and trained in Nicaragua. In short, when Soviet armies moved into Afghanistan in December 1979, American policy shifted decisively away from flirtation with detente and efforts to reach accommodation with Moscow.

The Reagan View of U.S. Interests Vis-à-Vis Moscow

Ronald Reagan not only pursued a hard-line policy toward the Soviet Union when he came to the White House in 1981; he also sharpened American anti-Soviet rhetoric to a point unknown since the early days of the Eisenhower administration. Reagan held the Soviet Union responsible for most of the trouble in the world and for running a bankrupt society which could not maintain itself without overwhelming military power. He predicted that the Marxist-Leninist system would fail in due course and said that the West must be strong enough to prevent the Soviet Union from achieving by force what it could not do by peaceful means. To many Americans and Europeans, Mr. Reagan's views were a return to the Cold War of the late 1940s and early 1950s. A big difference, however, was that a new generation of Europeans and Americans had grown up during this thirty-year period and were not as confident as was Mr. Reagan's generation that the Soviet Union could be contained with military power. Moscow's achievement of parity with the United States in strategic weapons during the 1970s and its overwhelming superiority in conventional arms in Central Europe made it appear to be a greater threat than ever. This perception promoted new peace movements in Western Europe and in the United States, demanding an end to the arms race and negotiations between the superpowers to reduce the threat of nuclear war. Thus, while the Reagan administration in 1981-82 was pushing through Congress the largest peacetime increases ever in the U.S. military budget and preparing to confront the Soviet Union on a worldwide scale, European and American opinion was increasingly divided on the wisdom of doing so. Beginning in the fall of 1981, the President made serious offers to renew SALT negotiations with the Soviet

Fig. 17. U.S. National Interests Vis-à-Vis the Soviet Union

Basic Interest at Stake	Intensity of Interest			
	Survival	Vital	Major	Peripheral
Defense of Homeland		U.S.S.R.		
Economic Well-Being			U.S.S.R.	
Favorable World Order		U.S.S.R.		
Promotion of Values			U.S.S.R.	

Union, and in accordance with his determination to bring about reductions in strategic nuclear weapons, he renamed the process START (Strategic Arms Reduction Talks). Thus, while greatly expanding U.S. conventional and strategic forces and publicly chastising the Soviet Union as an "evil empire" and a threat to world peace, Mr. Reagan proposed new plans to control the growth of nuclear weapons and reduce the likelihood of military confrontation.

The Reagan administration's view of the Soviet Union may be summarized as shown on the national interest matrix in Figure 17. The U.S. defense-of-homeland interest in regard to the Soviet Union is listed at the vital level because that country is capable, and may have the will, to inflict severe damage on the U.S. homeland. Because of this, every President must calculate the implications of a military confrontation with Soviet forces anywhere in the world, particularly in Europe, because this could escalate quickly into a strategic nuclear war. Therefore, the United States has a vital interest not only in having the most modern weapons available to deter a Soviet attack on the United States but in being able to sustain damage to this country while preventing the collapse of its society and institutions. A President also needs to pursue serious arms negotiations with the Soviet leaders; success in such talks is a vital U.S. defense interest because successful negotiations would reduce the possibility of nuclear war. Ironically, a vital defense-of-homeland interest for the United States means that while it must build and deploy the most awesome nuclear weaponry in order to insure that U.S. leaders cannot be intimidated by the Soviet Union or any other hostile power, it must also pursue serious arms control negotiations in order to stop the outbreak of such a war.

The U.S. economic interest in the Soviet Union is growing because American farmers and manufacturers see a large export market there. The reaction of U.S. wheat farmers and manufacturers of energy-related equipment to President Carter's economic sanctions against Moscow following the invasion of Afghanistan is indicative of this interest, which had been spawned during the 1970s when trade with Eastern Europe was encouraged. President Reagan's reversal of the Carter sanctions, despite his strong anti-Soviet rhetoric, shows that increased apprehension of Soviet military adventures is not strong enough to overcome the Republican Party's desire to provide export markets for its constituencies, such as western farmers. On the other hand, Mr. Reagan was firmly opposed to making financial credits available to the Soviet Union and East European countries, and he went through a serious confrontation in 1982 with European NATO leaders to underscore his point that the West should not finance the Siberian gas pipeline. With the lifting of martial law in Poland in 1983, Mr. Reagan eased some economic restrictions on that country but there was no sign that U.S. economic interests in Eastern Europe would grow so long as Eastern bloc countries were unable to pay hard currency for imports. The exception was grain, and the Soviet Union pays for that in hard currency.

The most critical area of conflict between U.S. and Soviet interests, as it has been since 1945, is in the world-order category—in those parts of the world that the Soviet leadership covets and that the United States is determined to deny to it. Specifically, Soviet leaders from Stalin onward have desired to extend Soviet influence over *all* of Germany in the West, Turkey and Iran in the South, Korea and Japan in the East; and they have also sought to neutralize China. These are near-term Soviet world-order interests, and Moscow has worked toward them steadily since 1945. Longer-term Soviet world-order interests include a dominant influence in Western Europe, Scandinavia, and the Mediterranean countries; friendly, cooperating oil-rich Arab states; a neutralized India and Southeast Asia; and an Africa that can be fully exploited for its minerals. In short, the Soviet Union desires to be the dominant imperial power in both Europe and Asia, just as it sees the United States being the dominant power in the Western

Hemisphere. That is what Soviet leaders mean by "equality" between the superpowers.

All American Presidents since Truman have steadfastly opposed the fulfillment of these Soviet world-order interests. The North Atlantic Pact, the Baghdad Pact, the Manila Pact, the ANZUS Pact, and the bilateral defense treaties with Japan, South Korea, Taiwan, and the Philippines were all designed to thwart the Soviet Union's determination to expand its influence in Europe and Asia after World War II. This U.S. grand containment policy began to crack in the 1950s: Egypt's Gamal Nasser decided to accept arms from the Soviet Union in order to support his ambitions for a united Arab world; India and Indonesia took the lead in sponsoring a nonaligned group of nations that maintained friendship with the Soviet Union while denouncing Western colonialism; Ho Chi Minh decided to join with the Soviet Union and China to oust France and then the United States from Indochina; and even in the Western Hemisphere, the Soviet Union embraced the new Marxist dictator of Cuba and eventually made him the accomplice of Soviet ambitions in Latin America and Africa.

The old containment policy has further eroded in the Middle East with the ouster of the Shah of Iran in 1979 and the Soviet invasion of Afghanistan ten months later. It threatens to break down also in Europe if West German public sentiment moves toward neutralism, and in Southeast Asia if China and the ASEAN countries are unable to contain Vietnam's territorial ambitions, supported by Moscow. Even in North America, Moscow is seeking to make things so uncomfortable for the United States in El Salvador that the United States will be obliged to shift attention and resources away from other areas in order to shore up interests closer to home.

Finally, the ideological struggle between capitalism and socialism, between freedom and oppression, between Christian values and atheism—to cite some of the ideological rhetoric used by conservative supporters of President Reagan—is not more than a major interest of U.S. policy-makers. This is because in the mid-1980s Marxism is no longer seen by most countries as an alternative to the free market system as a way of ordering modern society. Social welfare programs instituted in much of the First World during the past forty years have reduced disparities between rich and poor in Western societies, so that the untamed capitalism of Marx's time is now heavily regulated in most advanced countries. Thus, the Soviet Union's Second World has little appeal except in some backward Third World states. The real problem is more economic than ideological in these areas, and U.S. policy since President Truman enunciated his Point Four program has been to provide economic hope to underdeveloped countries as the best way of limiting the appeal of Marxism. However, this erosion of Marxism is offset by Soviet training and support for armed insurgents in many countries, where they may have the ability to impose Marxist-Leninist rule. That seems to be the pattern in Nicaragua and El Salvador, and in certain African countries such as Angola and Ethiopia.

U.S. National Security Council Policy toward the U.S.S.R.

The Reagan administration came to power in 1981 convinced that U.S. national interests around the world were in serious jeopardy for several reasons: the growing Soviet military power, the unwillingness of several European NATO countries to be realistic about Soviet objectives in the Middle East as well as Europe, and the indecisiveness shown by both Republican and Democratic administrations during the 1970s in dealing with the U.S.S.R. Mr. Reagan's National Security Council was composed of "realists" who fully agreed with Truman's assessment thirty-five years earlier that "force is the only thing the Russians understand": Secretary of State Alexander Haig, whom Reagan had chosen because of his long experience in the national security field and his rapport with European leaders resulting from his tour as supreme commander of NATO; Secretary of Defense Caspar Weinberger, a hardheaded administrator and long-time associate of Mr. Reagan; Director of Central Intelligence William Casey, Mr. Reagan's campaign manager during the 1980 presidential race, who had had long experience in the intelligence field; Richard Allen, a conservative academic who had been Mr. Reagan's foreign policy adviser during the election campaign and was appointed his Assistant for National Security Affairs. Vice President George Bush, who also had extensive experience in national security affairs—in Congress, in China, and as Director of the Central Intelligence Agency—played an important role in

National Security Council deliberations, as well. The President invited the U.S. permanent representative to the United Nations, Jeane Kirkpatrick, to join many NSC meetings. Mrs. Kirkpatrick, a conservative academic, was ideologically close to Mr. Reagan's own view of international Communism, and her views on U.S. policy in Latin America were given particular weight by the President. During the second year of the Reagan administration, the President replaced Richard Allen as National Security Adviser with William Clark, a long-time associate whom Mr. Reagan, while governor of California, had appointed to the California Supreme Court. Clark had been made Deputy Secretary of State in 1981 to give him training in foreign policy and national security affairs, with which he had had no previous experience. He shared the President's deep suspicion of the Soviet Union and the international Communist movement. When Judge Clark moved to the White House, the post of National Security Advisor was upgraded; unlike Richard Allen (who had reported to the President through Counselor Edwin Meese), Mr. Clark became one of the President's closest advisors. In the summer of 1983 he reportedly was the architect of Mr. Reagan's decision to deploy American military forces to Honduras and naval units to the waters off Nicaragua. In October 1983, President Reagan decided to appoint Clark Secretary of the Interior and replace him in the White House with Robert McFarlane, Clark's deputy at the NSC.

The President also replaced Secretary of State Haig in June 1982 with George Shultz, an economist and business executive who had served in several Cabinet positions during the Nixon Administration. Shultz replaced Haig at a time of considerable disarray in the administration's foreign policy: Israel had invaded deep inside Lebanon without prior knowledge of the United States; the European allies were furious with President Reagan for imposing sanctions against U.S. firms and their licensees for selling pipeline equipment to the Soviet Union; and there was bitter controversy within the administration over arms control negotiations.

Secretary of State Shultz, an academic by training and temperament, seemed less concerned with crisis management and day-to-day issues in foreign policy and viewed it as his major responsibility to formulate a cohesive, long-range policy for dealing with the Soviet Union. His objective was to define U.S. national interests in a way that would win bipartisan support in Congress and among American foreign policy elites. His most formidable task was articulating a long-term policy toward Moscow that would be both realistic and consistent, and could serve as the basis of comprehensive negotiations with the new Andropov leadership. After a year in office and after discussions with many world leaders, including Soviet Foreign Minister Andrei Gromyko, Shultz chose in June 1983 to address the Senate Foreign Relations Committee on the Reagan administration's considered view of U.S. relationships with the Soviet Union. His was the definitive statement of U.S. national interests in relations with Moscow.

In his prepared text, the Secretary said that "every postwar American President has come sooner or later to recognize that peace must be built on strength; President Reagan has long recognized this reality." Shultz recalled that in the previous two years the country had made a "fundamental commitment" to restoring its military and economic power as well as its moral and spiritual strength; having started on the path to rebuilding its strength, the Reagan administration was ready to engage the Soviet leaders in "constructive dialogue through which we hope to find political solutions to outstanding issues." The Secretary then elaborated how U.S. national interests were affected by Soviet objectives and policies:

> Certainly there are many factors contributing to East-West tensions. The Soviet Union's strategic Eurasian location places it in close proximity to important Western interests on two continents. Its aspirations for great international influence lead it to challenge these interests. Its Marxist-Leninist ideology gives its leaders a perspective on history and a vision of the future fundamentally different from our own. But we are not so deterministic as to believe that geopolitics and ideological competition must ineluctably lead to permanent and dangerous confrontation. Nor is it permanently inevitable that contention between the United States and the Soviet Union must dominate and distort international politics. A peaceful world order does not require that we and the Soviet Union agree on all the funda-

mentals of morals or politics. It does require, however, that Moscow's behavior be subject to the restraint appropriate to living together on this planet in the nuclear age. Not all the many external and internal factors affecting Soviet behavior can be influenced by us. But we take it as part of our obligation to peace to encourage the gradual evolution of the Soviet Union toward a more pluralistic political and economic system, and above all to counter Soviet expansionism through sustained and effective political, economic and military competition.[4]

Shultz went on to say that detente, which had been pursued in the 1970s, had not worked: "The policy of detente represented an effort to induce Soviet restraint. While in some versions it recognized the need to resist Soviet geopolitical encroachments, it also hoped that the anticipation of benefits from expanding economic relations and arms control agreements would restrain Soviet behavior." The Secretary added that "unfortunately, experience had proved otherwise. The economic relationship may have eased some of the domestic Soviet economic constraints that might have at least marginally inhibited Moscow's behavior. It also raised the specter of a future Western dependence on Soviet bloc trade that would inhibit Western freedom of action toward the East more than it would dictate prudence to the U.S.S.R." Shultz thus sided with the hard-line group which, in the early 1970s, had argued against detente because they believed it would weaken the West's resolve to resist Soviet pressure while having little tangible effect on Soviet pursuit of its ambitious world-order interests.

Shultz said the Reagan administration's policy was not based on a containment theory, as enunciated in the Truman administration and followed for the next twenty years. "Unlike containment, our policy begins with the clear recognition that the Soviet Union is and will remain a global superpower. In response to the lessons of this global superpower's conduct in recent years, our policy, unlike some versions of detente, assumes that the Soviet Union is more likely to be deterred by our actions that

4. "U.S.-Soviet Relations in the Context of U.S. Foreign Policy," *Department of State Bulletin*, July 1983, p.66.

make clear the risks their aggression entails than by a delicate web of interdependence."[5] Shultz thus underlined the Reagan administration's view that a large stick, rather than a large carrot, would be more effective in curbing such Soviet behavior that the United States considered prejudicial to its world-order interests.

In this major statement of U.S. policy toward the Soviet Union, which was specifically approved by President Reagan, Secretary Shultz touched on three basic U.S. national interests. Regarding defense-of-homeland, he stated: "The central goal of our national security policy is deterrence of war; restoring and maintaining the strategic balance is a necessary condition for that deterrence." At the same time, he said, the United States was accelerating programs to strengthen its conventional capabilities: "To deter or deal with any future crisis, we need to maintain both our conventional capabilities and our strategic deterrent." He also noted that arms limitation was part of the U.S. defense interest: "Strength and realism can deter war, but only direct dialogue and negotiation can open the path toward lasting peace."

Regarding economic well-being, Shultz said that "economic transactions can confer important strategic benefits and we must be mindful of the implications for our security." But he added that U.S. policy is not one of economic warfare against the U.S.S.R.; East-West trade conducted on the basis of commercially sound terms and mutual advantage "contributes to constructive East-West relations." It is noteworthy that on August 25, 1983, Secretary of Agriculture John Block signed a new five-year grain agreement with the Soviet Union, guaranteeing that supplies would not be interrupted for political reasons, as they had been by the Carter administration following the Soviet invasion of Afghanistan. Moscow agreed to pay for this grain in hard currency, however.

Shultz devoted a significant part of his testimony to world-order interests and recited a long list of trouble spots where the administration believed the Kremlin's leaders were behaving in a way that was not conducive to peace and cooperation with the United States. His statement summed up the Reagan view of Soviet actions affecting U.S. world-order interests: "We must address the threat to peace posed by the Soviet exploitation of

5. Ibid., 67.

regional instability and conflict. Indeed, these issues—arms control and political instability—are closely related: the increased stability that we try to build into the superpower relationship through arms control can be undone by irresponsible Soviet policies elsewhere.

In our numerous discussions with the Soviet leadership, we have repeatedly expressed our strong interest in reaching understandings with the Soviets that would minimize superpower involvement in conflicts beyond their borders." Secretary Shultz ended his prepared statement to the Foreign Relations Committee with this summary of where relations with the U.S.S.R. stood in the summer of 1983:

> We have spelled out our requirements and our hope for a more constructive relationship with the Soviet Union. The direction in which that relationship evolves will ultimately be determined by the decision of the Soviet leadership. President Brezhnev's successors will have to weigh the increased costs and risks of relentless competition against the benefits of a less tense international environment in which they could more adequately address the rising expectations of their own citizens. While we can define their alternatives, we cannot decipher their intentions. To a degree unequalled anywhere else, Russia in this respect remains a secret. Her history, of which this secrecy is such an integral part, provides no basis for expecting a dramatic change. And yet it also teaches that gradual change is possible. For our part, we seek to encourage change by a firm but flexible U.S. strategy, resting on a broad consensus, that we can sustain over the long term whether the Soviet Union changes or not.[6]

Shultz's clear and balanced statement of U.S. interests and policy toward the Soviet Union was based on two important premises: first, that the course of firmness and strength he said the United States would follow in dealing with Soviet aggressive behavior would be sustainable over a long period of time—not just during the Reagan presidency; and second, that the new Soviet leaders who emerged after Yuri Andropov would be more

6. Ibid., 72.

willing than their predecessors to curtail Soviet worldwide ambitions.

Although the Secretary predicted that the United States would sustain a firm but flexible strategy, regardless of whether the Soviet Union changed its policies, that remained to be seen, given the volatile political climate prevailing in the United States in 1983-84. Why should Soviet leaders not think that they will eventually achieve their international goals by being patient and simply letting the dialectic political forces within the United States gradually force an accommodation to Soviet superiority in international affairs? From a Soviet perspective, the correlation of forces will be in their favor if the United States elects a new President every four years, and the party out of power panders to public criticism of huge defense budgets and the threat of nuclear war.

If Secretary Shultz's analysis of U.S. interests in relation to the Soviet Union becomes the basis of a bipartisan formulation of U.S. policy, however, this new trend may continue into the 1990s regardless of which political party holds the White House, and notwithstanding the frequency with which the U.S. electorate changes Presidents. Soviet leaders may then have to scale down their ambitions or be prepared to run greater risks of armed confrontation with the United States. If we assume that Soviet leaders are as rational about the risks of nuclear war as are American leaders, the question then comes down to which side has the greater political will and staying power—in what Mr. Shultz sees as the continuing competitiveness of two superpowers with worldwide interests. That is why it is essential that Soviet and American leaders have a clear perception of what each side considers to be its vital interests—those for which they will go to war. If a miscalculation is made—like Nikita Khrushchev's in Cuba in October 1962—the two leaderships must have a fail-safe system for containing the confrontation before it escalates into a large and possibly catastrophic conflict. If linkage policies failed to work in the 1970s and if arms treaties and East-West trade did not encourage the Brezhnev leadership to curtail adventurous policies in Africa, Asia, and Central America, the Reagan formula modeled on the Truman prescription may be more successful. This implies that the United States must have sufficient military power to convince Soviet leaders that they cannot win easy victories in the Third World—such as Angola, Afghanistan, and Cambodia—and certainly not in Central America. This reasoned approach of Secretary of State George Shultz to U.S.-Soviet relations came crashing down in September 1983 as the result of the Soviet shooting-down of a Korean commercial airliner over Sakhalin Island. Moscow's decision to blame the incident on the United States, by charging that the plane was on a spy mission, infuriated official Washington and most of the world community, especially when Soviet Foreign Minister Gromyko subsequently said that his country reserved the right to shoot down any other airliner that crossed into Soviet territory. President Reagan's early response set the tone for U.S. official statements, in Washington and at the United Nations, and probably resulted in Foreign Minister Gromyko's decision not to attend the U.N. General Assembly session—although he cited restrictions against the landing of Aeroflot planes in New York as his reason.

On September 3, two days after the plane had been destroyed with the loss of 269 lives, Mr. Reagan said that "the United States and many other countries of the world made clear and compelling statements that express not only our outrage but also our demand for a truthful accounting of the facts." He denounced the Soviet Union for ignoring the tradition of the civilized world that "has always offered help to mariners and pilots who are lost or in distress." He continued: "What can we think of a regime that so broadly trumpets its visions of peace and global disarmament and yet so callously and quickly commits a terrorist act to sacrifice the lives of innocent human beings? What can be said about Soviet credibility when they so flagrantly lie about such a heinous act? What can be the scope of legitimate mutual discourse with a state whose values permit such atrocities? And what are we to make of a regime which establishes one set of standards for itself and another for the rest of humankind?"[7]

The Reagan administration seemed determined after this tragedy and the worldwide denunciations not to return to "business as usual" relationships with the Soviet Union. Yet Washington carefully stated that it would not cancel the recently concluded grain deal with Moscow, nor would it interrupt the arms reduction talks going on in Geneva. Although most NATO countries

7. *Washington Post*, 3 Sept. 1983, p. A22.

strongly denounced the Soviet Union and agreed to sanctions against Aeroflot flights into their countries, West European governments were insistent that arms control discussions must proceed because public opinion—particularly in West Germany—demanded these negotiations regardless of its revulsion over Soviet behavior in the Korean airline disaster. Therefore, the Reagan administration was not in a position to sharply alter its previous policies toward Moscow; but it turned up the volume of its anti-Soviet rhetoric to an unprecedented degree.

Summing Up

The United States and the Soviet Union since World War II have had quite different priorities in their basic national interests. The United States became deeply involved in promoting its economic and world-order interests worldwide because there were few threats to its defense-of-homeland interest. The Soviet Union, on the other hand, was obsessed with defense-of-homeland from 1945 until the early 1970s, when it reached nuclear parity with the United States. Its world-order and economic interests abroad have widened, however, as its fear of being attacked at home has lessened. Thus, the superpowers are today in the classic position of satiated and unsatiated competitors for international influence—not much different from Great Britain and Germany at the beginning of the twentieth century. That competition, unfortunately, resulted in a war that devastated European supremacy in world affairs and led, a generation later, to a second round that brought European civilization near to collapse. Whether the threat of nuclear holocaust will enjoin the new superpowers from pressing their competition to the brink of war is not certain; nevertheless, this threat has maintained the peace between them for forty years. Barring an all-out war, the great danger in the relationship during the next decade is that a test of wills may take place in an area in which both powers think they have vital interests at stake, and a local war will then turn into a larger one because neither side will believe it can afford to back down. This could happen in the Persian Gulf area, close to Soviet borders and therefore viewed by Kremlin leaders as rightfully within the Soviet area of influence and not to be contested by the United States. A similar situation in reverse applies to the unstable situation in Central America. This is not to say that war *will* occur in the Persian Gulf but rather that it is an area where the Soviet Union has great advantages in deploying force, if it chooses to do so, and where the United States would have few allies and great difficulty in bringing credible force to bear. That is why it is crucial that U.S. and Soviet leaders reach an understanding on how far each side is prepared to go in pressing its view of vital world-order interests.

9. Priorities among U.S. National Interests

During the 1970s, three Presidents of the United States tried to redefine U.S. national interests in a way that would be more consistent with U.S. capabilities and the willingness of the American people to use the armed forces to defend vital U.S. interests. The Guam Doctrine, later called the Nixon Doctrine, made it clear that countries allied with the United States, particularly those in Asia, would be expected to bear the brunt of ground combat if they were attacked by hostile forces and that the United States would rely on its air and naval power to support them. When Great Britain withdrew its forces from bases in the Red Sea, the Persian Gulf, Singapore, and Malaysia in 1971, the Nixon administration decided not to replace them, as President Truman had reluctantly done when Britain withdrew from Greece and Turkey in 1947. Despite proposals by some strategists to have the United States fill the perceived power vacuum left by London's decision to withdraw from "East of Suez," President Nixon decided instead to encourage the Shah of Iran to assume responsibility for security in the Persian Gulf area. He also sought agreement with Moscow to limit the presence of Soviet and American warships in the Indian Ocean. In Europe, Mr. Nixon pressed the NATO allies to accept more of the defense burden there. The detente policies initiated by the President and his foreign policy adviser, Dr. Henry Kissinger, led to the first strategic arms agreement with Moscow in 1972 and the Helsinki Accords in 1975 which set the postwar boundaries of the East European states. President Gerald Ford tried to limit U.S. commitments in East Asia, particularly after the Vietnamese Communist victory in South Vietnam in 1975; he also continued the policy of encouraging Iran to be the peacekeeper in the Persian Gulf area by selling it the most modern American military equipment. He continued the SALT process with the Soviet Union, signing an interim SALT II agreement with President Brezhnev at Vladivostok in 1974. President Jimmy Carter tried during 1977 and 1978 to reduce the U.S. troop presence in many parts of the world, particularly in Korea where he wanted a complete withdrawal of American ground forces. He pressed Congress to approve the Panama Canal treaties so that the United States could avoid sending a larger force to defend the canal against an antagonistic population, and he reduced U.S. military missions in many Latin American countries. In the Middle East, Mr. Carter exerted great efforts to achieve a peace between Israel and its Arab neighbors in order to prevent another Arab-Israeli war—one which he feared might engage U.S. and Soviet forces. But for all his efforts in Panama and at Camp David, Mr. Carter was unable to bring peace either to Central America, where the Sandinista revolution in Nicaragua in 1979 threatened to turn that country and El Salvador into Communist regimes, or to the Middle East, where the Iranian revolution in 1978-79 completely upset the delicate balance of power in the Persian Gulf. Neither could he prevent the Iranian hostage crisis and the Iran-Iraq war. Therefore, beginning in 1980 President Carter vastly expanded U.S. vital interests by declaring that the Persian Gulf area was "vital," thus setting in motion a greatly expanded U.S. military role in the Middle East—the opposite of what he had hoped to accomplish when he took office in 1977. President Reagan expanded U.S. military commitments and presence in the Middle East by creating the Central Command, including the Rapid Deployment Force, and by building military facilities in Egypt, Oman, Somalia, and Kenya—in addition to expanding U.S. bases on the Indian Ocean island of Diego Garcia. Mr. Reagan also dispatched U.S. Marines to Lebanon in 1982 in an effort to prevent renewed civil war there. In sum, presidential perceptions of U.S. national interests underwent a significant change in the twelve years between 1969 and 1981.

Priorities among U.S. Interests

This study has discussed many areas of the world in terms of their importance to U.S. national interests. The analysis is based on strategic, economic, political, and ideological factors that condition the way Americans view the world in the 1980s, taking into account the question of why certain areas of this planet seem to be highly important to us and why U.S. forces should be expected to engage in hostilities, if necessary, to defend them. Using the national interest matrix outlined in Chapter 1, Figure 18 summarizes the findings of the previous chapters regarding the relative importance to the United States of twelve geographical sectors of the globe. This breakout of U.S. world-wide interests suggests that most *vital* concerns of the United States are in the world-order category—areas that contribute significantly to international security and to the global balance of power. Four of the six vital areas are tied to the United States by defense treaties: North America, Western Europe, Northeast Asia (Japan and South Korea), and the Southwest Pacific (Philippines, Australia, New Zealand). One additional area, the eastern Mediterranean, has strong security ties to the United States; another, the Soviet Union, is a continental power which can significantly threaten U.S. interests on a global scale.

Figure 18 also suggests there are only two areas—North America and the U.S.S.R.—that vitally affect U.S. defense-of-homeland interests: that is, those that can seriously threaten U.S. territory. North America clearly is at the vital, and potentially at the *survival*, level of defense interest because of the long unprotected U.S. borders with Canada and Mexico, and the strategic proximity of the islands off the U.S. coasts (Cuba, the Bahamas, Iceland, and Greenland). The Soviet Union is also in the vital category because of its ability to seriously damage American territory by submarine or air attack. Similarly, two areas of the world are vitally imporant to the U.S. economy: North America, which contains two of the top three trading partners of the United States (Canada and Mexico); and Northeast Asia, which includes Japan, the second largest trading partner of the United States, and South Korea, which is among the top ten. In terms of promotion of values (ideology), only two areas qualify at the vital level: that is, those in which the United States has a deep commitment to the preservation (or building) of democratic institutions. These are Western Europe and North America. There is no suggestion implied here that the United States should disregard an interest in human rights and social justice in other regions of the world; it does mean that the U.S. government should have an

Fig. 18. U.S. National Interests by Geographical Area

Basic Interest at Stake	Intensity of Interest			
	Survival	Vital	Major	Peripheral
Defense of Homeland		N. America U.S.S.R.	W. Europe E. Mediterranean S.W. Pacific N.E. Asia S. America	S.E. Asia Persian Gulf N. Africa Southern Africa China
Economic Well-Being		N. America N.E. Asia	W. Europe E. Mediterranean Persian Gulf S.E. Asia S.W. Pacific S. America U.S.S.R. Southern Africa	N. Africa China
Favorable World Order		N. America W. Europe E. Mediterranean N.E. Asia S.W. Pacific U.S.S.R.	Persian Gulf S.E. Asia S. America N. Africa Southern Africa China	
Promotion of Values		N. America W. Europe	E. Mediterranean N.E. Asia S.W. Pacific S. America U.S.S.R. Southern Africa	Persian Gulf S.E. Asia N. Africa China

exceptionally high interest in seeing that democracy continues to flourish in Western Europe and in North America. This is especially important in Central America, which has had no real tradition of democracy and social justice since these small states obtained their independence from Spain. Yet it is essential that the attributes of democracy be implanted there. It should be clear from a look at this division of the world into vital, major, and peripheral interests that most U.S. national interests in the 1980s fall into the major and peripheral categories. This means that they should occupy considerable attention from U.S. policy-makers

Fig. 19. U.S. Worldwide Interests by Major Country

Basic Interest at Stake	Intensity of Interest			
	Survival	Vital	Major	Peripheral
Defense of Homeland	Canada Mexico	Britain Caribbean Basin U.S.S.R.	Australia Brazil China Egypt France Greece Israel Italy Japan Norway Philippines Saudi Arabia South Korea Turkey Venezuela West Germany	Argentina Chile India Iran Lebanon Nigeria Pakistan South Africa Thailand
Economic Well-Being		Canada Japan Mexico West Germany	Argentina Brazil Britain Caribbean Basin France Greece India Iran Israel Italy Nigeria Norway Saudi Arabia South Africa South Korea U.S.S.R. Venezuela	Australia Chile China Egypt Lebanon Pakistan Philippines Thailand Turkey
Favorable World Order		Australia Britain Canada Caribbean Basin Egypt France Greece	Argentina Brazil Chile China India Iran Lebanon	

Fig. 19 (continued)

Basic Interest at Stake	Intensity of Interest			
	Survival	Vital	Major	Peripheral
Favorable World Order (continued)		Israel Italy Japan Mexico Norway Philippines Saudi Arabia Turkey U.S.S.R. Venezuela West Germany	Nigeria Pakistan South Africa South Korea Thailand	
Promotion of Values		Australia Britain Canada France Greece Israel Italy Japan Mexico Norway Venezuela West Germany	Argentina Brazil Caribbean Basin Chile Egypt India Nigeria Philippines South Africa U.S.S.R.	China Iran Lebanon Pakistan Saudi Arabia South Korea Thailand Turkey

but should not become so crucial that a President is counseled to become militarily involved in them—unless they are directly threatened by the Soviet Union.

Figure 19 represents an attempt to classify thirty important countries around the world according to their importance to the United States, using the four basic interests described in Chapter 1 and suggesting the intensity of interest that each should entail for the United States in the 1980s.

Analyzing National Interest Priorities

In analyzing this breakout of U.S. national interests by country, it is important to make two qualifications. First, this study is based on the assumption that international relations are, in the final analysis, determined by the leaders and governments of sovereign states, not by international organizations, private institutions, or multinational corporations. This is not to say that these organizations have no influence on government (their influence is heavy), but rather that decisions about trade policy, military and economic assistance, the initiation of covert activities, the imposition of economic sanctions, and, finally, the decisions to engage in warfare are made by sovereign governments (see Chapter 2). Policy decisions by U.S. leaders are based on their perceptions of U.S. national interests. Second, there is no known way to predict how a particular U.S. administration will view the national interest when it is faced with a specific issue or crisis and must make a decision about the policy tools a President should employ to achieve policy objectives. The scholar's task is not to predict what a President will think or do, but rather to lay out a reasonable picture of what U.S. interests *ought to be* in terms of our historical experience, our economic and political needs, and our security requirements, consistent with both our ability and willingness to defend them in case of war. This discussion of where U.S. defense, economic, world-order, and ideological interests lie in the 1980s is based on an *objective* analysis of why certain countries and regions are very important to the United States and a *subjective* judgment about how intensely the United States should be willing to defend its interests in relation to those countries. I do not claim this to be the only methodology for arriving at sound judgments about how the United States should decide its foreign policy and military strategy, but I do believe that the national interest approach suggested—particularly the matrix approach used to show the relative priority of countries in terms of basic U.S. interests—is a useful and perhaps a valuable way to plan U.S. national security policy. What follows is my effort to summarize the most important U.S. national interests in the 1980s, using the four categories of interest described in Chapter 1 as the framework for discussion.

Defense of Homeland

Figure 19 suggests that there are only four major countries in the world that *vitally* affect the defense of the United States:

Canada, Mexico, Britain, and the Soviet Union. (The Caribbean Basin is a collection of small countries in Central America and the islands of the Caribbean.) Recalling that defense of homeland is concerned with protection of the territory, population, and political system of the United States, it is easy to see that Canada constitutes at least a vital and probably a survival defense interest. This is because Canada's territory and air space are critical to the defense of the continental United States in any conflict involving the only other power capable of inflicting massive damage on the U.S. homeland—the Soviet Union. Mexico is a vital defense interest, and probably a survival one in case of war, because of its long, relatively uncontrolled border with the United States and its rapidly growing, impoverished population. This could pose a serious threat to the western United States if a war broke out in Central America or Mexico and millions of refugees tried to escape to the United States. Britain is a vital defense interest because of its strategic position in the North Atlantic athwart the sea routes that Soviet missile-carrying submarines must cross in order to approach the U.S. Atlantic coastline. In addition, Britain has naval and air resources that are essential for patroling the North Atlantic. Although not listed here, Iceland also must be considered a vital defense interest of the United States because the crucial U.S. military base located at Keflavik monitors Soviet submarine and air traffic in the North Atlantic. Greenland is similarly of vital strategic importance. Canada, Greenland, Iceland, and Britain are therefore crucial to the defense of U.S. territory because of their location and their ability to detect and monitor Soviet ship and aircraft movements near the U.S. coastline. The Soviet Union is a vital U.S. defense interest because it could destroy large segments of the U.S. homeland.

The numerous countries listed as *major* in the defense-of-homeland category all have an alliance or close defense relations with the United States. They are not, however, at the same level of importance to the *defense of U.S. territory* as the countries listed above. This is not to downgrade their importance to the security of the United States; it simply means that their contribution is not *directly* related to the defense of U.S. territory; their vital importance lies in the "favorable world order" category (see below). Argentina, Pakistan, Saudi Arabia, and Thailand, for example, have very little impact on the defense of North America. Turkey, on the other hand, performs a key function for defense of the U.S. homeland: it provides U.S. intelligence services with crucial listening posts from which vital Soviet strategic information can be obtained through electronic surveillance.

Economic Well-Being

As with defense-of-homeland interest, only four major countries are *vitally* important to the United States economically. Two of them—Canada and Mexico—are also in the defense category. They are joined here by Japan, the second most important U.S. trading partner and among the world's strongest economies; and West Germany, the most important economic and financial power in Europe and one of the top U.S. trading partners. Saudi Arabia, whose petro-dollars invested in U.S. banks and whose decisive influence within the OPEC bloc give it great economic influence, is probably a major rather than a vital economic interest to the United States. It might be argued that Great Britain ought to be a vital U.S. economic interest because of London's importance as a world financial center. However, the decline of the British economy over the past twenty years and the government's abandonment of special Commonwealth economic arrangements in favor of the European Common Market in the 1970s make Britain less influential to U.S. economic interests. The same is true of France and Brazil; both are important economic powers whose importance may grow in the future, but whose economic strength is not vital to the United States today.

Clearly the non-Communist world is far more interdependent economically than was the case ten or twenty years ago, and it may therefore be an oversimplification to judge U.S. economic well-being as vitally dependent on four countries, and affected very importantly by only another seventeen. It can be argued that none of them is among the poor Asian and African states that form the bulk of the "have-not nations," which joined together during the 1970s to demand a far greater effort by the northern industrialized nations to aid their development. Some of these countries, such as Zaire and Zimbabwe, are suppliers of key raw materials to the United States. Nigeria, by contrast, is listed as a major economic interest because it is the most important economic power in Africa. It is likely that other developing countries will become major U.S. economic interests during the next five or ten years, but in the mid-1980s the countries listed in the vital and major categories constitute the areas to which the United States must give greatest economic priority for the foreseeable future. The country giving the United States the most serious economic problems is Japan, which has become an economic superpower in the last fifteen years. Government policy has enabled Japanese companies to target certain industries in the United States for special competition, particularly in autos, electronics, cameras, and even pianos. Using the free trade practices followed by the United States, Japanese manufacturers have penetrated the U.S. market in these and other fields in a major way, resulting in the decline of large U.S. industries and the layoff of hundreds of thousands of U.S. workers in 1981-82. Despite the Reagan administration's strong efforts to dissuade Congress from enacting restrictions against imports of Japanese products, the U.S. auto industry, the auto unions, and many members of Congress now favor specific legislation limiting Japanese imports, under the rubric of "fairness" in trade practices. A strong possibility exists that Congress, under Democratic Party pressure, will enact restrictive legislation against Japan's products. Several Democratic candidates for president in 1984 indicated support for such legislation in order to placate American labor.[1]

World Order

The furtherance of a favorable world order has been a U.S. mission since the end of World War II. As a result, the United States has entered into numerous military alliances and concluded many defense agreements with countries in every part of the world. Some of them, most notably the fourteen European NATO partners and Japan, are clearly vital world-order interests because they contribute greatly to international security and to the world balance of power between the Soviet Union and the non-Communist countries. Others, like Saudi Arabia and the Philippines, contribute little except their land and strategic position. The problem for American policy-makers has been to dis-

1. See Sidney Blumenthal, "Drafting of a Democratic Industrial Plan," *New York Times Magazine*, August 28, 1983, p. 31.

tinguish between those countries that are truly *vital* and those that are important but not vital to the world-order interests of the United States. If some are vital, is this because they provide modern, credible military forces that contribute measurably to the world-wide balance of power? Or are they believed to be vital simply because their location seems to be important to maintaining the strategic balance with the Soviet Union?

Figure 19 lists eighteen countries whose territory and military forces are so important to the world balance of power and international security that they must be considered vital world-order interests of the United States. In North America they are Canada, Mexico, Venezuela, and the countries of the Caribbean; in Europe they include Britain, France, West Germany, Norway, and Italy; in the eastern Mediterranean they are Turkey, Greece, Israel, and Egypt; in the Persian Gulf there is Saudi Arabia; and in East Asia they are Japan, the Philippines, and Australia. These are the anchors, so to speak, around which the United States projects its power worldwide. Most of these states have substantial military forces and contribute importantly to the regional balance of power in their areas. Others—among them China, Brazil, South Korea, Nigeria, and Thailand—are important friends of the United States but are not vitally important to the projection of U.S. military power in the world—even though they contribute to political stability in their areas. The Soviet Union is a vital U.S. world-order interest because it has the capability, and desire, to upset the world order in ways that are detrimental to the United States—as it did by sending Soviet forces into Afghanistan in 1979, and Cuban forces with Soviet advisers to Angola in 1975 and to Ethiopia in 1977.

One country on this list of vital world-order interests, the Philippines, contributes no forces to the security of areas outside its borders and nothing except its land to the U.S. worldwide balance of power. Yet this island country is considered vital because the United States maintains two of its most important strategic bases there: Clark Air Force Base and Subic Bay Naval Base. The United States agreed in 1983 to greatly increase the amount of aid provided to the Philippines as "rent" for these bases, a total of $900 million. However, the Marcos government's martial law has engendered increasing opposition within the country. The assassination of opposition leader Benigno Aquino in August 1983, upon his return to Manila from the United States, shocked the Philippine population as well as many Americans, and Marcos's political position became more difficult because of suspicion that his government had arranged the killing. President Reagan canceled a state visit at the end of 1983, and the question began to be raised whether the Philippines could continue to be viewed as a vital U.S. interest if the Marcos policies turned the population toward extremism and anti-Americanism.

Egypt, although it has no defense alliance with the United States, has been a vital world-order interest since the late 1970s when it made peace with Israel and agreed to cooperate militarily with the United States in the defense of the Persian Gulf. Egypt has the largest and best trained army in the Arab world, and it could be a key military force if war broke out in the Persian Gulf or in East Africa. Saudi Arabia and Israel are vital world-order interests for similar reasons.

Promotion of Values

An important part of American policy, historically and currently, is the promotion of American ideas of individual freedom and democratic institutions abroad. While no one argues that the United States should go to war solely to protect democratic governments around the world, there certainly is a strong correlation between most U.S. defense alliances concluded since World War II and the democratic nature of governments in the countries included in the U.S. defense umbrella. Nearly all the countries listed as vital world-order interests in Figure 19 are democratic countries by U.S. standards. The exceptions are the Soviet Union, the Philippines, Turkey, and Egypt. Therefore, a general rule in American foreign policy should be that countries considered to be vital U.S. world-order interests for balance-of-power reasons should be at least *major* ideological interests as well. Such countries should be urged by the United States to sustain and improve their democratic institutions because this is important in building internal security against Communist and other totalitarian ideology. Although President Carter overemphasized human rights in conducting his foreign policy, all U.S. Presidents need to suggest to allied governments, preferably in private, the strong U.S. belief that allied countries should not only allow but encourage free speech and a free press, as well as regular, fair elections in which all elements of society can participate.

There are a few countries whose democratic institutions are so important to the United States that it would cause great alarm in Washington if their governments were overthrown by a *coup d'état*. These are strong U.S. allies whose adherence to a democratic form of government is vital to U.S. ideological interests worldwide: Britain, France, West Germany, and Italy in Europe; Japan and Australia in the Far East; Canada, Mexico and Venezuela in the Western Hemisphere. With the possible exception of Mexico these few countries are strongly wedded to democratic institutions—even though West Germany, Italy, and Japan have enjoyed it only since the late 1940s. It is an important part of the U.S. national interest to insure that democracy in these countries flourishes, not only as a benefit to the peoples concerned but also as an example to other nations of the advantages of strong democratic institutions based on the rights of individual citizens to choose their leaders.

United States Policies in Relation to Interests

This survey of the world in the mid-1980s, in terms of U.S. interests, leads to the conclusion that the United States is over-committed internationally. U.S. forces are stretched to a dangerous degree, not only in Western Europe, where the United States maintains a personnel total of some 326,000, but also in the Middle East, Indian Ocean, Southeast Asia (Philippines), and Northeast Asia (Japan and South Korea). In fact, the twelve carrier battle groups that the U.S. Navy currently has in commission are not considered sufficient to carry out all the commitments the Navy has to maintain in every ocean of the world.[2] There is general agreement that the U.S. Army, numbering 785,000 personnel, is under strength in terms of the growing

2. In 1983 there were twelve U.S. attack carriers in commissioned service, six assigned to the Atlantic and Mediterranean fleets and six to the Pacific fleet. The Navy normally keeps three carriers on the East coast of the United States and three on the West coast, for overhauls or training maneuvers. The Secretary of the Navy proposed to Congress in 1983 that this number be increased to fourteen carriers in order that the Navy could adequately take care of increased responsibilities in the Indian Ocean and the Caribbean. Congress accepted this plan.

commitments it has been given in the Rapid Development Force (now part of the Central Command) and its growing responsibilities in the Caribbean and Central American region. The Reagan administration pledged that it would not reinstitute the military draft, although it is doubtful whether the all-volunteer force—even with increased enlistments during 1982-83—would be capable of manning an expanded Army, Navy, and Air Force in case of a serious international crisis. In addition, the Reagan administration faced growing congressional opposition in 1983 to large increases in defense spending while U.S. budget deficits were running at $200 billion per year and after cuts in domestic programs in the early 1980s resulted in serious domestic political repercussions. This was particularly true after the Democratic Party increased its majority in the House of Representatives in the 1982 midterm elections.

It seemed clear in 1983, both from the size of U.S. military forces and the opposition to President Reagan's requests for a 10 percent increase in defense expenditures that the United States was overcommitted in the world in terms of how much defense the country was willing to pay for and what countries it was prepared to fight for. The latter factor was reinforced in September 1983 when Congress debated giving the President authority to keep sixteen hundred U.S. Marines in Lebanon for another eighteen months.

Of the vital interests suggested in Figure 19, there is probably no doubt that the American people and Congress will eventually be persuaded that Central America—the long forgotten area on the U.S. doorstep—must be accepted as a serious U.S. security problem and that military and large economic aid must be granted these countries to give them a semblance of hope for the future and make them less susceptible to the Marxist-Leninist doctrines being pressed on them by leftist forces.

In Europe, there is little doubt that the United States will continue to honor its commitment to protect Western countries against Soviet blandishments so long as they desire American protection. But neutralism in Denmark, West Germany, the Netherlands, and Greece could shatter the NATO consensus if pacifist or neutralist forces gain control of these governments. The same is true for Great Britain, although the shattering of the Labour Party in the elections of 1983, which was due to its sharp leftward drift, make it likely that the Conservatives will remain in power for some time and thus give Britain a stronger role in NATO.

Similarly, there is no doubt that the United States will in the foreseeable future defend Japan against Soviet pressures. Nevertheless, Japan's reluctance to build up its armed forces to a size commensurate with its economic interests and political aspirations opens the possibility that the U.S. Congress will impose sanctions on Japan's continuing economic penetration and domination of certain U.S. markets and that this kind of action will in turn harm the U.S.-Japan political relationship. If Prime Minister Nakasone remains in power and is able to move parliament to substantially increase the country's armed forces and defense effort, particularly if Japan increases its import of U.S. products as part of a military expansion, this will probably defuse the growing anti-Japanese sentiment in Congress.

The United States will no doubt defend South Korea again, as it did in 1950, if it is attacked by North Korean forces. However, this commitment does not require the stationing of 40,000 U.S. ground forces in Korea, especially when U.S. Army personnel are in great demand elsewhere. Before the end of the 1980s, it should be possible for the United States, Japan, and China to provide jointly for South Korea's security, with the U.S. ground contribution being reduced to a small force of about 5,000. It should not be necessary for the United States to retain the primary responsibility to defend South Korea thirty years after the end of the Korean War, especially when China and Japan are moving toward greater economic cooperation and both have the Soviet Union as their principal adversary. The United States should therefore adjust its military role in Northeast Asia downward and encourage Japan and China also to increase their military cooperation.

In Southeast and Southwest Asia, the Persian Gulf, eastern Mediterranean, southern Africa, and South America (minus Venezuela and Colombia), U.S. interests are overextended and will become more so unless U.S. political leaders resist the pressure to permit U.S. aspirations to outrun this country's willingness to incur financial and human costs. This is not to say that the United States has minimal interests in these regions or that the American

people would have no concern if countries in those areas succumbed to Communism—either through internal subversion (as
in Afghanistan in 1978), civil war (as in Angola in 1975-76), or free
elections (as in Chile in 1970). The United States had a major
national interest in all of those countries and would have a similar
one in others that might come under military pressure from
Cuban, Vietnamese, or Libyan forces—to name several national
groups that fit the category of surrogates for the Soviet Union.
The essential point here is that although most threats to Third
World countries generate substantial U.S. economic and military
aid and political action by Washington, it is a completely different
question to ask whether the United States should send its *own*
forces to defend such a country if it has no specific defense
alliance with the United States. For example, although the U.S. is
committed by the Rio Treaty to defend any South American
country if attacked from outside, it is doubtful that the United
States should defend Argentina if it is attacked by Brazil or Chile,
or vice versa; this is because U.S. interests in South America are at
the *major*, not vital level. President Reagan's reluctance to send a
large U.S. force to Lebanon in 1982-83 to preserve that country's
independence, as President Eisenhower did in 1958, suggests that
Lebanon in the 1980s is so unstable internally that Washington is
unwilling to stake its prestige on declaring it a vital interest.
Southeast Asia was downgraded to a major U.S. interest by
President Nixon in 1969 when he came into office, and President
Ford upheld that judgment when he replaced Mr. Nixon. This
accounts for the fact that Washington did not intervene when
Hanoi launched its final offensive in South Vietnam in 1975, in
clear violation of the Paris Agreements of 1973. For similar reasons, President Carter decided not to offer any help to Cambodia
when it was invaded by Vietnam in 1978.

The area where it is most difficult for American political leaders in the mid-1980s to determine U.S. vital interests is in the
Indian Ocean and the Persian Gulf. President Carter declared this
to be a *vital* interest in 1980 for two reasons. First, he believed that
the United States, Western Europe, and Japan were vitally dependent on the continued flow of oil from the Persian Gulf and that
this flow would be jeopardized if revolution swept the area—as
had happened in Iran—and oil were used as a political weapon by

the controlling states. Second, the United States could not tolerate having the Soviet Union extend its political influence southward toward the Indian Ocean and bring the Arab countries, plus Iran, into its sphere of influence. President Reagan reiterated this position when he took office in 1981, and he expanded the U.S. Rapid Deployment Force. By 1983 the United States had established military facilities in a number of countries adjacent to the Persian Gulf area, and it conducted joint military exercises with several countries in the region.

There is no question that the Persian Gulf is very important to the United States and to the whole Western world because of its oil; what is doubtful is whether the oil in this area is *so* important that U.S. armed forces should be engaged in a major war there if the Soviet Union decides to take advantage of political turmoil in Iran and Iraq to extend its influence southward—perhaps by persuading Iran to give it a naval base on the Persian Gulf. If the Soviet Union does not use its own forces but employs diplomacy, aid, and subversion to convince Iran and other Persian Gulf countries to deal with Moscow rather than Washington, should the United States try to prevent this with the use of its own forces? I don't believe so. There is a strong likelihood that a large majority of Congress and the public would oppose the use of U.S. forces in the Persian Gulf under such circumstances, and the War Powers Act of 1973 gives Congress the option of refusing to sanction such a move. The congressional debate in September 1983 on keeping 1600 Marines in Lebanon is symptomatic of the strong domestic resistance any President will encounter in seeking Congressional approval to use force in the Persian Gulf.

If, as I believe it will, the United States continues to be reluctant to use armed forces in the Middle East, the question must then be asked: why is the President planning to deploy forces where it will be extremely difficult for them to fight and prevail? The reason is that the presence of U.S. forces along the periphery of the Persian Gulf may slow down the erosion of Western influence there, an erosion resulting from the replacement of the Shah's regime in Iran by a revolutionary Islamic one. Buying time may help other countries in the region to strengthen their political regimes and make them less likely to be undermined by revolutionaries encouraged by Iran or the Soviet Union. Deployment of

U.S., French, Italian, and British forces to Lebanon—and to the Indian Ocean—might have cautioned Moscow against using its own forces to exploit an attractive opportunity in Iran, Iraq, or Pakistan, or to support a South Yemen effort to overthrow the Saudi monarchy.

The danger is that if the United States positions a sizable fighting force in the Indian Ocean, as well as in Egypt and Oman, the propensity to use it in case of local conflicts or internal strife will be very great. The host countries will not understand why U.S. forces are not used against hostile neighbors until Soviet forces are engaged. That was the problem that President Reagan confronted in Lebanon in the summer of 1983 and early 1984, when U.S. Marines were not reinforced and used in support of the Lebanese Army to defeat the militias of various political factions that refused to accept a political settlement of Lebanon's internal problems. By keeping the Marines at sixteen hundred men, the President could maintain that their mission was "peace-keeping." In the Persian Gulf area, it may be very difficult for a President to refrain from intervening in local wars because large forces under the Central Command are being positioned to inter-vene there. As occurred in Southeast Asia twenty years earlier, the desire to use American forces in combat, rather than have them sit on the sidelines, becomes overwhelming when local troops are engaged and one faction is being aided by an outside enemy. In Vietnam, the enemy was North Vietnam and China; in the Persian Gulf it could well be Iran, with Soviet backing if not full participation.

Summing Up

It is time for the United States to face the reality that it does not have the means or the will to defend more than North America, Western Europe, Japan, the Philippines, Australia, Turkey, Isra-el, and Egypt in the foreseeable future. We may not even be willing to defend Israel and Egypt if they are unable to bring about real peace between themselves and among the Arab coun-tries. The attitude of Americans toward the world has changed fundamentally since President John Kennedy said in January 1961 that Americans would go anywhere and pay any price to defend freedom. We are not returning to the isolationism of the 1930s, I believe, but as a people we are less willing to bear the defense burdens of the world than we were twenty years ago. A careful reshaping of American military strategy to fit a more modest conception of our vital interests is not only prudent in the mid-1980s; it is an absolute political necessity if this country is to avoid courting disaster as an overcommitted giant.

10. Epilogue

The early months of 1984 saw a number of significant international events that directly affected U.S. national interests and foreign policy, and some others that were important but less significant to the well-being of the United States. These key events were: the continuing emplacement of U.S. medium range nuclear missiles in several European countries; the death of Soviet leader Yuri Andropov and his replacement by Konstantin Chernenko; the withdrawal of American peace-keeping forces from Lebanon and the continuation of civil war there; the growing U.S. military involvement in Central America; and, perhaps most ominous, the escalation of the Iran-Iraq war in the Persian Gulf. Other important but less notable events were: the warming of political and economic relations between the United States and the Peoples' Republic of China, symbolized by the visit of President Reagan to Peking; the disunity shown in the European Common Market and the growth of neutralism in several NATO countries; the return to democratic government in Argentina following the overthrow of the military dictatorship; and the nonaggression treaty signed between South Africa and Mozambique, which opened the possibility of peace also in Namibia. In addition, there were three important developments within the United States that had a direct bearing on its defense of homeland, economic, and world order interests. These were: the spectacular growth of the American economy while inflation remained at a moderate level; the steady expansion of the U.S. military arsenal, both in strategic and conventional weaponry; and the renewed willingness of the U.S. Government to use covert actions and economic pressure, as well as military aid, to effect policy changes in other countries. Despite the momentary decline of

U.S. prestige in the Middle East resulting from withdrawal of Marines from Lebanon, the mood of the American people and its government in the spring of 1984 was one of self-confidence, in contrast to the "malaise" that President Jimmy Carter complained about during the latter part of his tenure.

The U.S. withdrawal from Lebanon was probably inevitable once the Reagan Administration decided in 1983 that it was not prepared to send a much larger military force to impose its will on the warring Lebanese factions and on Syria, the principal outside supporter of the anti-government militias. Israel had made its decision in August 1983 when it pulled its forces back from Beirut and left American peacekeeping forces exposed to hostile Lebanese factions. Although some in the Reagan Administration, notably Secretary of State George Shultz, favored keeping the Marines in Beirut and reinforcing them, it was unmistakably clear by February 1984 that the American public was strongly opposed to a U.S. military presence in Lebanon and that the Democratic leadership in Congress was prepared to exploit this sentiment against Mr. Reagan in an election year. Had the President waited longer to extricate the American force from its militarily exposed position, Lebanon would have loomed ever larger as an election issue at a time when Mr. Reagan's political prospects were otherwise generally favorable.

The withdrawal from Lebanon had its political price in the Middle East, however. Pro-Western countries such as Jordan, Egypt, and Saudi Arabia viewed the action as a sign of American weakness. King Hussein of Jordan, despite earlier assurances to President Reagan, decided not to participate in preliminary peace talks with Israel. The prestige of Syria was considerably increased by the American decision, and other Arab countries were obliged to pay greater attention to Syria's interests not only in Lebanon, but also in the Palestinian issue and in the Iran-Iraq war. The U.S. withdrawal also had an effect on the ruling Likud coalition government in Israel. The opposition Labor Party called for the total withdrawal of Israeli forces from Lebanon, and this stand promised to become an important issue in the July 1984 Israeli general elections.

Finally, the withdrawal from Lebanon rekindled a ten-year-old debate within the United States about the War Powers Act and the role of Congress in deciding when and how the President may use U.S. military forces outside the United States. In April 1984, the Reagan Administration launched a drive to repeal this legislation, which had been passed over a presidential veto in 1973. Secretary of State Shultz called it an infringement on the President's constitutional power to define and defend U.S. national interests abroad, and the issue seemed certain to be debated in the 1984 presidential election campaign.

The brutal Iran-Iraq war neared the completion of four years, and a strong possibility emerged in the spring of 1984 that Iran would overwhelm Iraq's defenses by human wave attacks and then move on to Baghdad. Iraq used air power against Iran's oil ports and bombed commercial ships moving out of its harbors. More dangerous, however, was Iraq's use of chemical weapons against Iranian forces. Although the Baghdad government denied it had used chemical agents, United States and United Nations observers verified their use and President Reagan called for a worldwide ban on the manufacture and detonation of these weapons. Nevertheless, Iraq seemed determined to employ whatever weapons were available to defend its homeland against Iranian troops. As the largest and most dangerous conflict going on in the world in 1984, the Iran-Iraq war had the potential of escalating and drawing in other countries—not excluding the Soviet Union and the United States. President Reagan warned Iran on several occasions not to interfere with the shipping of oil from the Persian Gulf to international markets; if the Khomeini government nevertheless tried to block the oil traffic by mining waters or bombing a tanker, this could quickly lead to armed conflict with U.S. naval forces stationed near the Strait of Hormuz. The question of what would happen to Iran when the Ayatollah Khomeini died was another issue. If civil war erupted in Iran, should the United States become involved with aid to one of the factions? That remained one of the most serious questions that would face the American President in the not distant future, if not in 1984 then surely in 1985 or 1986.

By far the most divisive foreign policy issue within the United States in early 1984 was Central America, and what should be done about El Salvador and Nicaragua. This was not as much an East-West issue as it was an internal political one within the United States. Clearly, the Soviet Union was not prepared to go to war with the United States over Nicaragua or El Salvador, any more than it was about to defend Grenada when the United States invaded it in October 1983 to protect American citizens. The real issue was whether the American public and Congress were willing to permit the President to use strong measures, including military force, to insure that communist revolutions did not sweep over all of Central America and then threaten the stability of Mexico. In April 1983, President Reagan staked out his position that Central America was a *vital* interest to the United States and that he planned to provide large amounts of both economic and military assistance in an effort to prevent the collapse of non-communist regimes—even though existing governments left much to be desired in terms of human rights and social justice. The Kissinger Commission, set up by the President to give him bipartisan recommendations on what should be done, delivered its report in January 1984; but this comprehensive study was promptly criticized by the Democratic leadership in Congress because it generally supported President Reagan's policies. A related issue was whether Congress should continue to finance covert assistance to Nicaraguan rebels (contras) who were increasingly effective in disrupting Nicaraguan port facilities and harassing Sandinista military forces in northern and southern Nicaragua. At issue was whether this covert aid was for the purpose of overthrowing the Sandinista government (which the rebels intended) or whether it was meant only as harassment, to persuade the government in Managua to change its ways and stop supporting insurgents in El Salvador (which Congress preferred). In early April 1984, the U.S. Senate debated these issues in detail and gave the President a resounding victory in terms of economic and military aid to El Salvador and covert aid to Nicaraguan rebels. The Democratic-controlled House of Representatives was not as forthcoming, but there were signs that congressional opposition to the President's policies in Central America was eroding, as the American public became aware of the stakes involved in this area near the U.S. southern border, and of the extent of Cuban involvement in support of insurgent forces in the region. In contrast to Lebanon, where American public opinion persuaded the President to withdraw U.S. forces, on Central America the American public seemed receptive to the idea that stronger U.S. measures were required to protect this vital area.

The relationship of the United States and Western Europe will in the long run be the most fundamental of all U.S. world order interests, but the political climate on both sides of the Atlantic early in 1984 left much to be desired. President Reagan's hard-line policies had clearly eroded European confidence about the future of East-West relations. While European and American governments took satisfaction from the successful deployment of U.S. Pershing II and cruise missiles, there was an undercurrent of apprehension among many sensible Europeans about whether the United States could be trusted with the fate of Europe in a nuclear age. On the one hand, there seemed to be growing doubt about whether *any* American President would risk nuclear war for the sake of Western Europe; and at the same time, there was growing fear that American policy toward the Soviet Union might goad Moscow into taking actions that would precipitate a conventional war in which Europe would be destroyed whether nuclear weapons were used or not. Despite these doubts, a change in alliance relationships did not appear imminent so long as the leaders of Britain, France, West Germany and Italy remain strong "realists"; the danger lay in the fact that opposition parties in Britain, West Germany, the Netherlands and Denmark were moving toward neutralist positions in the East-West struggle for world influence and pledged themselves to pursue anti-nuclear and neutralist foreign policies when they return to government power—probably before the end of the decade. If either West Germany or Britain abandoned NATO's strategy based on nuclear deterrence and sought accommodation with the Soviet Union, this would have a profound effect not only in Europe but also in Africa, the Middle East, and Latin America. Indeed, Western Europe is the most vital interest of the United States outside North America, and the loss of these strong allies would significantly upset the world balance of power to the detriment of the United States. East Asia may soon become more important as a vital economic interest, but it does not compare with Europe in political influence in most parts of the world.

Finally, the Soviet Union remained an enduring competitor of the United States for world power and influence, and it gave no sign of slackening its determination to stay in the great power race. The transition from Yuri Andropov to Konstantin Chernenko was a smooth one, and the Politburo seemed to have set in

place the cast of characters who will lead the next government—
which could occur within the next several years. The very large
Soviet naval exercises in the Atlantic in April 1984 and the
Kremlin's continued hard-line policy against renewed nuclear
weapons negotiations indicated a toughness of attitude that ran
counter to arguments made by some Reagan Administration
officials that the Soviets would have to negotiate a nuclear arms
deal when it became clear they could not divide the West over the
Euromissile issue. Although the Kremlin seemed willing to talk
about renewal of cultural and scientific exchanges and the re-
opening of trade links, there was no real evidence early in 1984
that Moscow was prepared to change its policy on the relationship between Pershing II and SS-20 missiles and thereby
concede that U.S. medium range weapons were in Europe to stay.
Soviet leaders seemed convinced that additional political mileage
could be squeezed out of European public opinion on the nuclear
weapons issue, particularly in West Germany where anti-nuclear
groups continued their campaign and the Social Democrats decided to join rather than fight them.

In 1984, perhaps more than usual, the world waited for the
U.S. electorate to decide who would lead the United States in the
next four years and for signals of the kind of policies the new
Administration would pursue. The leadership in Moscow apparently decided after the Korean plane tragedy in September 1983
that they would not deal with Mr. Reagan until it was clear
whether he would be president another four years. West Europeans were torn between discomfort over Mr. Reagan's tough
policies toward the Soviet Union and concern that another candidate might be a less effective alliance leader. Ronald Reagan was a
known quantity, Europeans said, one who at least followed a
consistent policy. Consistency in American foreign policy, instead of the ups and downs and turns of the 1970s, was what most
of the world looked for in 1984. A key question thus emerges: If
Ronald Reagan is reelected in November 1984, will he necessarily
continue the policies established in his first term or decide on
significant changes in the way the United States looks at and deals
with the rest of the world? If Walter Mondale gets the Democratic
nomination and is elected, will he abandon the policies set in
motion by Mr. Reagan or continue the "peace through strength"
philosophy? As we look at the future of American foreign policy,

we may ask: Are U.S. national interests in the 1980s coming into sharper perspective so that the new President and Congress can forge a foreign policy consensus? Or are the divisions in the country around perceptions of national interest still so deep that any president will have to struggle mightily to set a steady foreign policy course during the remainder of the 1980s?

My view is that we are seeing the reemergence of a consensus in foreign policy that will produce a new, more pragmatic view of U.S. national interests. This will entail a move away from the globalism of the past thirty years and give the President a mandate to be tough-minded about establishing priorities among the many foreign claims on this country's economic resources, military power, and psychological strength. There is no reason why the United States should not be able to continue as a great world power and at the same time take a detached view of some areas and issues in the world that are either beyond the ability of the United States to change (Lebanon is an example) or so tenuous in terms of the U.S. stake that they are not worth a confrontation with the Soviet Union (Poland and Afghanistan, for instance). If one believes, as I do, that the Kremlin's leaders are not resigned to world war and are interested in ways to reduce tensions, it surely would be a wise course to keep open negotiating channels at every level and to explore fully the areas of mutual interest. Clearly, the United States must have a strong defense and a strong desire to defend its interests while negotiating; but neither Soviet nor American leaders will be able to drive the other side into a surrender or humiliation—no matter how much military power they hold. Therefore, prudence strongly suggests that Washington and Moscow should be willing to think about measures of accommodation in 1985 and beyond—in their mutual self interest.

Index